NEW FORMATIONS

EDITOR:
Scott McCracken

REVIEWS EDITOR
Timothy Bewes

EDITORIAL ASSISTANT
Helen Pendry

EDITORIAL BOARD:
Timothy Bewes
Laura Chrisman
Jeremy Gilbert
David Glover
Cora Kaplan
Neil Lazarus
Mandy Merck
Scott McCracken
Alasdair Pettinger
Bill Schwarz
Jenny Bourne Taylor
Wendy Wheeler

ADVISORY BOARD:
Ien Ang
Angelika Bammer
Tony Bennett
Jody Berland
Homi Bhabha
Victor Burgin
Lesley Caldwell
Hazel Carby
Erica Carter
Iain Chambers
Joan Copjec
Lidia Curti
Tony Davies
James Donald
Simon Frith
Stuart Hall
Dick Hebdige
Colin Mercer
Edward Said
Renata Salecl
Gayatri Chakravorty Spivak
Judith Squires
Valerie Walkerdine

New Formations is published
three times a year by
Lawrence & Wishart
99a Wallis Road, London E9 5LN
Tel: 020-8533 2506
Fax: 020-8533 7369
Website:www.l-w-bks.co.uk/
formation.html

ADVERTISEMENTS:
For enquiries/bookings contact Va
Lawrence & Wishart

SUBSCRIPTIONS:
UK: Institutions £120, Individuals £40.
Rest of world: Institutions £120; Individuals £40.
Single copies: £14.99 plus £1 post and packing
Back issues: £14.99 plus £1 post and packing for
individuals; £34.99 plus £1 post and packing for
institutions

CONTRIBUTIONS AND CORRESPONDENCE:
Send to: The Editor, *new formations*
European Studies Research Institute
University of Salford, Salford M5 4WT
s.mccracken@salford.ac.uk

BOOKS FOR REVIEW:
Send to: Timothy Bewes
Reviews Editor, *new formations*
12 Weymouth Street, London WIW 5BY
timothy.bewes@btinternet.com

new formations publishes themed issues, themed sections
and discrete articles. Contributors are encouraged to
contact the editor to discuss their ideas and to obtain a
copy of our style sheet, which can also be obtained on
our website at http://www.l-w-bks.co.uk/style.html

Manuscripts should be sent in triplicate; experts in the
relevant field will referee them anonymously. The
manuscripts will not be returned unless a stamped, self-
addressed envelope is enclosed. Contributors should
note that the editorial board cannot take responsibility
for any manuscript submitted to *new formations*.

ISSN   0 950 237 8
ISBN   0 85315 96 02

Text design and setting by Art Services, Norwich
Printed in Great Britain at the University Press,
Cambridge.

NOTES ON CONTRIBUTORS

Bob Bennett has taught - and danced - in the US and Nigeria, and currently lectures in Communication, Culture and Media at Coventry University where he leads modules on Dance in Everyday Life, The Body, and Trans/gressions.

Tony Bennett is Professor of Sociology at the Open University. His recent publications include *Culture: A Reformer's Science* (1998) and (with M. Emmison and J. Frow) *Accounting for Tastes: Australian Everyday Cultures* (2000). He is also co-editor of *Culture in Australia: Policies, Publics, Programmes* (2001) and of *Understanding Everyday Life* (2001).

Clare Birchall is Tutorial Fellow in Media Studies at Sussex University. She recently completed her DPhil thesis, a poststructuralist reading of conspiracy theory, from which she has published several articles. Her next work will be concerned with the accidental in television, under the working title *Is this still TV?*

Fred Botting is Professor of English at the University of Keele. He has published *Making Monstrous, Gothic,* and *Sex, Machines, and Navels*. With Scott Wilson he has written *Holy Shit: The Tarantinian Ethics, Bataille* and co-edited *Georges Bataille: A Reader* and *Georges Bataille: A Critical Reader.*

Patrick Brantlinger is Rudy Professor of English and Victorian Studies at Indiana University. His most recent books are *The Reading Lesson: The Threat of Mass Literacy in Nineteenth-Century British Fiction* (1998) and *Who Killed Shakespeare? What's Happened to English Since the Radical Sixties* (2001).

Carolyn Burdett is Principal Lecturer in English at the University of North London. Her book *Olive Schreiner and the Progress of Feminism: Evolution, Gender, Empire* was published in 2001.

David Cunningham teaches English Literature at the University of Westminster. He has been a guest editor of the *Journal of Architecture* and has published previously on Beckett, Adorno and the neo-avant-garde. He is currently co-editing a collection of essays on post-war avant-garde movements.

Grant Farred is an Assistant Professor in the Literature Programme at Duke University. He is editor of *Rethinking C.L.R. James* (Basil Blackwell, 1996), and author of *Midfielder's Moment: Coloured Literature and Culture in Contemporary South Africa* (Westview, 1999) and of *What's My Name? Vernacular* (forthcoming, University of Minnesota Press, 2002).

Jeremy Gilbert teaches Cultural Studies and Media Studies at the University of East London, and sits on the editorial board of *new formations*. He is the co-author of *Discographies: Dance Music, Culture and the Politics of Sound* (Routledge, 1999), and co-editor of *Cultural Capitalism: Politics After New Labour* (Lawrence & Wishart 2001).

Raiford Guins is Visiting Assistant Professor of Film Studies at the University of California, Irvine, and US Principal Editor for the *journal of visual culture*.

Kate Ince is Senior Lecturer in French Studies at the University of Birmingham. She has published widely on French literary and theoretical writing and feminist criticism and theory, and written a study of Orlan, *Orlan, millennial female* (Berg, 2000). She is now working on French cinema.

Suhail Malik writes on visual arts, life sciences and philosophy and teaches in the Department of Visual Arts, Goldsmiths College, University of London.

Mandy Merck is Professor of Media Arts at Royal Holloway, University of London. Her most recent book is *In Your Face: Nine Sexual Studies* (NYU 2000). Her next publication will be the editorial collection *The Art of Tracey Emin* (Thomas & Hudson, 2002).

Joanne Morra is Senior Lecturer in Historical and Theoretical Studies at Central Saint Martins. She has published on Bruegel and translation, contemporary art and critical theory, and is a Founder of the cultural theory journal *parallax* and the Principal Editor of the new *journal of visual culture*. With Marquard Smith, she is the Guest Editor of this themed issue of *new formations*.

Andrew Patrizio is Director of Research in the Faculty of Art & Design, Edinburgh College of Art, from where he edits *292: Essays in Visual Culture*. He is Associate Curator at the Laing Art Gallery, Newcastle and is writing a book on artist Stefan Gec for Black Dog Publishing.

Aura Satz is an artist completing a PhD at the Slade School of Fine Art. She teaches part-time at the Slade and History of Art at UCL, and contributes to *Tema Celeste, NY Arts Magazine* and *EDGE*. She recently devised 'The Ubermarionette', an installation-performance of live puppets and prosthetic/phantom limbs.

Marquard Smith teaches in the School of History of Art, Film and Visual Media at Birkbeck College, University of London and is Visiting Curator/Research Fellow for the Osteogenesis Collection at the Science Museum in London. He is a Founder of the journal *parallax*, a Founder and the Editor-in-Chief of the *journal of visual culture*, and co-editor of *the limits of death*. With Joanne Morra, he is the guest editor of this themed issue of *new formations*.

Bernard Stiegler is Director of Research at the Institut National de L'Audiovisuel, Paris. The first half of his two volume *la technique et le temps* has been published by Stanford as *Technics and Time I*. His is also the author (with Jacques Derrida) of *Echographics of Television*.

Scott Wilson is Director of the Institute of Cultural Research, University of Lancaster, and a Managing Editor of the journal *Cultural Values*. His publications include *Cultural Materialism*, and, as co-editor, *Diana: The Making of a Media Saint*. With Fred Botting, he has written *Holy Shit: The Tarantinian Ethics, Bataille*, and co-edited *Georges Bataille: A Reader* and *Georges Bataille: A Critical Reader.*

CONTENTS
NUMBER 46 SPRING 2002

The Prosthetic Aesthetic

THE PROSTHETIC AESTHETIC

Marquard Smith and Joanne Morra

In considering the bonds between modernity, technology and the body, there is no better place from which to begin than from the figure of prosthesis. This themed issue of *new formations* brings together a series of articles that approach and question prosthesis in general, and do so specifically in relation to aesthetics. Hence the convergence that is our title, 'The Prosthetic Aesthetic'. Implicitly engaging with the etymological derivations of each concept, the aesthetic and the prosthetic, these articles re-articulate the ways in which we 'perceive' (Greek *aisthetikos*) the 'place' (Greek *prosthesis* from *prostithemi*) of the prosthetic within the culture of modernity. Building on work carried out across the Humanities and Social Sciences over the last ten years or so, these texts extend our thinking on the relationship between aesthetics, the body, and technology as an a priori prosthetic one.

This past decade has witnessed the emergence and dissemination of discussions around prosthesis as an historical, philosophical, technological, political, ethical, and medical concern. The subject of prosthesis has been raised in the discourses of cultural history, critical theory, philosophy, literature, cyberculture, and the visual arts.[1] There is also a large body of knowledge that has contributed to debates surrounding prosthetics, while not necessarily being on prosthetics as such. 'The Prosthetic Aesthetic' places itself squarely within this literature and at the same time offers something in addition to it. For while there is a great deal of writing on prosthetics and its associated concerns, this is one of the first collections to examine the confluence of the body, technology and prosthetics in an aesthetic and visual forum. As such this issue considers various aspects of visual culture including ornamentation, drawing, photography, body tracing, performance, theatre, body art, sculpture, installation art, television, video, and (digital) film. The modalities of these visual media are examined through the discourses of philosophy, psychoanalysis, media studies, history, feminist theory, art history, critical theory, and medicine as a means of unpacking certain types of consequences borne of prosthesis. Instances of these prosthetic concerns that are presented here include the issues of consciousness, compositing, the organic versus the machinic, the post-human, autobiography, indexicality, desire, the Other, the phenomenon of the phantom limb, deficiency, puppetry, and gestation.

Together, these articles are concerned with the visual and aesthetic aspect of prosthetics as a means of contributing to an understanding of the problems, challenges, and possibilities that prosthetics has to offer visual culture, and the ways in which visual culture - as a resolutely prosthetic concern - can offer new ways of understanding the formation

1. See for instance work by Parveen Adams, Tim Armstrong, Lisa Cartwright, Howard Caygill, Mark Dery, Sander L. Gilman, Elizabeth Haiken, Sarah Kember, Celia Lury, David T. Mitchell and Sharon L. Snyder, Sadie Plant, Vivian Sobchack, Bernard Stiegler, Allucquère Rosanne Stone, Rosemarie Garland-Thomson, Mark Wigley, David Wills, and writings in the journal *Technema: Journal of Philosophy and Technology*.

and function of prosthesis.

A number of the articles published here were presented in one form or another at a conference we organised at the Institute of Contemporary Arts, London, in April 2000 entitled 'Between Bodies and Machines: The Prosthetic'. Thanks go to Heidi Reitmaier, then Head of Talks at the ICA for being such a great host and to Barry Curtis at Middlesex University for its financial support of this event. Thanks also go to Jeremy Gilbert and Scott McCracken at *new formations* for their presence, both real and spectral, during that event and to *new formations* for their encouragement of and patience with this project. Special thanks go to the speakers at the ICA event and to all the contributors in 'The Prosthetic Aesthetic'.

November 2001, London

Transcendental Imagination in a Thousand Points

Bernard Stiegler

Horkheimer and Adorno saw in Hollywood cinema, joined to radio and magazines, the risk of an actual catastrophe for human spirit, caused by an apparatus of alienation whereby 'Automobiles, bombs, and movies keep the whole thing together',[1] an aesthetic barbarity 'subordinating in the same way and to the same end all areas of intellectual creation, by occupying men's senses from the time they leave the factory in the evening to the time they clock in again the next morning'.[2]

How would these philosophers, who were already hard put to imagine the impact of the then recent invention of television, have described the life of the worker, or the worker on the dole, who in France today spends almost four hours watching television? And how would they have reacted to the advent of digital networks? Given the irrefutable fact that in the not too distant future these networks will affect profoundly the whole spectrum of the mass media and especially television, incorporating it into a new system they would undoubtedly have described as a world-wide apparatus of 'alienation' whereby television becomes tele-action in the wake of a tele-society marching unhindered toward the 'market society' so preoccupying to European social-democrats.

1. Theodor Adorno and Max Horkheimer, *Dialectic of Enlightenment*, John Cumming (trans), London, Verso, [1944] 1979, p121.

2. Ibid., p131.

***

A few years ago, I wrote the following on the irreducible materiality of the image:

> The image in general does not exist. What we call the mental image, along with what I am going to call here the image-object, something always found in a story and inscribed in a technical history, are two sides of the same phenomenon that can no more be separated from each other than the signified and the signifier, which used to define the linguistic sign. Jacques Derrida's critique of the opposition of these two concepts - the postulating of the signifier as a contingent variation of an ideal invariant - is beyond challenge. Just as there is no 'transcendental signification', there is no mental image in general, no 'transcendental imagery' existing prior to the image-object. There remains the question of the transcendental imagination, which I will not take up here.

Now is the proper time to address this question of transcendental imagination.

The undeniable difference - which is not, however, the same thing as an antithesis - between mental image and image-object, means that they are always involved with one another, neither being able to diminish the other's inherent difference. The most immediately obvious difference is that what is objective is lasting, while what is mental is ephemeral. Likewise a memory-object is lasting ... while a 'mental' memory is remorselessly, rapidly, effaced: living, lived memory is fundamentally unstable and always leaves us in a lurch. Death is nothing other than the total wiping out of memory.[3]

3. B. Stiegler, 'L'image discrète', in J. Derrida and B. Stiegler, *Echographie de la télévision*, Paris, Galilée, 1996.

From the thesis positing *retentional finitude* as the principle of all philosophical analysis, I derived, in the first two volumes of *Technics and Time*, the concepts of epiphylogenesis and tertiary memory.[4] I set out to show that when Heidegger, in his critique of the Husserlian view of time, which nevertheless informs his own view, posits that 'the being we ourselves are' is always an heir, is always preceded by a factical already-there, by a past it has not experienced and which therefore is not its own, but which must become its own past (for such is time - see *Being and Time* §6) the consequence, which is not acknowledged in *Being and Time*, is that *beyond the primary and secondary retentions analysed by Husserl, there have to be tertiary retentions*, that is to say, technical traces able to make this factical past accessible to *Dasein* as a past which is not its own, which it has not lived, and which nevertheless must become its own, which it must inherit as its own history. Such is historiality (*Geschichtlichkeit*).

4. B. Stiegler, *Technics and Time 1: The Fault of Epimetheus*, Stanford, Meridian, 1998; B. Stiegler, *La Téchnique et Le Temps: La Désorientation*, Paris, Galilée, 1994.

What I call tertiary memory, Heidegger always called *Weltgeschichtlichkeit*. He did not, however, allow it to belong to the originary sphere of 'authentic' temporality, even though this question is at the heart of the Kantian mysteries surrounding the question of the transcendental imagination.

***

'Culture' and 'spirit' only begin with the fact of technics. This point of view will have serious consequences during the critique I will undertake of Horkheimer and Adorno's concept of cultural industry.

Our two philosophers characterise this concept in reference to what Kant calls the schematism of the pure concepts of understanding.[5] Kantism distinguishes two sources from which is deduced the possibility of knowledge for the human subject: sensibility and understanding. Schematism, conducted by the imagination, is what allows sensibility and understanding to unite, which is to say, in the same stroke, that which allows for the unity of consciousness itself. Now, since cultural industries are industries of the imagination, Horkheimer and Adorno depict the industrialisation of the imagination in terms of an industrial exteriorisation of the power to schematise, and by the very fact, in terms of a reification, an alienating becoming-object (*chosification*) of knowing consciousness:

5. In the first chapter of the 'Analytic of Principles', in *Critique of Pure Reason*, Norman Kemp Smith (trans), New York, Macmillan, 1965, p177.

Industry has deprived the individual of his function. The first service offered to industry's customer is to schematize everything for him. According to Kant, a secret mechanism operating in the depths of the soul prepares immediate givens so that they may adapt to the system of pure reason. Today, the secret has been divulged.[6]

6. Adorno and Horkheimer, *Dialectic of Enlightenment*, op. cit.

The unifying function of the imagination would thus be, after a fashion, short-circuited, eliminated by an industrialisation of culture literally numbing its customer-subjects, and alienating in the most radical of ways the free subject of reason, which it would in fact enslave. Hence the general 'marketing' of cultural commodities would necessarily be the unleashing of the most irrational elements of the society: the most irrational, the least cultural and the most unreasonable: the most *barbarian*.

Horkheimer and Adorno thus accuse cinema of paralysing the imagination and more broadly the discernment of the spectator to such a degree that he or she is no longer capable of distinguishing perception and imagination, reality and fiction. Their discourse at this point could readily be applied to the domain of virtual reality and electronic games:

The more cultural industry succeeds through its techniques in rendering reasonably accurate likenesses of real objects, the easier it is to have people believe that the exterior world is but the sheer extension of the one discovered on film. The sudden introduction of sound has completely subordinated the process of industrial reproduction to the pursuit of this goal. Real life should not be able to be distinguished from film.

***

Granting this, there remains the obligation of explaining why and how consciousness can to this extent be intimately transpierced and controlled by the unwinding of a film, and what truth of consciousness and 'real life' is then revealed through cinema. A film is a temporal object, in the Husserlian sense of the term. It is with a critical analysis of the Husserlian theory of time that an account can be given of the power of cinema over consciousness.

The analysis of a melody as temporal object will enable us to understand the operation of the consciousness of this melody, to the extent that this consciousness is itself a temporal flux. Husserl discovers within this flux *primary retention*: in the 'now' of a melody, in the present moment of a musical object that flows away, Husserl shows how the present note can be a note, and not just a sound or a noise, only inasmuch as it retains in itself the preceding note which remains present in it, and which in turn has retained in itself the preceding one, and so on.

This *primary retention*, which belongs to the present of perception, must not be confused with *secondary retention*, which would be for example the melody I heard yesterday, and which I can hear again in imagination by the play of memory, and which thus constitutes the past of my consciousness.

Husserl, before Adorno and Horkheimer, says perception and imagination are not to be confused.

And he is right. With this distinction between primary and secondary retention, Husserl makes a crucial discovery. But this distinction soon becomes an opposition: primary retention will have nothing to do with secondary retention. Now, it is obvious that the fact of having heard a melody, whose memory is conserved by secondary retention, modifies the conditions of the flowing away of this same melody on a second audition of the same interpretation. The primary retentions are in this case retained by consciousness following criteria of selection which obviously depend on the secondary retentions of temporal objects previously perceived by the same consciousness. Were this not the case I would always hear the same thing at each audition.

Husserl absolutely refuses to envisage a composition of primary and secondary retentions, and he will, therefore, oppose them. Secondary retentions stem from the imagination, while primary retentions are part and parcel of perception: were Husserl to admit a surdetermination of the latter by the former, he would have to admit that perception is always haunted by imagination and, in this sense, inhabited by fictional reality. Husserl must rule out the possibility that perception, only be cinematographic, and that the perceived is nothing other than the screen of this film. He therefore excludes a fortiori from his analyses what I have called tertiary retention, and in particular the phonogram.

Tertiary retention is this prosthesis of consciousness without which there would be no spirit, no haunting return, no memory of unlived or non-lived past, no culture. The phonogram is such a prosthesis, but of a remarkably singular kind, in that, as a recording of a trace in an object (here an analog recording), it in turn obviously overdetermines the articulation of primary and secondary retentions.

More generally, the technical history of tertiary memories (that is, in the final analysis, the history of the *Weltgeschichtlichkeit*) overdetermines the human history of primary and secondary memories. Thus, it is only from the technical possibility of the analog recording of a melody, dating from the invention by Thomas Edison and Charles Cros of the phonograph, that it is possible for the same consciousness to listen twice to the same melody, in the same interpretation - to have twice over the experience of the same temporal object, and in the same stroke to realise that the same temporal object repeated twice gives up two different experiences and thus, by this very fact, to be able to state that the play of primary retentions, that is, the phenomenon itself, is each time a different one despite the identity of the object retained, and that repetition, therefore, always yields up a difference.

The experience of such an identical repetition of a temporal object only becomes possible, for the first time in the history of humanity, with the invention of Cros and Edison: their phonograph profoundly transformed the play of memory, imagination and consciousness. This transformation continues with cinema, then with television and the *Kulturindustrie* in general - exteriorising and reifying in the same stroke the work of a supposedly 'transcendental' imagination.

How was that *possible*?

***

In the 'Transcendental Analytic' of the *Critique of Pure Reason*, Kant sorts out three different syntheses: of apprehension, reproduction, and recognition.[7] I will now show how closely linked they are to primary, secondary and tertiary retentions, and how the role played by tertiary retentions (in the constitution of consciousness, a role unacknowledged by Kant) is responsible for the power of cultural industries to 'schematise everything for their customers'.

7. Kant, *Critique of Pure Reason*, op. cit., pp129-151.

My basic thesis on the 'Transcendental Analytic' comprises two complementary arguments: The passage from the 1781 edition, version A, to that of 1787, version B; bears witness to Kant's failure to articulate the three syntheses of imagination set out in A, and repeated in B, onto the transcendental unity of apperception (with imagination slipped into a subsidiary position, and the understanding regaining its absolute authority). What is neither thought out or clearly expressed in A (no more so than in B, but in the later case the problem is solved by regressing from the level of A so as to eliminate the contradiction), is the difference holding between primary and secondary retentions (later delineated by Husserl). Kant systematically amalgamates them, as the syntheses of apprehension and reproduction.

The 'spontaneity of the understanding' is the principle of a 'triple "synthesis"':

> For knowledge is (essentially) a whole in which representations stand compared and connected ... A synthesis must always correspond to a synopsis; receptivity can make knowledge possible only when combined with spontaneity. Now this spontaneity is the ground of a threefold synthesis which must necessarily be found in all knowledge; namely, the apprehension of representations as modifications of the mind in intuition, their reproduction in imagination, and their recognition in a concept. These point to three subjective sources of knowledge, which make possible the understanding itself - and consequently all experience.[8]

8. Ibid., pp130-31.

The question of this threefold synthesis, and in the first place of the first synthesis, that of apprehension, is the question of time: if the manifold of intuition is to be ordered, the reason is that all our representations 'belong to inner sense', 'all our knowledge is thus finally subject to time, the formal condition of inner sense. In it they must all be ordered, connected, and brought into relation'.[9] This is why, within the manifold, intuition must

9. Ibid., p131.

'distinguish time in the series of impressions'. This distinction of temporal succession, at the heart of the intuition of any phenomena whatsoever, is the work and the accomplishment of the synthesis of apprehension.

Next Kant specifies the definition of the synthesis of reproduction: 'Representations which have often followed or accompanied one another finally become associated, and so are set in a relation whereby, even in the absence of the object, one of these representations can, in accordance with a fixed rule, bring about a transition of the mind to the other'.[10]

10. Ibid., p132.

What Kant is describing here is what Husserl analysed as *secondary retention*. Now, at the end of this paragraph, Kant's problem arises: he confounds this capacity of reproduction with that of primary retention. As a result, he must posit that the synthesis of reproduction is retention in apprehension itself:

> But if I were always to drop out of thought the preceding representations (the first parts of the line, the antecedent parts of the time period, or the units in the order represented), and did not reproduce them while advancing to those that follow, a complete representation would never be obtained ... not even the purest and most elementary representations of space and time could arise.[11]

11. Ibid., p133.

In other words, Kant makes that very mistake Husserl will accuse Brentano of making. Kant is obviously referring to primary retentions whereas he believes he is describing the synthesis of reproduction, as that which renders apprehension possible: 'the synthesis of apprehension is thus inseparably bound up with the synthesis of reproduction'. Kant thinks he is describing the synthesis of reproduction exactly when it is apprehension at stake, as the phenomenon of primary retentions, which quite precisely must not be confused with secondary retentions constitutive of the essence of the synthesis of reproduction.

Kant confuses two forms of retention, that is, two forms of synthesis. Now, it is precisely this confusion, occurring in 1781, that makes the exposition so unclear, obliging him to rework the transcendental deduction. Indeed, it is not clear exactly what is meant, in 1781, by the synthesis of apprehension. What else can the obligation that the manifold 'must first be run through' represent (for this is yet another definition of the synthesis of apprehension) if not the *retention of that which is run through by that which is now running through the manifold*? The only way Kant could clearly distinguish between this and a secondary retention (a reproduction in the 'absence of the object', which he also defines as the synthesis of reproduction) would be if he could consider the first synthesis as the *conversation of the already past in the still present* and as the *protention of that which is still to come*.

Now intervenes the third synthesis, that of 'recognition': 'For in so far as (our modes of knowledge) are to relate to an object, they must necessarily agree with one another, that is, must possess that unity which constitutes the concept of an object'.[12] The synthesis of recognition establishes and maintains the coherence of consciousness with itself in so far as it is a flux, and a flux whose unity is to be guaranteed: this flux cannot contradict itself. This unification of the flux overdetermines as synthesis of recognition the unification of the syntheses of apprehension and reproduction whereby an object can be presented to consciousness by the simple fact of the recognitional unification of the flux of consciousness: 'It is clear that ... the unity which the object makes necessary can be nothing else than the formal unity of consciousness in the synthesis of the manifold of representations. It is only when we have thus produced synthetic unity in the manifold of intuition that we are in a position to say that we know the object'.[13] This unification of consciousness with itself, through its objects, is the projection of apperception that Kant calls transcendental in so far as it corresponds to the a priori necessity expressed by a rule (a concept):

12. Ibid., pp134-35.

13. Ibid., p135.

> But this unity is impossible if the intuition cannot be generated in accordance with a rule by means of such a function of synthesis as makes the reproduction of the manifold a priori necessary, and renders possible a concept in which it is united ... This unity of rule determines all the manifold, and limits it to conditions which make unity of apperception possible ... But a concept can be a rule for intuitions only in so far as it represents in any given appearances the necessary reproduction of their manifold, and thereby the synthetic unity in our consciousness of them.[14*]

14. Ibid.

In short, the transcendental unity of consciousness is also that of its objects, and therefore, that of the unity of the world in general. The concept unifies the diversity of what is re-produced in the empirical realm as its essence and its necessity, but only in so far as the latter are pro-duced by the concept. From out of the re-production of the past manifold, the concept abstracts its still to come unity: re-production is at a more profound level pro-duction because the concept implements the a priori legality of the temporal flux constituted by the categories. This is the way in which this recognitional unification, which is also that of the very flux of consciousness, prepares, on the basis of a reproducible past, the unitary future of the flux and the objects constituted therein.

But why affirm at this point the necessity of what I have called tertiary memory? Are Kant's three syntheses indeed the translation, in the total phenomenon of consciousness, of Husserl's three retentional forms, and the translation of what necessarily binds them into one? I will now address these questions.

**

The first two syntheses owe their unity to the third synthesis of 'recognition', which inserts the first two forms of synthesis, that is, the first two retentional forms, into the unified flux of consciousness, a unity that Kant calls the *unity of apperception*. In other words, the third synthesis is in charge of the *compatibility* of all primary and secondary retentions constitutive of the warp and woof of consciousness *qua* always the same consciousness, however diverse the primary and secondary streaming through it, giving it form and imparting to it its principle of becoming. The third synthesis aggregates and edits the first two (which in some respects can be considered rushes and inserts) into one united temporal flow. This process is constitutive of what may be called the cinema of consciousness, projecting - being already protracted - toward the future.[15]

15. See Jean-Luc Godard, *Introduction à une véritable histoire du cinéma*, Vol.1, Paris, Albatros, 1980, p145.

Now can anyone possibly not see that as the flux of Kant's own consciousness - which of course he uses as the object and model of the activity of any consciousness - unfolds it becomes constituted in its unity in the course of the writing of those works that make up his work? How can one possibly not see that 1) this unity is not given, but is promised, and 2) the force of the work lies in its *materialised* unification of the elements of consciousness constituted by the *literal* tertiary retentions of this work, and 3) that 'Kant' is only the name of the work's *author*, the rest being of small importance? Such a situation, giving rise to Kant's authority, is possible only because the primary and secondary syntheses of imagination are essentially synthesizable by this flux (of consciousness) of syntheses that make up the 'objective' memory of a book, or film.

There are two versions of the *Critique of Pure Reason* - two write-ups, that is, two archives or syntheses of the history of the consciousness of Kant himself, and through it, of *the history of philosophical consciousness* - the first of which is published in 1781, and the second in 1787, each with a distinct preface, and significant modifications of the 'Transcendental Analytic' taking place in the second edition, especially in the section 'Transcendental Deduction of the Concepts of the Understanding'. Now, what does the second preface tell us about what to make of the first write-up modified by this second edition/write-up? To recap drastically, we are told that the *second edition changes nothing in the first*, except that the former is more explicit, and that consequently, the first edition remains completely valid despite the differences in write-ups. More precisely, the preface tells us that this second edition has tried out some 'corrections': 'These improvements involve, however, a small loss, not to be prevented save my making the book too voluminous, namely, that I have had to omit or abridge certain passages, which, though not indeed essential to the completeness of the whole, may yet be missed by many readers as otherwise helpful'.[16]

16. Kant, *Critique of Pure Reason*, op. cit., p35.

How surprising these statements seem when one remembers the profound contradiction between the two editions of the *Critique*! Now, these contradictions, concerning the role of the third synthesis and that of the imagination, are indeed the sign of a problem Kant has with the problem of contradiction - the contradiction of the self with itself, which is the very temporality of the self, what Deleuze called its 'chasm'. Yet the preface to the second edition rolls on tranquilly, explaining that 'The (now) more intelligible exposition, which, though altering absolutely nothing in the fundamentals of the propositions put forward or even in their proofs, yet here and there departs so far from the *previous method of treatment*, that mere interpolations could not be made to suffice'.[17]

17. Ibid.

The two editions thus do differ considerably, 'here and there', but this is simply a formal discrepancy: nothing fundamental is affected. This seems so true that Kant's editors published both editions in one, as is still done today in most modern translations, and Kant suggests as much: 'This loss, which is small and can be remedied by consulting the first edition, will, I hope, be compensated by the greater clearness of the new text'.[18]

18. Ibid.

In short, there are deep, serious contradictions between the 1781 and 1787 editions, but Kant insists on maintaining at all costs the unity of the flux of his own consciousness in the course of the passage of these six years. What else happened than the simple passage of time? During the passage, events took place, and especially a public critique of the *Critique*, which would oblige Kant to rework it,[19] that is, to rewrite the history of his own flow of consciousness 'before the reading public'.

19. The second edition is the opportunity for Kant 'to remove, wherever possible, difficulties and obscurities which, not perhaps without my fault, may have given rise to the many misunderstandings into which even acute thinkers have fallen in passing judgment upon my book', ibid., p33.

Consciousness can only become self-consciousness providing it is able to exteriorise itself, to become objective in the form of trances whereby it becomes accessible to other consciousnesses. Although Kant, no more so than Husserl, resorts to some sort of tertiary retention, it is obvious that the *literal recording* of Kant's flux of consciousness, in so far as it leads to the writing of the *Critique of Pure Reason*, is the essential condition of the analysis of the activity of consciousness the work aims to be. The thought of Kant can only present itself to us in the form of a book - or to himself for that matter, except that in his case the presentation developed in the very course of its writing, its editing - before him: on the screen of the sheet of paper *qua* support of his thought, a true *crutch of the understanding*.

That is why, in 1996, I placed the following sentence from Kant as the epigraph to my work *Technics and Time: Disorientation*: 'I mean by the public use of our own reason that which is done as expert before the general reading public',[20] that is, obviously, to the extent that one writes oneself. We know that Kant never wrote a line by chance: he cannot set and identify the unity of apperception of the consciousness he is otherwise than through the possibility of inscribing, conserving and ordering the primary and secondary retentions (that is, the syntheses of apprehension and reproduction) effected by the imagination of his forgetful consciousness (whose memory is finite[21]), in the form of tertiary etentions (the written sentences whereby *The Critique of Pure Reason* takes shape). Inscribed, set down, conserved, these sentences can be reread, criticised, analysed, objectified, selected, and put together in new combinations. Conserving, discerning, comparing and finally editing in the unity of a book which is also the unity of his thought, that is what Kant can do with these sentences in so far as they are the objective materialisations of his primary and secondary retentions, which can thus be

20. Stiegler, *Techniques and Time*, op. cit.

21. Just as the intuition of the human subject is finite, that is, only passive, unlike God, whose intuition is productive and whose memory, in Leibniz, is infinite.

22. Conservation, comparison and discernment are exactly the fundamental functions of imagination as Kant lists them in the *Anthropology*. But reference should be made also to the Husserlian analyses of the role of writing in the constitution of mathematical ideality, which I comment upon in *Désorientation*, op. cit.

23. The expression is used by Leibniz in reference to the advantages of writing.

24. Kant, *Anthropology*, op. cit., p149.

25. Including today, with the analog and digital technologies of live productions and real time, this immediate past of what past as media event, that I did not live, and that nevertheless inserts itself in the presentness of my present. See here *Désorientation* op. cit..

manipulated.[22]

From 1781 to 1787; Kant has all the time he needs[23] to re-examine the past flux of his own consciousness, and to seek the persevering unity of the flux of his consciousness to come, to the extent that he was able to set down, identify and unite the manifold of his thought by materialising it. He thus becomes the object of himself, and can thus become the object of a re-flexive critique by which he can affect himself: he can thus and only thus proceed to the examination of the conditions of his own possibility which are also the conditions of possibility of all his objects. These are the very conditions whose 'most extreme possibility' Heidegger would accuse Kant of neglecting.

Critique analyses and synthesises. But this is only possible because critique can manipulate, and here, manipulate time, that is, the play of primary and secondary retentions through their tertiary materialisations. Now these critical materialisations of inner sense are just as susceptible of being manipulated by the culture industry given that, for it, the consciousness of people is its raw material, objectifiable and reifiable because originarily outside of itself. And this is why a critique is again necessary. In other words, Kant can and must write that all phenomena are in me, that is, 'are determinations of my identical self ... only another way of saying that there must be a complete unity of them in one and the same apperception'.[24] The self is in the middle of 'itself', that is, in the middle of its objects and prostheses, a milieu which, by the same token, is not only itself, but its other. And this other precedes it, it is an already-there, a past the self has not experienced,[25] and which can become its past only by becoming its future. This structure of prosthetic precedence, founding the possibility of tertiary memory and memories, is the projective support of consciousness. It is what allows all consciousnesses which have preceded it to inherit its past - witness ourselves here: as the reading public of Kant's works - it is also what allows for the projection of a future. This is what we shall explore now in a study of the question of schematism, which will bring up the question of version B of the 'Transcendental Deduction'.

***

In order for intuitions to be subsumed under concepts, during the synthesis of recognition,

> There must be some third thing, which is homogenous on the one hand
> with the category, and on the other hand with the appearance ... such a
> representation is the transcendental schema ... pure a priori concepts
> ... must contain a priori certain formal conditions of sensibility ... which
> constitute the universal condition under which alone the category can
> be applied to any object.[26]

26. Ibid., pp181-82.

'This condition ... is the schema of the concept ... Since, however, the synthesis of imagination aims at no special intuition, but only at unity in the determination of sensibility, the schema has to be distinguished from the image. If five points be set alongside one another, thus, ..., I have an image of the number five' or 5, or V. This image is empirical and therefore contingent (since the number can be represented by any of these images) and is thus something altogether different from the fact of thinking this number. Such a thought is 'the representation of a method whereby a multiplicity, for instance a thousand, may be represented in an image in conformity with a certain concept, rather than the image itself. For with such a number as a thousand the image can hardly be surveyed and compared with the concept'.[27]

27. Ibid.

Indeed, it is not blatantly obvious that in the following *figure* there are a thousand (1000) dots:

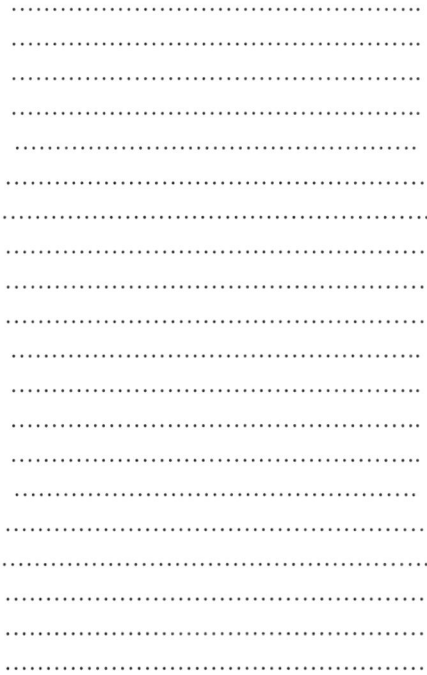

Although the Greek for this figure is *skhema*, it is not a schema in the Kantian sense, but only an image. But then why would the geometric figure, originally image and trace (*graphein*) be called, in Greek, *skhema*? And to what extent is a number like a thousand possible, as a method in conformity with 'a certain concept' for the consciousness of which it is the object, without an image?

The answer is to no extent whatsoever straightforward. The number supposes, in fact always, some sort of tertiary retention (whether the case be that of the fingers of a counting child, the body of a witch, an abacus or a system of alphanumerical writing) which alone can allow numbering and objectifying. This capability has a history, in the course of which it one day becomes possible to conceive (in the course of a process) of the number 1000. There was a time, quite recent compared to the long history of humanity, when the number 1000 was literally inconceivable to the consciousness of mankind, not yet equipped to think it.

Kant can only speak of the number 1000 (or the figure/image image) because he has at his disposition technical and materialised systems of notation which allow for the manipulation of symbols and to set down by means of this image (resulting in the word 'thousand' which is itself an aural image) the result of an operation of the understanding consisting in the conjoined operation of internal and external sense.

The synchronisation of internal and external sense here conditions the activity of the understanding, which in the same stroke is submitted to the passive synthesis of its 'tools'. In fact, number in general can only be conceived providing it is figured in a system of traces called a system of numeration, which always refers to a gesture consisting itself in a manipulation of symbols whose nature is external - and there can be no mental arithmetic that does not result from the secondary interiorisation of a calculation by symbolic manipulations, that is, by manual behaviour.

'One never wearies of mentioning the first humans starting to count by awkwardly drawing stick figures on the sand of beaches and deserts', writes Geneviève Guitel.

> It is also possible to engage in an art consisting in the regular notching of a stick ... in order to conserve the memory of a number ... Each of these material translations of a number apply the principle of correspondance ... but ... the situation is altogether different when, for each sheep of the herd, a clay marble is placed in a receptacle ... or when an individual, relying on expressive mimicry, uses his body as a machine designed to retain the number of fish caught. In the first case we have an abstract image of a herd of sheep: one clay marble per head. There is no need here to know how to name the initial integers; this accounting can be done silently ... the receptacle can be placed in the archives of the superintendant, but he must know how to count whereas the shepherd is incapable.[28]

28. M.G. Guitel, *Histoire comparée des numérations écrites*, Paris, Flammario, 1975, pp19-20.

The conception of a number results from gestures implementing by their accomplishment a principle of correspondence. These gestures allow for the production of an image which is certainly abstract, but which is an image-abstract- object as support and condition of the projection of a mental abstract image. The conception of the number one thousand supposes written enumerations, a stage of abstraction coming out of the manipulations of symbols called 'written numeration of position' where it is clear that the schema supposes the image, even when the possibility of the image would suppose, in reciprocal fashion, the possibility of the schema - the possibility of schematisation in the sense Kant strives to give it, that is, as a process of projection of inner sense into the tertiary memories, that is, the images accessible to external sense.

Such reciprocity is called by Simondon a transductive relation, although the author criticises the hylomorphism of much Kantian thought.[29] It is necessary to distinguish the schema from the image, but nevertheless there is no manifestation of the schema without an image, mental or not. When Kant, in proposing an image for the integer five, traces five points on a line, inserting this sketch ..... into a sentence, he unfortunately forgets that the word five is already an image, hailing from a very old history.

I shall say once again today and henceforth in the name of the question of the transcendental imagination: there is no mental image without an image object. Like the image of the flock of sheep as an abstract representation materially constituted by a set of marbles, the first numbers as abstract entities are first of all very concrete memory supports: the flux of consciousness, in which the number constitutes a determination of internal sense, in which there follows one after the other units forming a totality which is numerable and synthesisable in the unity of apperception, that flux of consciousness is retentionally finite. As the memory of its own flowing away, it quickly fails and must rely on external supports, on prostheses of memory which would also be the fetishes of imagination and the projection screens of all its phantasms.[30] These retentional prostheses impart to the flux of consciousness (that is, to consciousness itself, for it is only flux) spatial intuitions of the flowing away of its temporal intuitions. This is why *ars memoria* are possible.

These spatial intuitions have the advantage of being able to be retained 'objectively' while allowing the flux to be *abbreviated*: it is possible to cursively read the 'number' depicted by the dots above, but such a reading would be long, and always subject to error, whereas in the written number 1000, an image has been substituted for the cursive operation of the unfolding of time; it has been abstracted from this unfolding to become its equivalent, once consciousness has engaged in long series of exercises - to begin with the one consisting of the counting of fingers.

It is this general equivalent whereby space gives figure to time that allows what Marx calls the 'general equivalent' of capital: money allowing for the accumulation of abstract value because it can be manipulated, such money is time. The tertiary memory, of which money is the most abstract form, allowing for abstraction based on the principle of correspondence, opens in the same stroke the systematic exploitation as system of spatial equivalences (the images of the numbers) of temporal operations (enumerations as fallible flowings away of the flux of consciousness).

***

But if I were always to drop out of thought the preceding representations (the first parts of the line, the antecedent parts of the time period, or the

29. Jacques Rivelaygue explains that the Kantian category is a 'relation which constitutes its terms': this is exactly the definition of Simondon's tranductive relation.

30. Such images, always in the process of fetishisation, are also hallucinatory images of the prosthetised living body supporting the flux of consciousness, the body of the other (the alter ego) and bodiliness as such.

31. Kant, op. cit., p133.

units in the order represented), and did not reproduce them while advancing to those that follow, a complete representation would never be obtained: none of the above-mentioned thoughts, not even the purest and most elementary representations of space and time, could arise.[31]

This is Kant describing primary retention, but he believes he is inside the synthesis of reproduction; he therefore does not see what secondary retention is: precisely not primary retention. I have shown why the retentional finitude of the flux of consciousness induces the necessity of a third form of retention whose consequence is here the following: if the *figured* synthesis, the *synthesis speciosa*, becomes in the 1787 edition the true synthesis of productive, not only reproductive imagination - that is, transcendental imagination - if therefore this synthesis is what enables a line to be mentally drawn to construct space, this faculty which is also the principle of geometric construction could never do without the line in space: without the hand.

32. 'A new light flashed upon the mind of the first man (be he Thales or some other) who demonstrated the properties of the isosceles triangle. The true method, so he found, was not to inspect what he discerned either in the figure, or in the bare concept of it, and from this, as it were, to read off its properties; but to bring out what was necessarily implied in the concept that he had himself formed a priori', ibid., p19.

Thales, whose revelatory experience is convoked in the 1787 preface, could never reason geometrically[32] without gestures depicting pure space, that is, the a priori conditions of empirical space, in this empirical space itself. If Thales constructs the figure, and is not content with simply following it, he constructs a figure without which there would be no concept. The construction of the concept is that of the figure and conversely - it is of course accompanied by discourse, but the discourse is itself inscribed letter by letter: the requirement that it be set down is all the more stringent given that the figure keeps in sensitive space the trace of a line of reasoning of pure space, that is, on the a priori conditions of the possibility of intuition. As was the case for numeration, there can be no possible thought without figurations which are also traces, gestures of thought as it must work through its inscriptions in space, which allow to uncover in the intuition of the empirical given a pure intuition of the formal conditions of this empirical intuition - which are, as we have underscored above, the crutches of the understanding, and not only of belief.[33]

33. For, as Kant wrote, there are crutches of belief - I take up this theme in a commentary on Derrida: *La fidélité aux limites de la déconstruction*, forthcoming from Cambridge University Press.

Pro-duction is a figuration and the second edition defines it as a figured synthesis (*synthesis speciosa*). If the figure were not essential here, not absolutely essential, then why qualify this synthesis as 'figured': why translate *speciosa* by *figurliche*? (To figure, to give figure to, is the meaning of the verb *skhematizo*). We are examining the question of the conditions of the constitution of the schema and the role played in it by the image. Kant posits that the schema precedes the image: I hold that they are co-emergent, that is, in a transductive relation. Image and schema are the two facets of an identical reality constitutive of an historical process conditioned by the epiphylogenetic structure which refers to the general system of tertiary memories forming the milieu of consciousness, its world as the spatialisation of the time of past and passing consciousnesses *qua Weltgeschichtlichkeit*.

Heidegger calls the third synthesis that of the future, that is, of the project. But this cannot be understood unless it is granted that the facticity of the past of *Dasein* is what opens up the very possibility of its future (in 'the most extreme possibility') because this past is originally tertiarised, that is, synthesizable as a prosthesis. A true critique of the *Critique of Pure Reason*, a 'new critique' if you will, must confront this question of originary exteriorisation. This is what makes inheritance possible. Heidegger sees in all linear conceptions of time, dominant in both versions of the *Critique of Pure Reason* the typical expression of metaphysics in general. But he does not see that the real problem with the third synthesis is here in so far as it supposes exteriorisation (*Weltgeschichtlichkeit*). This question is originarily linked to that of the protentional inachievement and inadequation of the flux with itself, and is the only place where something like sharp judgement and the risk of decision can occur. Because there is inadequation of consciousness to itself, and différance in the Derridean sense, there can be a process of individuation in the Simondonian sense. This inadequation occurs in the situation of inachievement in 'the most extreme possibility'.

As projective, the synthesis of recognition, holding together as it were, the past and the future of the flux, trying to make them compatible, if not sheerly adequation (barring which there would be no opening up to the future), compresses the whole stakes of the inadequation of the flux of consciousness of Kant with itself. This is why in the second edition, this projective apparatus is transformed into a simple agent of the understanding. A secret agent, hidden in the recesses of the soul.

When adequation becomes effective, there is no longer unachievement or inadequation. The individual then bequeaths this accomplished inadequation, as it were, to the posterity of his or her heirs - in the form of tertiary memories. From out of this tertiary inadequation, these memories attempt to open a future in the unachievement of all things, which never ceases to strive toward achievement ... through prostheses: the question of unachievement is precisely the question of prostheticity - always in the promise and yet in the adequation of an absolute future.[34]

34. See on this point *La fidélité aux limites de la déconstruction*.

***

The digital integration of the cultural industries through the convergence of the information, audiovisual and telecommunication technologies is the new framework of production and broadcast of 'tertiary retentions', and a new milieu for the spirit. In the course of the twentieth century, the milieu of the spirit has become that of an industrial exploitation of the times of consciousness. It is not a question of a monstrous evolution whereby 'schematism' would all of a sudden jump outside of consciousness: consciousness was never self consciousness other than by projecting itself outside itself. But in this era of information industries, and in particular analog and digital technologies making it possible, this exteriorised and materialised consciousness becomes the material for manipulations of flux and for projections of masses in such ways that a pure and simple annulment of 'self consciousness' by its exteriorisation not only becomes possible but would appear highly probable: this is what is to be thought in the homogenising synchronisation of the fluxes of consciousness by audiovisual temporal objects.

This synchronisation is also responsible for the manipulation of consciousnesses in the era of audiovisual, mass industrial temporal objects. The critique of this manipulation, in other words, cannot be a denunciation of a denaturing of consciousness by cinema - this is what allows cinema and television to maintain their control. Consequently, the critique of cinema and television as social phenomena capable of destroying consciousness itself (this is what I elsewhere have called the question of an ecology of spirit) calls for a new critique of consciousness itself, a redeployment of the Kantian endeavour.

The 'general equivalent' as the condition of the market in which, with the cultural industries, the time of consciousnesses has itself become a commodity, is conditioned by the general equivalence of primary-secondary time in its tertiary spatialisations, which can be manipulated, stocked, exchanged, and capitalised. In the industrial becoming of culture, consciousness itself is up for sale. This can always be decried as barbarian degeneracy, a monstrous state of affairs: but it is only the strict consequence of the finitude of fluxes of consciousness in general, of their originary prostheticity. Any struggle against this possibility implies its acknowledgement, that is, implies the conclusion of the preceding analyses: THERE IS NO SPIRIT WITHOUT AN OBJECTIVE RETENTIONAL MILIEU; THE HISTORY OF THIS MILIEU IS ALSO A HISTORY OF TECHNICS, THAT IS, TODAY, A HISTORY OF INDUSTRY. The future of the spirit cannot only consist in a geopolitics of cultural technologies that would also be an ecology of the spirit. A politics of consciousness (but what else is politics if not, preeminently, a politics of consciousness?) is necessarily a politics of technics.

Translated by Georges Collins

This paper, given at the ICA in London on April 15 2000, appears here in a slightly modified form.

From Senseless Acts of Violence to Seamless Acts of Visibility: 'Film Censorship' in the Age of Digital Compositing

Raiford Guins

The equipment-free aspect of reality here has become the height of artifice ... [1]

Walter Benjamin

REMEDIATING FILM CENSORSHIP

Since the late 1970s cinema has undergone a remediation. To consider the effects of new media on cinema is to cautiously conceive of a restructuring of the ways in which films have been made traditionally. Following Jay David Bolter and Richard Grusin's lead in *Remediation: Understanding New Media*, cinema now 'absorb[s] computer graphics into its traditional structure'.[2] That is, as their use of the term remediation suggests, film production, most notably Hollywood cinema, is currently being refashioned by computer 'centred' mediation in all aspects of production. Put in dramatically different terms, 'cinema becomes a slave to the computer' according to Lev Manovich.[3] Perhaps it is more accurate to state that the masters have simply designed more efficient shackles to control their property. Either way, the consequences for cinema remain the same: 'graphics, moving images, sounds, shapes, spaces, and texts become computable ... simply sets of computer data ... media become new media'.[4]

As a result of this refashioning, the expression 'digital cinema' has emerged as an umbrella phrase to cover the many technologies redefining cinema at present. It is important to acknowledge that digital cinema is neither a single apparatus, nor an inherently unified set of applications, but a broad way of identifying the numerous techniques, objects, software and programs, often independent of one another, resulting from the digitisation of existing media. Once data, or more specific to how we have conceived of traditional filmmaking, once live-action footage is converted into numerical data, it attains equal malleability to its counterpart non-photographed, computer generated images; and as converted and stored data the 'physical-reality' captured by a camera becomes easier to modify through a score of different computer programs. 'In digital filmmaking', Manovich explains, 'shot footage is no longer the final point but just raw material to be manipulated in a computer, where the real construction of a

1. Walter Benjamin, 'The Work of Art in the Age of Mechanical Reproduction', in Hannah Ardendt (ed), *Illuminations*, London, Fontana Press, 1992, p226.

2. Jay David Bolter and Richard Grusin, *Remediation: Understanding New Media*, Cambridge, Massachusetts, MIT, 2000, p147.

3. Lev Manovich, *The Language of New Media*, Cambridge, Massachusetts, MIT, 2001, p25.

4. Ibid.

5. Lev Manovich, 'What Is Digital Cinema?', in P. Lunenfeld (ed), *The Digital Dialectic: New Essays on New Media*, Cambridge, Massachusetts, 1999, p181.

scene will take place'.[5] While the subjects of new media and digital cinema, just to use an already common term, are vast and pose complex questions for representation and realism, as well as questions for the very identity of cinema, I would like to intentionally limit my interest and excitement for these subjects to inquire after the impact that digital image manipulation has had (and dare I suggest will have) on practices of film censorship. If cinema is in grave danger of losing its identity, the same loss perhaps applies to film censorship: an eroding term that no longer seems to adequately account for the policing and management of film content.

Digital image manipulation works through the techniques of processing and compositing. Processing (also known as sampling) involves the digitisation and storage of non-converted imagery. Compositing, the focus of this essay, includes the superimposition, movement, rearrangement, removal, repairing, cleaning, and smoothing of images in order to foster a 'seamless', continuous and believable product for mass consumption. For example, the stunt wires and harnesses that allowed *The Matrix*'s Trinity (Carrie-Anne Moss) to not only get the jump on her pursuers, but to create one of the most memorable as well as parodied scenes in recent cinema, is a highly polished indicator of digital compositing's ability to erase traces of the required equipment for orchestrating the actual stunt from the final image. Simply stated, special effects are made more believable once their apparatus is rendered invisible. In this instance, digital compositing serves the shot, the character's performance, and *The Matrix*'s narrative. In another instance, digital compositing makes it easier to modify data so that an MPAA (Motion Picture Association of America) rating can be achieved (usually an R instead of an NC-17)[6] without the disruptions in the continuity and

6. R= Under 17 requires parent or adult guardian; NC-17= no one 17 and under admitted.

integrity of a film's narrative that can result from poor editing. The inclusion of computer generated figures to block a particular shot of the orgy scene in Stanley Kubrick's *Eyes Wide Shut* (1999) is one such example of digital compositing being used to censor/classify, and is discussed later in this essay.

To begin assessing the impact of these changes, I would like to pose a question: *does the remediation of cinema insist upon a reconsideration of how film censorship operates through digital compositing?* Implicit within the proposed question is the general position that the censoring of films via digital image manipulation is radically different from the censoring operations exercised through an exclusively analog medium dependent upon the splicing together of celluloid strips to mask deleted frames. This position ought to function as a starting point from which to gauge the question; merely pointing to this difference does not begin to digest the full extent of this remediation. In fact, I would like to make good on this introduction's heading and offer this essay as an active work in progress, perhaps an aperitif for what all indications suggest will be an outstanding banquet of change. After all, our sweet tooth for new media has only begun to sense the possibilities and promises of digital cinema.

This question, I suggest, is worth asking now and in this particular forum on prosthetics - a forum within which additions to an existing form change the character, appearance, performance and way of knowing what is being modified - for a number of reasons. In trying to respond to this question, the article is intended to work alongside current scholarship on digital cinema and new media. It is not intended to fault those who have, for whatever reasons, not considered film censorship (a subject of study given over to long and mostly descriptive histories, tales of moral panic, sensationalism, and self-righteous polemics). Asking this question hopes to acknowledge continually that film is a heavily policed object and cannot be divorced from the diverse power relations converging in the form of film censorship. If digital compositing makes it easier to seamlessly control the image, then this is not without repercussions for how power works on, as well as, through the image. To this end, the next section will consider, the metamorphosis of film censorship's 'concrete' measures and policing practices from analog models into digital image manipulation.

Numerous writers, (including Tom Gunning, Lev Manovich, Andrew Darley, Jay David Bolter, Richard Gursin, and Angela Ndalianis) have drawn convincing analogies between digital cinema and early cinema history to account for the attractions displayed on screens at the beginning and end of the twentieth century. Their work pressures a consideration of exactly how practices of film censorship are reconfigured within this analogy. The return to 'the cinema of attractions' thesis produces both similar and divergent effects on an understanding of film censorship as practiced through digital compositing. In the final section of this essay, I attempt to carve out a few directions through which the implications of their analogy may be pursued.

WHAT YOU CAN'T SEE WITH YOUR EYES WIDE OPEN

Within the fields of film, media, and visual studies much has been made about the computer-generated images deployed on a particular scene in Stanley Kubrick's *Eyes Wide Shut*. Both Barbara Creed's 'The cyberstar: digital pleasures and the end of the Unconscious'[7] and Jon Lewis' book-length study of US film censorship, *Hollywood v. Hardcore: How the Struggle over Censorship Saved the Modern Film Industry*[8] claim that in order for *Eyes Wide Shut* - a film already obsessed with visual knowledge - to secure an R rating from the MPAA, digitised figures had to be superimposed on a medium-shot of the lengthy orgy scene to strategically block an explicit shot of a man and woman fucking. This action was apparently deemed unacceptable for this rating. The inclusion of computer-generated figures - a cloaked man and nude woman seated next to one another - purposely intercepts the spectator's ability to see. On the R rated version, all one can see, all that one is allowed to see, takes the form of two virtual actors obscuring an evening's worth of libertine banality. Had this intervention not taken place, leaving the film in its 'unaltered' version, it would have received an NC-17

7. Barbara Creed, 'The cyberstar: digital pleasures and the end of the Unconscious', *Screen*, 41, 1 (2000).

8. Jon Lewis, *Hollywood v. Hardcore: How the Struggle over Censorship Saved the Modern Film Industry*, New York, New York University Press, 2000.

rating and its exhibition and profit-making potential would have been severely restricted.

At the opposite end of cine-aesthetics is another, and tellingly different, instance of an intervention taken to directly police film content. In the UK, the BBFC was involved in the removal of around one minute worth of original footage from *The Evil Dead* (Sam Raimi 1983) in order to receive a certificate for video release. Although this removal was conducted on the videocassette version of Raimi's film which automatically poses an additional set of concerns for how the BBFC regulates what enters the private sphere, it does, nonetheless, provide an excellent example by which to distinguish the different operations affecting each title. Within the full minute deleted, one scene in particular stood out for the BBFC: the jabbing of a pencil into a victim's leg by a zombie-like creature (it's always difficult to determine the exact entity in Raimi's films). Once inserted, the zombie proceeded to repetitively wiggle the pencil in the open wound. In the final cut of the film only one wiggle appeared.

In reference to Kubrick's final film, Lewis is lightheartedly dismissive when discussing the brief alteration to the orgy scene. He writes, 'it's a silly little change in a silly and long scene'.[9] The main premise of *Hollywood vs. Hardcore* is that film censorship serves an economic function. Film censorship, rather than remain fixated on the image, 'only incidentally and superficially regards specific film content'.[10] While Lewis does breath a certain fresh air into the stale debates of US film censorship, I am neither convinced that direct actions taken to police the image can be easily dismissed, nor led to believe that these actions are somehow insignificant. I would agree with Lewis that a change has occurred; however, this change is far from frivolous. Unlike the sequence that Tom Cruise's character uncomfortably experiences (and desperately envies) in *Eyes Wide Shut*, the procedure invoked to 'cut' Raimi's film did not involve digital compositing. *The Evil Dead* was re-edited rather than 'cleaned' as digital compositing now makes possible.

So what precisely are the differences between analog and digital means of manipulating a film to achieve a particular rating? When conceiving of film censorship as an activity a dominant image quickly materialises: a pair of scissors - glistening blades open and at the ready. Murray Schumach's classic study of film censorship, *The Face on the Cutting Room Floor*, Baxter Phillip's *Cut: the Unseen Cinema*, and more recently, Tom Dewe Mathews' *Censored* all promote this visual metaphor as the instrument through which to imagine film censorship.[11] Schumach's text shows scissors actually cutting through a celluloid strip, whereas Phillips' cover pictures celluloid pieces cascading from the blades of scissors. In these depictions, the ever-present pair of scissors signifies two sets of meanings: the cut as authoritarian and the process most associated with the censoring of films, and the cut as an editing technique in the production process.

The authoritarian 'cut' of film censorship has been perceived as indiscriminate, often clumsy: a slovenly enterprise of inconsistency and

9. Ibid., p1.

10. Ibid, p2

11. See Murray Schumach, *The Face On The Cutting Room Floor: The Story of Movie and Television Censorship*, New York, William Morrow and Company, 1964; Baxter Philips, *Cut: the unseen cinema*, New York, Crown, 1975; and Tom Dewe Mathews, *Censored*, London, Chatto and Windus, 1994.

idiosyncratic irregularity. The censor's cut is construed as violent and oppressive. Films severely cut to achieve a rating are commonly regarded as having been 'butchered', 'hacked apart', and 'shredded to pieces' in their approved state. The second meaning is also quite specific. When films are re-edited to fit neatly into a particular rating, the editing style most adhered to is continuity editing. Those given this task are not actively engaged in championing the montage practices of Vertov, Bazin, or Eisenstein! In this instance, elation is absent and assemblage does not become the ammunition of modernist art. After the frames that contain the questionable shots are cut, the remaining shots are spliced together to give the impression that the footage is continuous. Unlike the shocks and surprises found in modernist montage, continuity editing endeavors to 'create a smooth flow from shot to shot'.[12] Continuity requires precision to minimise the unsightly appearance of seams.

12. David Bordwell and Kristin Thompson, *Film Art: An Introduction*, New York, McGraw-Hill Inc., 1993, p261.

The scissors' dual meanings are played out well in Giuseppe Tornatore's *Cinema Paradiso* (1989). Recall the haphazard editing in the films exhibited within the local cinema of *Cinema Paradiso*. A bell rung by the village priest indicated what specific footage had to be removed for acceptable public viewing. Often the audience would recognise incongruent frames and linear distortions within a film's narrative, and respond with boos and hisses. Not only was the medium revealed to the audience in the cinema by the disruption to narrative continuity, so was the censoring action evidenced by the noticeable absence of frames.

While the image of scissors is a powerful one, I would argue that it is no longer a pertinent signifier for comprehending film censorship's remediation. The emblematic pair of scissors owes its powers of signification to analog media. Digital technology redefines the editing process. As stated previously, digital cinema is a phrase that houses many disparate parts. Traditional film making techniques once kept apart are now joining forces to assist in production. It is necessary to cite Manovich at length to explain this union:

> Previously, editing and special effects were strictly separate activities. An editor worked on ordering sequences of images together; any intervention within an image was handled by special-effects specialists. The computer collapses this distinction. The manipulation of individual images via a paint program or algorithmic image processing becomes as easy as arranging sequences of images in time. Both simply involve 'cut and paste'. As this basic computer command exemplifies, modification of digital images (or other digitized data) is not sensitive to distinctions of time and space or of differences of scale.[13]

13. Manovich, 'What Is Digital Cinema', op. cit., p179-181.

Time and space are large contingencies in both analog and digital editing. Camera centered filmmaking is dependent upon progression; a strip of celluloid consists of individual advancing frames. Analog's cut, while inevitably affecting the spatial relations of a particular shot or scene, performed an eradication of time by removing specific frames that were part of a linear order. Manipulation was limited to the process of removal. An editor could 'cut', this we know, but the ability to 'paste' prior to user-friendly operating systems was known only in terms of a fine cohesive used to join perforated strips together.

The composite allows for greater control over what is placed in individual frames and entire scenes. Modification is easier, faster, and more precise: images can be combined, recombined, inserted (the virtual actors from *Eyes Wide Shut*), erased, painted, dragged, duplicated, distorted, cleaned, and of course, cut. Yes, the new techniques of digital cinema can conjure convincing cinematic moments: a crowded dock for an optimistic maiden voyage in the *Titantic* (1997), Presidential acknowledgement from John F. Kennedy in *Forrest Gump* (1994), and an intense training programme with your very own robot in *Lara Croft: Tomb Raider* (2001). At the same time, however, these identical applications work to hide the seams of censoring actions. The seamlessness of digital cinema has prompted many writers to highlight this feature as its most definitive. For example, Andrew Darley writes that digital techniques, 'ensure the seamless combination of the disparate source images within the frame or shot';[14] and Creed proclaims, 'the flow of computer-generated images has a greater potential to appear seamless'.[15] Digital compositing, like the cut of analog censorship, attempts to cover ruptures. Its abilities in this area are much more convincing; no trace is left. How can one discern what has been taken out of a certain shot like the audience of *Cinema Paradiso*, when most likely additional images have been inserted into individual frames as in *Eyes Wide Shut*?

Yet, is this the correct question to ask? What does knowing that an image has been modified, or manipulated for purposes of censorship reveal? Is this the hard proof by which to demand our constitutional 'freedom of speech'? The scare quotes should elude to my thoughts on this question. Basically, the search for missing moments has been made redundant. The reel comprised of censorship's stolen kisses in *Cinema Paradiso* loses its charm when it simply takes up space on one's hard drive. If, as I am suggesting here, film censorship is truly experiencing a remediation, then our relationship to it, its object of concentration, and how it shows its operations have changed. Digital compositing is a far cry from the 'parental advisory' warnings vandalising CD and record covers. Its task is to convince the viewer that its images are photorealistic and continuous; and this includes those images purposely inserted for securing a rating. Because compositing is rendered seamless, the question to ask is: what does this seamlessness look like?

'MAKING IMAGES SEEN':
FILM CENSORSHIP'S CINEMA OF ATTRACTIONS

For the most part, new media's profound implications for how films are currently made and understood have been informed by references to early

14. Andrew Darley, *Visual Digital Culture: Surface Play and Spectacle in New Media Genres*, London, Routledge, 2000, p18-19.

15. Creed, 'The cyberstar', op. cit., p84.

cinema history. Contemporary films reliant upon and promoted on account of digital technologies are said to mark a return to the principles that structured the infancy of cinema. For many, these principles are encapsulated by Tom Gunning's term for the epoch before 1906-1907: the cinema of attractions. Unlike narrative driven films that predicate realism on the effacement of the medium by investing believability and authenticity on a film's fictional structure, formal conventions, and an investment in an actor's performance, the cinema of attractions predicated its performance on its ability to display and exhibit images in an astonishing yet convincing manner. The relationship between astonishment and credibility was based on the 'star' of early films, namely the machinery that enabled the production of the spectacle on offer. 'Early audiences' Gunning writes, 'went to exhibitions to see machines demonstrated (the newest technological wonder, following in the wake of such widely exhibited machines and marvels as X-rays or, earlier, the phonograph), rather than to view films'.[16] These same principles and practices, the mechanical extension of vision in new ways and onto new surfaces, and the elaboration of the medium's persuasive potential resting hand in hand with its extraordinary capabilities are, by recent accounts, the attraction of digital cinema.

16. Tom Gunning, 'The Cinema of Attractions: Early Film, Its Spectator and the Avant-Garde', in T. Elsaesser and A. Barker (eds), *Early Cinema: Space Frame Narrative*, London, BFI, 1990, p58.

Often accused of sacrificing narrative to the gods of computer-generated images - Pixar and Industrial Light and Magic - the analogy between Gunning's claim and the so-called 'effects cinema' of today has been furthered recently in Angela Ndalianis's, 'Special Effects, Morphing Magic, and the 1990s Cinema of Attractions'. Writing on the existing tension for film audiences and critics alike that special effects overshadow the traditional reliance placed on the supremacy of narrative by Hollywood conventions, Ndalianis articulates the emphasis placed on the visual over the literary as a defining feature of effects cinema:

> Contemporary effects cinema is a cinema that establishes itself as a technological performance, and audiences recognize and revel in the effects technology and its cinematic potential. Rather than centering the action solely around a story, this is a cinema that emphasizes display, exhibitionism, performance, and spectacle.[17]

17. Angela Ndalianis, 'Special Effects, Morphing Magic, and the 1990s Cinema of Attractions', in V. Sobchack (ed), *Meta-Morphing: Visual Transformation and the Culture of Quick-Change*, Minneapolis, University of Minnesota Press, 2000, p258.

Whether or not audiences do indeed 'revel in the effects' is very much open for debate. Instead of accounting for all the films that fit Ndalianis' description from *Armageddon* (1998) to *Toy Story 2* (1999), one only has to briefly consider any summer cycle since the late 1970s. At the time of this writing, for instance, *Lara Croft: Tomb Raider*, *Planet of the Apes*, *Pearl Harbor*, and *The Mummy Returns* occupied multiplexes the world over and certainly attest to Gunning and Ndalianis' arguments.

Much indebted to Tom Gunning's seminal analyses of early cinema history, Bolter and Grusin dedicate considerable space within their genealogy of new media to situating the cinema of attractions thesis into their exegesis.

They consider Gunning's work to be illustrative of how for digital cinema, and the argument is extended to all visual events produced by new media, 'the logic of hypermediacy can assert itself within the logic of immediacy'.[18] Hypermediacy refers to the activity of making audiences aware of the medium that they are experiencing, and this awareness of the medium itself becomes a part of the content being consumed. In contrast, immediacy strives to keep audiences unaware of the medium. Immediacy has so forcefully characterised the codes of narrative film that a glimpse of the filmic medium in operation, such as the visibility of support wires in a stunt sequence or the boom in a tender exchange of vows, often compromises viewers' experience of a film. In this context, noticing the medium detracts from the 'film' - understood as the content of its story.

18. Bolter and Grusin, *Remediation*, op. cit., p155.

Bolter and Grusin's claim for new media, the insertion of hypermediacy into the logic of immediacy, therefore presents something of a paradox. At first glance, it appears that one must imagine a simultaneous recognition and failure of recognition on the part of viewers. Upon further inspection, however, the contemporaneity of hypermediacy and immediacy within a single film points to the effect of new media on the expectations that structure the codes of cinematic realism. In keeping with my earlier statement of purpose, the remainder of this article will feel out the implications of remediation to film censorship. It will attend to the widespread claim that the frame of reference within which to discuss new media is the cinema of attractions, and by extension the impact of new media on the codes of realism that structure expectations for a film.

By invoking cinema as an attraction, Gunning relates the new medium of the late nineteenth century to other developing forms of modern mass leisure industries and spaces, ranging from amusement parks to vaudeville. Darley, who also acknowledges Gunning's importance for digital cinema, stresses that 'cinema has a much closer affinity with the tradition of popular entertainments than it does with painting, literature or the theatre ...'[19] Although no particular style, technique or school is invoked, Manovich contrasts Darley's claim, stating that the new cinema involves 'a particular branch of painting - painting in time. No longer a kino-eye, but a kino-brush'.[20] Manovich's decision to evoke a kino-brush in his discussion of digital cinema positions it in relation to precinematic practices for creating images manually. Digital production combines editing and special effects techniques in order to convincingly modify any aspect of the image, no matter how large (the Titanic), or how small (its passengers). The camera makes room for computer graphics programmes. Whereas for most of its existence, cinema was practised as a recording process, 'its role was to capture and to store visible reality',[21] the kino-brush marks the return to older forms of visual production set aside due to cinema realism's heavy investment in narrative. Like the cinema of attractions' emphasis on exhibition and display, digital cinema establishes itself on special effects, showing rather telling.

However, an emphasis on Manovich's kino-brush, which alludes to pre-

19. Darley, *Visual Digital Culture*, op. cit., p46.

20. Manovich, 'What Is Digital Cinema', op. cit., p192.

21. Ibid., p192.

cinematic techniques, is appropriate to a discussion of contemporary censoring practices because we are witnessing radical new developments in the form of technological means for policing cinema. At the turn of the last century, the seemingly recalcitrant object of cinema was largely policed through direct physical and municipal responses. Just prior to the period within which Gunning claims that cinema was 'willing to rupture a self-enclosed fictional world for a chance to solicit the attention of the spectator',[22] this enthusiastic attention also witnessed the removal of *Dolorita's Passion Dance* (1894) from peep show exhibition in the mid-1890s due to its then racy dance performance. Given that vaudeville, itinerant performances like fairs and carnivals, and amusement parks were the first entertainment institutions to incorporate films into their variety acts, the moving images shown varied, lacked a permanent home until the emergence of nickelodeon parlours, and consisted of short loops. The physical removal of films considered morally objectionable by outraged patrons, state officials, or moral reformers watching over popular entertainment, was perhaps the only response possible. Films at the turn of the century mostly consisted of one shot to show the captured movements. Editing was still in its extreme infancy, not yet a staple of filmmaking let alone conceived of as a method for censoring films in the name of public morality.

22. Gunning, 'The Cinema of Attractions', op. cit., p57.

The arrival of narrative film, recognised to begin with *The Great Train Robbery* (1903), produced longer films and utilised editing to convey a story. The ability to convey a story coupled with the growing prominence of permanent places for film exhibition prompted further actions. For example, New York City's Mayor George McCellan closed all city nickelodeons on Christmas Eve 1908, and the outcome of *Block* v. *Chicago* (1909) upheld police inspection and licensing of all films exhibited within the city of Chicago. In that same year a local-level attempt at prior restraint - films were to be previewed by a committee prior to exhibition in New York City - became the National Board of Censorship of Motion Pictures. In 1915 the board was renamed the National Board of Review. Its task, like the local committee before it, was to preview films prior to public release in order to 'protect' US audiences from matters considered potentially obscene by securing ideals of decency and morality through the medium of film. Here film itself becomes the primary object of inspection and surface for regulatory measures to be carried out.

It was not until the 1920s, that the 'Hays Office' officially known as the Motion Picture Producers and Distributors Association of America led by Will H. Hays, prescribed a set of guidelines to promote its policy of self-regulation. Under self-regulation, studios were asked to submit scripts to the Hays Office for review. Prior to release of the finished product, the Hays Office advised studios whether or not their materials were morally appropriate according to its 1927 'Don'ts and Be Carefuls' list of suspect themes and practices. These and other cautionary measures solidified self-regulation in the form of The 1930 Production Code (also known as The

Motion Picture Production Code).

To reiterate, measures used to police cinema during the early twentieth century did not rely on editing techniques. The prominent pair of scissors regularly associated with the cut of censorship did not become an actuality until much later in the form of national self-regulation. Measures most employed to regulate film exhibition prior to the establishment of formal review associations included: the removal of specific films, the closing down of spaces for exhibition, and unofficial age restraints. Keep them out, close them down, or get it out were the prevailing sets of actions used to police cinema. The reason that I draw attention to these points is to demonstrate that although production practices of digital cinema may involve a return to the concerns of pre-narrative film, the censorship practices of this early period are diametrically opposed to those employed today through digital compositing. Yet, there is a return.

Censorship of digital cinema participates in the exhibitionary characteristics of the cinema of attractions. Censorship is itself part of the technology and marvel on display. Or more specifically, digital cinema transforms censorship from a visibly invasive action on the body of the film into a special effect: from senseless acts of violence to seamless acts of visibility. In this process of remediation, digital compositing collapses the practices of editing with those of special effects so that censorship comes to participate in the promotion of believability through the seamless operations that compositing perfects.

If the kino-brush is in fact the new tool for modifying images, then film censorship amounts to a form of painting. It would appear that we are witnessing a shift from the censor's scissors to the composeter's brush. At this point, I would like to make an aside to an intriguing little point in Walter Benjamin's much cited essay, 'The Work of Art in the Age of Mechanical Reproduction'. Given the richness of Benjamin's essay, one might be inclined to pass over the conceit through which he compares the relationship of painting and film to reality. He proposes that the camera operator manipulates reality as intimately as the surgeon handles the organs of the person upon whom she operates. For Benjamin then, the surgeon's technique is credited as more significant than that of the painter, whose work does not broach the natural distance between herself and her object. The painter's effect on the reality she represents is thus compared to the magician's approach to healing. Specifically, Benjamin argues that whereas the magician can only heal by touching the surface, 'by the laying on of hands', the surgeon 'cuts into the patient's body' and thus greatly reduces the distance maintained by the magician.[23]

23. Benjamin, 'The Work of art in the Age of mechanical Reproduction' op. cit., p227.

Yet with the benefit of hindsight that new media confers on scholars of technology, one might be inclined to suggest that Benjamin underestimated the power of the magician, and by extension the power of the painter - especially the painter who wields a kino-brush. With a kino-brush touching the surface in the service of censorship, painting effects a far more intimate relationship to what is presented than the cut.

Analog censorship can only practice on the body lying in its operating theatre. The censor's scissors like the surgeon's scalpel can only perform an invasive procedure of eradication on the materiality of a body. Such cuts always bespeak a form of destruction, for no matter how precise a scalpel's incision, surrounding tissue is always damaged. Unlike digital compositing, which is capable of acting on the body of the 'film' without leaving evidence, analog censorship's dependence on the cut always leaves scars - minute traces of its presence and gracelessness.

This is not to suggest that digital censorship is to be taken lightly or viewed as an innocent descendant of the more visibly violent cut. Although the magician has a relatively small impact on the materiality of the body she heals through the laying on of hands, her act may effect a major change in the condition of her subject for it speaks to the subject's belief in the magician's authority - the source of her power. One might also add, that the very authority that purports to heal a sick body is always the source of the power that she expresses.

Digital cinema throws our habitual understanding of cinema as a photographic recording into suspicion, and forces us to reconsider cinema as a form of painting practised by a 'kino-brush'. Here individual images are easily modified through remediation: the painter's brush gives way to the mouse and the precise stroke gives way to 'cut and paste' modification. Processes of digital image manipulation and synthesis, the technical apparatus' continuing ability to efface all traces of itself, as well as a further engagement with the concepts of representation and realism in the age of seamless digital reproduction are the necessary foci through which to track how film content is packaged for consumption and modified to ensure MPAA approval.

When censorship becomes a convincing effect of the virtuosity of filmic production, especially in the form of a seamless composite, emphasis has shifted from encountering traces of what has been removed to the proliferation and perfection of what can be seen. Digital censorship may not cut, yet it does perhaps carry the potential for its own form of violence, one characterised by an amorphous overabundance of production. The two virtual actors in *Eyes Wide Shut* are only one such example, yet their presence marks the *absence* of a cut. It paints over the disruption to continuity that would have otherwise existed, and may perhaps point to a painting over of the type of debates that have traditionally characterised film censorship.

BETWEEN BODIES WITHOUT ORGANS AND MACHINES WITHOUT DESIRE: DELEUZE-GUATTARI'S ELISION OF PROSTHETIC ACTUALITY

Suhail Malik

The enhancement of the human or organic living body by material prosthetic additions is for some an already dated notion of how technical conditions and operations transform the experiences, capacities and possibilities of that body. Prosthetic modification has reached a certain plateau with the figure of the cyborg and its now familiar promise of transformation and invention in political, cultural and theoretical registers. Hardt and Negri articulate the position more rigorously than most in *Empire*:

> The anthropological metamorphoses of bodies are established through the common experience of labour and the new technologies that have constitutive effects and ontological implications. Tools have always functioned as human prostheses, integrated into our bodies through our labouring practices as a kind of anthropological mutation both in individual terms and in terms of collective social life. The contemporary form of [anthropological] exodus ... demand[s] that tools become poietic prostheses, liberating us from the conditions of modern humanity ... Donna Haraway's cyborg fable, which resides at the ambiguous boundary between human, animal, and machine, introduces us today, much more effectively than deconstruction, to these new terrains of possibility - but we should remember that it is a fable and nothing more. The force that must instead drive forward theoretical practice to actualise these terrains of potential metamorphosis is still (and ever more intensely) the common experience of the new productive practices and concentration of productive labour on the plastic and fluid terrain of the new communicative, biological and mechanical technologies.[1]

1. Michael Hardt and Antonio Negri, *Empire*, Cambridge MA, Harvard University Press, 2000, pp217-218.

Despite the political lure of the 'fable' of the transformative power of prosthetics, it remains limited because it is a theoretical fiction, in contrast to the 'new productive practices' just mentioned. The technological realisations of such practices mean that the 'cyborg metaphor constructed around machine components' permeation into organic structures has, in its informational aspects, remained in a state of arrested development in the thinking of the Industrial Age and, in any case, is no longer adequate to describe what is currently transpiring'.[2] The emergence of digital network systems and virtuality since the late 1980s (that is, since the writing of Haraway's 'Cyborg Manifesto') means that the 'permeation' of human activity

2. Gerfried Stocker, 'New Images of Mankind', in G. Stocker & C. Schöpf (eds), *Ars Electronica 99: LifeScience*, Vienna & New York, Springer, 1999, p23.

and technical operations is, as Hardt and Negri propose, now predominantly vectored through the circuits and processes of dematerialised and affective labour.[3]

In these conditons, the extension of the organic is now more likely to be informational than material, to the extent that it might now seem as though the standard image of the prosthetic has had to be discarded. But, in fact, the cyborg *is* a materially enhanced organic body, and its construction is dependent upon highly regulated information feedback mechanisms between organic and technical orders of operation. Thus, the prosthetic remains an interpenetration or integration of the organic body/system with the technical apparatus/system - even if it is in a reversed version of the standard unilateral notion of the prosthetic as an extension of the organic:

> research and theorising on the digital revolution have concentrated on the application of mechanical components to and into the biological body - and this with considerable success when one considers the reality of modern medicine and prosthetics … - whereas a different mode of going about these tasks has emerged as a result of progress in biology. With ever-increasing frequency, success is achieved by introducing biological components into the mechanical environment. Bioinformatics - in current usage 'wet computing' - has become an important bearer of hopes in the field of computer technology.

> The spectrum extends from innovative bacteriological data storage media with enormous storage capacity and access speed all the way to Affymetrix's DNA chips, by means of which it is already possible to simultaneously analyse and digitally process over 40 000 genes and expressed sequenced tags.[4]

Add to this the electrocomputational analysis of organic material, the theory and experimental successes in using DNA molecules as electrocomputational switches, thus opening the way for sub-organically based nanocircuitry,[5] and it becomes clear that the 'Industrial Age' notion of the cyborg is rendered obsolete not so much by its redundancy as by its exacerbation.

In such circumstances, the anthropocentric or biocentric notion of the prosthetic, wherein it serves to enhance extant sensory, muscular or even affective powers, or where it is taken to be a supplement for a lack (however rigorously these terms may be determined), is clearly surpassed in two senses. First, the technical apparatus is no longer just an adjunct to the organic living *body* in the sense of an integrated biological system. Its conjugation now exceeds that dimension of organisation and is effected in a coherent system with (proto-)organic matter of all orders of complexity and systemic integration. Second, in the developments of prosthetics beyond the order of the body capable of living, neither the bio-organic nor the technical side now has *de jure* precedence or priority in their conjunction. The prosthetic

3. Michael Hardt and Antonio Negri, *Empire*, op. cit., p217.

4. Stocker, 'New Images of Mankind', op. cit., pp23-24.

5. David Whitehouse, 'DNA Computers Take Shape', <http://news.bbc.co.uk/hi/english/sci/tech/newsid_60000/600323.stm>, 2000; Qinghua Liu, Liman Wang, Anthony G. Furtas, Anne E. Condon, Robert M. Corn, Lloyd M. Smith, 'DNA Computing on Surfaces', in *Nature*, 403 (2000), pp175-179.

is instead a *two-way* channel that may 'enhance' the technical system with biological or organic parts as much as the more traditionally known contrary.

Without an 'origin', without a presupposable basis or condition, or a tendential purpose for the integration of organic and technical augmentations, prostheses then propose, if they do not already effect, an increasing contiguity between the organic and the technical orders of material organisation. This development is sometimes called a 'hybridisation' of the organic and technical. Such a designation, however, disguises what is most problematic and difficult here: the *demand* to explain, recognise and comprehend what exactly is going on *in fact*, in the interlocking of organic and technical orders of material organisation. 'Hybridisation' is far too loose and naturalistic a category and name to determine how and in what respects that contiguity is actually being produced. A more precise designation of their common milieu and its development is given by characterising it instead as a *general complex of organisation*. This latter designation has the added advantages of explicitly signalling: first, the material dimension of organisation as the specific methodological and material issue in the development of the organico-technical milieu that prostheses realise; and, second, that the *fact* of the organico-technical milieu is also a *complex* in that its categorical determinations no longer enjoy their historically sedimented demarcations.

The advantage, then, of determining the actuality and effectivity of prosthetics in terms of a general complex of organisation is that, as a complex, prostheses destabilise and alter traditional theoretical and historical categories. But if that actuality itself comes to be recognised through the deployment of categories, the problem is then one of how the general organic-technical milieu that prostheses instanciate and signal is to be recognised and understood, never mind mobilised. And if recognised, in what terms is it to be recognised if the traditional bases for such comprehension are transformed by that very actuality? Though these questions are common to any invention, prostheses demand their specific formulation in terms of organisation: that is, how to comprehend the historical, material, physical, collective, conceptual, and ideational sliding of the organic and the technical into one another?

Bernard Stiegler has recently argued that the very intentionality that characterises the technical order - as involving anticipation, pro-tention and so on - is itself a result of technicity.[6] This serves to remove the anthropocentric condition for technics and makes the human an apprehending consciousness indebted to technicity as much as technicity is indebted to human protention in action: in traditional Aristotelean terms, the ends that are the cause and justification for the technical construction. Although Stiegler's move is radical as regards the traditional status, principles and causality conventionally attributed to anthroponoesis in relation to the technical, it remains on the traditional side of the standard discrimination of the *organic* and the technical, since Stiegler characterises the latter as

6. Bernard Stiegler, *Technics and Time I: The Fault of Epimetheus*, R. Beardsworth & G. Collins (trans), Stanford Ca., Stanford University Press, 1998 [1994].

'organised non-organic matter'. 'Prosthetics' then remains a relatively stable term for Stiegler, even if its status and power is dramatically transformed. By contrast, the present argument proposes that this determination - which is a condition for Stiegler's argument and beyond - is problematised by both the actuality of the prosthetic and its future. This problematic requires a return to the question of how the destabilisation of the categories and actualities of the organic and the technical are to be comprehended at all.

Conventionally, prosthetics involves the conjunction of two distinct orders of organisation: the distinction being that the technical order is a material organisation that is intentionally produced while (as Stiegler agrees) the organic order is not. This standard and doctrinal separation of orders of organisation corresponds to the methodological and epistemological schema that set up the major debates in the life sciences of the eighteenth and nineteenth centuries, and which, in muted forms, still haunt lifesciences today. The principal axis of the debate is between mechanism and vitalism. Mechanism stipulates material and efficient causes (the latter in the guise of forces) to be conditions sufficient for a complete determination of present and future states of a material system. This is the basis of modern and contemporary physics, chemistry, engineering and technoscience in general. Vitalism posits a specific quality for the living that is irreducible to material and efficient causes. Although vitalism has dropped out of favour under the continued attack of mechanists and the correlative demise of teleology as an explanatory cause for natural material processes, the distinction between the 'merely mechanistic' and the living system continues, at least insofar as the explanatory framework for the latter is increasingly considered as not particulate but structural, intrasystemic and 'networked' - organisational, in a word.[7]

This latter distinction between the organic and the technical lies behind the cross-integration of these categories of material organisation, in that prosthetics is effected as a technically driven operation. But that distinction is also undone by prostheses in their contemporary and future actuality, in that the organic no longer remains a merely 'unintentional' order of material organisation but is co-constituted with the intentionality of the technical. The point here is that the categorial problematic of the actuality of prosthetics is no less one of the continued distinction of epistemological and explanatory doctrines by which the constitution of material organisation is understood. Again, then, prosthetics does not just trouble the distinction between the organic and the technical *in fact* but also in their categorial registration. What categories are there, then, for comprehending what prosthetics propose?

At present the discussion of indistinction between the technical and the organic is heavily indebted in the arts and humanities to Deleuze-Guattari and especially to their notion of the 'machinic phylum'.[8] The rest of this article considers whether Deleuze-Guattari's conceptualisation of the machine *does* provide some theoretical or conceptual leverage on what

7. Stuart Kauffman amongst others tries to synthesise the mechanistic with the specificity of ordered living systems (see *At Home in the Universe: The Search for Laws of Complexity*, Harmondsworth, Penguin, 1995). For an extensive historical account of how this mechanistic sytemisation of biology has developed since Darwin see David Depew and Bruce Weber, *Darwinism Evolving: System Dynamics and the Genealogy of Natural Selection*, Cambridge MA, MIT Press, 1995, Chs 13-15.

8. Gilles Deleuze and Félix Guattari, *A Thousand Plateaus: Capitalism and Schizophrenia*, tr. B. Massumi, Minneapolis, University of Minnesota Press, 1987 [1980]. Translations throughout have generally been slightly modified.

prosthetics proposes. To be clear from the outset: the intention here is not to affirm Deleuze-Guattari's theory, which is found to be inadequate to the conditions of prosthetic actuality. Despite its accomplished argument, its effectivity and force, its institutional and extra-institutional success and, at the time of writing, its increasingly doctrinal status, Deleuze-Guattari's 'machinic phylum' and its attendant conceptual apparatii is seen to *elide* a comprehension of what is involved in the organico-technical milieu. The task of finding a conceptual framework that is adequate to the plastic and categorial transmutations effected by prosthetics remains.

Yet the 'machinic phylum' looks at first to be such a conceptual framework. Deleuze-Guattari define it as: 'the flux of movement-matter [*matière-mouvement*], the flux of matter in continuous variation, conveyer of singularities and traits of expression. The operating and expressive flux is as much natural as it is artificial'.[9] The machinic phylum includes the continuity between the organic 'phylum' and the technical one and is moreover the conceptualisation of a *material* process and transformation, of 'destratified, deterritorialised matter',[10] which is, in its flux, only quasi-conceptualised. Both characteristics are right for the indeterminable categoriality of prosthetics. But, again, more specificity than is offered by this definition is required. The question is *how* does such a 'matter in movement' conjoin the phyla we are concerned with? *How* is the machinic phyla instanciated as the organico-technical milieu? These are, moreover, questions about whether the concept of the machinic phylum allows for an explanation of the material process of prosthetic actuality.

A fuller determination of the machinic phylum can be found in what Deleuze-Guattari call the 'desiring-machine', the constitution of which is presented in detail in *Anti-Oedipus*.[11] The theoretical and methodological compatibility between the desiring-machine and the complex articulation of prosthetics discussed above is clear in that, for Deleuze-Guattari, the former surpasses the distinction between mechanism and vitalism: 'Neither mechanism nor vitalism has really understood the nature of desiring-machines, nor the double necessity to introduce production in desire as much as desire in mechanics'.[12] As with the prosthetic, the desiring-machine straddles the conventional categories of the technical and the organic and undermines the epistemological and ontological solidity of these terms in distinction to one another.

The now common recourse to Deleuze-Guattari as conceptualists of the organico-technical milieu can be explained here: it relies on the hypothetical determination of prosthetics as desiring-machines. For that, prosthetics has to be considered in relation to what Deleuze-Guattari call the machine. Though the identification may seem to be an obvious one - what is the prosthetic in its technicity if not a machine of sorts? - it is not as immediate as all that since, as Deleuze-Guattari insist, for them the machine involves desire. And the determination of prosthetics in terms of desire is less than evident. Making that clear requires going into Deleuze-Guattari's argument in some detail.

9. Ibid., p409.

10. Ibid., p407.

11. Gilles Deleuze and Félix Guattari, *Anti-Oedipus: Capitalism and Schizophrenia*, R. Hurley, M. Seem & H.R. Lane (trans), Minneapolis, University of Minnesota Press, 1983 [1972].

12. Ibid., p44.

First, for Deleuze-Guattari the machine is a (perhaps paradoxical) system of associative breaks: cuts in 'material flows' that are also associative linkages. It is on the basis of these cuts and linkages - also the point at which a notion of the prosthetic seems to be successfully articulated - that Deleuze-Guattari introduce desire as a constitutive part of machinic production. Second, the organico-technical milieu - the general complex of organisation - can be characterised in terms of what Deleuze-Guattari call the 'whole' or, more famously, 'the body without organs'. The latter is a production of the desiring-machine that speaks to the totality of the system of associative breaks while remaining immanent to them. In other words, it presents the totality of the machine and its (desiring) production without totalising it in transcendental, dialectical or overarching ways. This allows Deleuze-Guattari to get out of the opposition or distinction in kind between the organic and technical orders of organisation, between mechanism and vitalism, which in turn seems to open up a way of capturing conceptually the organico-technical complex that prostheses actualise. However, the conclusion to this essay demonsrates that Deleuze-Guattari preclude any such elaboration for the very reasons that they seem to open it up (an opening that characterises their philosophy altogether).

The uncommon sense of Deleuze-Guattari's determination of the machine is clear from their definition of it as 'a *system of cuts* (*coupures* ['breaks'])'.[13] What is crucial about this definition is that it *generalises* the notion of the machine in terms other than those of technics, technology, mechanistics, construction or ends. It is instead a categorial definition of the machine. But even with this abstract definition, machinic production is materially and locally determined: 'It is never an issue of considering the cut as separated from reality; the cuts operate in the variable dimensions following the character under consideration. Every machine, in the first place, is related to a continual material flow (*hylé*) that it slices'.[14] Furthermore, the cut or break that characterises the machine is also a 'stitching' together of 'material flow'. The machine then does not intervene on a pre-existing flow of matter but, rather, *constitutes* a flow, and this continuity of the material flow is an 'ideal' one: 'far from opposing the cut to continuity, the cut conditions th[e] continuity [of matter]: it implies or defines what it cuts into as an ideal continuity'.[15] The continuity of the material flow through the cutting of the machine is its productivity. Machinic production thereby implies the interconnected sytematicity of machines, which is the continuity of the machinic phylum:

> The machine produces an interruption of a flux only insofar as it is connected to another machine that supposedly produces this flux. And doubtless this second machine is in its turn really a cut. But it is such only in relation to a third machine that ideally - that is to say, relatively - produces a continuous, infinite flux. Thus, the anus-machine and the intestine-machine, the intestine-machine and the stomach machine, the stomach-machine and the mouth-machine, the mouth-machine and the

13. Ibid., p36.

14. Ibid., p36.

15. Ibid., p36.

flow of milk of a herd of dairy cattle ('and then … and then … and then … '). In a word, every machine is the cut of the flux in relation to the machine to which it is connected, but is also the flux itself, or the production of a flow, in relation to the machine to which it is connected.[16]

16. Ibid., p36.

The relevance to a theoretical comprehension of prosthetics is clear: the prosthetic is in this sense a machine in that it 'cuts' into the organic and produces a material continuity between it and the technical. But, on the basis of the machine as Deleuze-Guattari propose it, there is nothing to decide here in the priority of the organic and the technical: the prosthetic equally cuts into the technical 'material flow' by virtue of adjoining the organic flow to it. That is, the organism is itself an organic machine that cut-breaks into the technical 'flow' (process might be a better word) and, in so doing, joins (onto) it and the 'material flow' of technics. Given this equivalence, the notion of the prosthetic as a unilateral 'extension' of the (usually human) organic is seen to be an anthropocentric determination of what prosthetics involve. Prostheses are also and equally an extension/cut of the organic flow into the technical. Deleuze-Guattari's notion of the machine seems to work well for thinking about prosthetics by beginning with its organico-technical categorial indeterminability, rather than arriving at it.

This equivalence between organic and technical orders of material organisation is, however, only obtained by allowing for the paradoxical constitution of machinic operation and the phylum it produces. The paradox is that the machine's break-cut-slice of the material flux, the 'schiz' of Deleuze-Guattari's famous schizo-analysis, is no less an associative linking across different registers of material flow. The paradox of a break-cut that is associative can be maintained without falling into incoherence (wherein the cut would completely disassociate any flux) by re-articulating the status of the machine with respect to the flows: any machine is only ever a *partial* object because by cutting into material fluxes it produces a larger flow, *and* that cut detaches the flow from itself, producing flows that are heterogeneous to themselves. As Deleuze-Guattari put it the material flows are then:

> chains that are the seat of detachments in all directions, schizzes everywhere that are valued in and of themselves and above all must not be filled in. This is thus [a] characteristic of the machine: detachment-cuts (*coupures-détachments*) that are not to be confused with deduction-cuts (*coupures-prélèvements*). The latter bear upon continuous fluxes and are related to partial objects. The former concern heterogeneous chains, and as their basic unit use detachable segments or mobile stocks, like building blocks or flying bricks.[17]

17. Ibid., pp39-40.

Although there are two distinct characteristics of the machine's cut which are 'not to be confused', it is nonetheless the case that since the machine constitutes the continuous flux by its cut, the 'deduction-cut' is constituted in and by the 'detachment-cut'. Or, in another register, the schizo-production of heterogeneous chains is also the constitution of partial objects that are themselves cut into. Something of the usual understanding of the prosthetic can be quickly recognised here as a schizzing machine and partial object in two aspects. First, that the technical prosthesis cuts into and stitches together the material organisations of the organic and technical fluxes; second, that the prosthesis has the status of a partial object for either flux independently *and* also for the thence extended enchained organico-technical flux. The production of the ideal continuity of the material flux by the machine qua schizzing partial object, of the product that is productive, is what Deleuze-Guattari propose to be the generation of *desire*: 'at the limit point of all the transverse or transfinite connections, the partial object and the continuous flux, the cut and the connection, are confounded: everywhere there are flux-cuts out of which desire wells up, flux-cuts that are the productivity everywhere operating the graft of producing onto the product'.[18]

18. Ibid., pp36-37.

Desire is neither external to nor other than the operation of the schizzing machine. The machine, as Deleuze-Guattari affirm it, is a desiring-machine. The more immediate point is that, with Deleuze-Guattari, prostheses as desiring-machines then have to be more precisely recognised as a prosthesis-schiz or, to abbreviate, a *prostheschiz*. Put the other way, this latter term can be used to designate the DeleuzoGuattarian sense of what prosthetics realises. The ideal continuity of fluxes it indicates converges with much of the argument outlined in our introductory remarks on the challenge of prosthetics to the established sense of clearly demarcated epistemological (conceptual and cognitive) and ontological (material and processual) categories of the organic and the technical (amongst other so-called binaries). If an overturning of both of these material and conceptual categories and demarcations is associated with the cyborg, here it is directed specifically towards the general complex of organisation that prostheses instanciate in their actuality.

The problem that now arises is that, if the notion of the prostheschiz is adequate to the actuality of prostheses as constituting the general complex of the organico-technical milieu, this begs the question as to how *organisation* (and its transmutations) is addressed in the concept of the desiring-machine. This requires an exposition of Deleuze-Guattari's formulation of the totality produced by a desiring-machine. Through this exposition, Deleuze-Guattari's theorisation of the desiring-machine - of what in this context we have called the prostheschiz - can be seen to be one that has no leverage on the actuality of how prostheses change the categorisations of the organic and the technical as specific yet distinct orders of *material* organisation. In other words, their theory has no leverage on the actuality of the organico-technical milieu.

Deleuze-Guattari present the notion of totality as it produces and is produced by the desiring-machine by taking Proust's *Recherche* as an instance of a desiring-machine. Constituted in its holes, discontinuities and interlocking sections, Deleuze-Guattari propose that Proust's 'literature machine' *produces* a whole (*le tout*) which does not encapsulate its parts but is no less a part like the others, a synthesising communication between the products which are then no less productive. Proust's writing maintains that 'the whole itself is a product which is itself produced as nothing more than a part alongside other parts, which it neither unifies nor totalises, but which it applies to in then establishing aberrant communications between noncommunicating vessels, transversal unities between elements that retain all their difference within their own dimensions'.[19] This is of course only an instance of the operation of a desiring machine in its three characteristics: products that produce (the whole), chains of detachment-cuts ('paths of communication between noncommunicating vessels'), and a residual subject of the machine (the elements retain all their differences).[20] This is why the theory of the desiring-machine is not integrative, dialectical or totalising. The whole is not larger than, nor transcendent to, nor does it overarch, the elements which produce it. It is simply produced *in addition to* those elements and at the same level as them. This immanentism is of course Deleuze-Guattari's appeal for contemporary (quasi-anarchic) pluralistic sociopolitical theory and practice and, as will be confirmed in a moment, for theories that attempt to conceptualise self-organisation more generally.

The whole is, in short, the ideational continuous flux produced by the desiring-machine. This 'body without organs'

> is produced as a whole, but in its place within the process of production, alongside the parts that it neither unifies nor totalises. And when it applies itself to them … it induces transversal communications, transfinite summarisations, polyvocal and transcursive inscriptions on its own surface, on which the functional cuts of partial objects do not cease to be recut by the cuts in the signifying chain … The whole is not only with all the parts; it is contiguous to them, itself a product apart from them and applying itself to them.[21]

In the more local terms of the prostheschiz, the whole can be identified as the general organisational complex of the organico-technical, the body without organs of the organic and the technical, a body that is produced by the prostheschiz between them.

The identification made here can be confirmed in the conceptual categorial register through Deleuze-Guattari's own argument, since the body without organs is the condition for the critiques of mechanism and vitalism cited earlier. The point here is that neither of these classical theories is able to comprehend the *production* of the whole but can only *posit* it as either external to, prior to, or superadded to the parts of which it is constituted: 'As a general rule, the problem of the relation between parts and the whole still remains badly posed by classical mechanism and vitalism, so long as

19. Ibid., p43.

20. Ibid., pp36-41.

21. Ibid., pp43-44.

the whole is considered as a totality derived from the parts [structural unity in mechanism], or as an original totality from which the parts emanate [as in vitalism], or as a dialectical totalisation'.[22] As much as mechanism or vitalism (or modern science and its correlate conceptual structures as propounded in philosophy) cannot comprehend desiring machines, so, going the other way, the concept-ideal of the desiring-machine allows the relation between parts and whole, between partial objects and the continuous flux, to be comprehended otherwise than by those modern (and sometimes classical) doctrines. That is, the prostheschiz qua desiring-machine allows for the organisation of *both* the organic and the technical to be understood as produced rather than derived (as in mechanism or technology) or primary (as in vitalism or ecologism). Moreover, it means that the doctrinal conflict between mechanism and vitalism, wherein one domain attempts to reduce and explain the other in its own terms, this conflict is surpassed. Thus beckons a theory appropriate to the general complex of organisation, of the organico-technical in its material and organisational complexity.

22. Ibid., p44.

But if we restrict ourselves to the specific distinction and relation between the living and the technical the question remains: *how* does the notion of the desiring-machine get beyond the dualism of mechanistics and vitalism? If the prosthetic inaugurates a passage from one to the other, the issue now, which is at the core of our concerns, comes down to the question of how and on what register prostheschizzes detach the material flows, the machines of the living and the technical, from themselves and adjoin them to one another, producing the organico-technical whole. How, that is, do prostheses produce the organico-technical body without organs? Does it do so conceptually or in fact. The one *and* the other?

For Deleuze-Guattari, these are questions about the inherence of desire in the machine. They argue that whatever incompatability is proposed between desire and the machine is set up by both mechanism and vitalism on the basis of the *unity* that each proposes as the condition for the living system:

> But how can we speak of machines in the microphysical or micropsychic region, *there where there is desire* - that is to say, not only in its functioning, but formation and autoproduction? A machine functions according to the previous attachments of its structure and the positioning of its parts, but does not set itself into place any more than it forms or reproduces itself. This is even the point that animates the usual polemic between vitalism and mechanism: the machine's ability to account for the functionings of the organism, but its fundamental inability to account for its formations. Mechanism abstracts from machines a *structural unity* in terms of which it explains the functioning of the organism. Vitalism invokes an *individual and specific unity* of the living, which every machine presupposes insofar as it subordinates itself to its persistence and extends the latter's autonomous formations on the outside. But it should be noted

that, in one way or another, the machine and desire thus remain in an extrinsic relationship, either because desire is itself a system of mechanical causes, or because the machine is itself a system of means in terms of the aims of desire.[23]

23. Ibid., pp283-284.

The doctrines of mechanism and vitalism establish the whole of the living organism, the unity of organisation, on diverse conditions. Both of these determinations require machines and desire to be concepts and actualities extrinsic to one another. Clearly, then, if the notion of the desiring-machine is to have any conceptual or material-practical power then another conceptual armature is required. By default of merging the diverse notions of the machine and desire this will also be the conceptual armature for the organico-technical whole or body without organs (organs such as the organic in distinction to the technical, for example), for what we are calling the general complex of organisation.

This other concept/production of the whole is developed by Deleuze-Guattari on the basis of Samuel Butler's method of dispersion of postulates, where 'each of these arguments [is carried] to an extreme point where it can no longer be opposed to the other, a point of nondifference'.[24] Here it is the distinction in principle and in fact between a composed structural unity and a posited individual unity that is to be dispersed. What is undermined is the traditional notion of the machine as 'never more than an extension of the organism', that is: the machine as a prosthesis with an anthropic or organic provenance which it is then said to enhance or extend. Through the method of dispersion the machine is comprehended instead *at the level of the social* as a 'limb' equivalent to any organic one. Butler contends that

24. Ibid., p284.

> [machines] really are limbs and organs lying on the body without organs of a society, which men will appropriate according to their power and their wealth, and whose poverty deprives them as if they were mutilated organisms. On the other hand, he is not content to say that organisms are machines, but that they contain such an abundance of parts that they must be compared to very different parts of distinct machines, each reacting to the others, machined in combination with the others.[25]

25. Ibid., p284.

That is, the organism is not a machine composed of parts (organs) but is rather produced as a whole by many different machines, each of which is a body, such that the organism is something like an interacting population of machines and their parts.

By running the comprehension of the organism and the machine into one another, so that each is determined in terms of the other, Butler undoes the distinction in kind between the machine and the organism. 'What is essential is this double movement run to the limit by Butler. *He shatters the vitalist argument by putting into question the specific or personal unity of the organism, and the mechanist argument even more decisively, by putting into question the structural unity of the machine*.[26] Accordingly, the doctrines of mechanism and vitalism lose their purchase and constitutive role in the epistemology and practice of the production of material organisation.

26. Ibid., p284.

Hence, by 'shattering' the distinction between the two modalities of unity into an indifference, Butler (and Deleuze-Guattari with him) enables the productive-material and conceptual passage between the living organism, which vitalism claims is specific to it, and the machine, which is claimed in its specificity by mechanism. There are not then any *unities* of organisation, but rather multiplicities that constitute the whole that is then neither determinably organic or technical:

> in the … profound or intrinsic direction of multiplicities there is interpenetration, *direct communication* [emphasis added] between the molecular phenomena and the singularities of the living, that is to say, between the small machines dispersed in every machine, and the small formations swarming in every organism: a domain of indifference between the microphysical and the biological, there being as many living beings in the machine as there are machines in the living.[27]

27. Ibid., p286.

Here, then, is a positive and determinate characterisation of the prostheschiz and its production: the 'interpenetration', the 'direct communication', the channel between the machine and the organic - or, in the terms Deleuze-Guattari are more directly interested in, between the machine and desire - such that the two are now indeterminable and indisassociable: 'Once the structural unity of the machine has been undone, once the personal and specific unity of the living has been deposed, a direct link appears between machine and desire, the machine passes to the heart of desire, the machine is desiring and desire, machined'.[28] Production (and the whole) subsequent to the shattering of unities is then only at a level free of such unities. It is multiplicitous, at the level that Deleuze-Guattari famously call the molecular. By contrast, production at the level of the categorial unities specified by mechanism and vitalism can then be characterised as molar. Using these determinations, the prostheschiz proposes a molecular production of such a body[29] in an organico*machinic* milieu. On the other hand, the extrinsic relation between the machine and the organic or desire constituted by such molar aggregates foresakes the whole that is the body without organs in favour of discreet unities (such as the organic counterposed to the machinic). The prostheschiz can then be characterised as a production of a body without organs, a body that is specifically organico*machinic*, and this can also serve to characterise the general complex of organisation. However, this more precise clarification of the how and what a desiring-machine can be makes clear the untenability of a DeleuzoGuattarian approach to comprehending the general complex of material organisation that the prothesis *in fact* proposes.

28. Ibid., p285.

29. Ibid., pp285-286.

The inadequacy of the desiring-machine as a theory of prosthetics is manifest at precisely the point where the difference between molar and molecular production is drawn. The problem is that while molecular machines are the multiplicitous production of the whole, Deleuze-Guattari delimit *technical* machines from this order of production. They determine the technical to be a *molar* order of production that belongs to the order of unities and these block the production of the body without organs:

> It is only at the submicroscopic level of desiring machines that there exists a functionalism - machinic arrangements, the machining of desire (engineering); for, there alone, functioning and formation, use and assembly, product and production are confounded. All molar functionalism is false, since the organic or social machines are not formed in the same way that they function, and technical machines are not assembled in the same way they are used, but imply precisely the determined conditions that separate their own production from their distinct product.[30]

30. Ibid., p288.

Technical machines do not produce themselves, since their functioning is not also their formation, their products are not also their own production and they refer to an exteriority to themselves. Technical machines are not autoproductive. They are not desiring-machines. Their production is not a molecular one. Nor does the 'molecular' refer to size or scale, despite Deleuze-Guattari's own predilections. It is not as though nanotechnology is going to render the theory of the desiring-machine any more actual than the traditional industrial-scale machine might. If anything, technical machines block the operation of desire. They countermand the production of desiring-machines, of the body without organs, which, even if it is an organico*machinic* multiplicitous whole for Deleuze-Guattari, cannot be an organico-technical whole for that very reason.

The technical machine can only be considered within the regime of *molecular* production if, unlike Deleuze-Guattari, technics is reconceptualised beyond its traditional determinations. Given that limitation, and without offering an alternative comprehension of the organico-technical complex that takes its technicity into account, it is clear that any notion of the prosthetic as a channel or invagination of the organic and the technical must remain for Deleuze-Guattari external to the theory and to the production of the desiring-machine. As then must any comprehension of the general complex of organico-technical organisation. In other words, even if Deleuze-Guattari's theory of the desiring-machine were adequate to a theorisation of the integration of *affect* and consciousness, such a validation of their conceptual apparatus would not allow an understanding of the specificity and actuality of prosthetics as a productive channel for the 'interpenetration' of organic and technical material organisation.[31]

31. *A Thousand Plateaus,* op. cit., p398.

Prosthetic actuality, taken as a technical production and what that implies in terms of a general complex of organico-technical organisation, is, in sum, not the kind of multiplicitous production Deleuze-Guattari affirm. For Deleuze-Guattari, there can be no 'prostheschiz' that refers to or captures anything of the prosthesis because the latter is technically organised. Equally, it can then be said that Deleuze-Guattari's theory has no bearing either on the historical and materially determined actuality and concept of prosthetics or on *any* prospective drawing together of the organic and technical orders of material organisation. Furthermore, Deleuze-Guattari determine technical machines to be of the order of molar production because they determine the technical as being constituted in and through capitalism. Capitalism is for them an axiomatic order of production in that it is structured by the law of diminishing profit. As such, it is unable to attain the stage of total schizomolecular production that defines the desiring-machine. As is well known, the affirmation of desire is for Deleuze-Guattari both a politico-economic critique and a surpassing of capitalism. That this is also a critique of the technical machine is not so well appreciated. It follows that the critique of Deleuze-Guattari mounted here is less comfortably positioned in relation to anti- or counter-capitalist positions, since it is capitalism that has been responsible for the development of the technical machine to the point where we can now speak of an organico-technical milieu.[32]

32. Suhail Malik, 'Is the Internet a Rhizome? Cyberspace and the Deleuze-Guattari Machine', in *Mute* 7, Winter 1997.

Without another notion of the technical machine, Deleuze-Guattari's theory of the desiring-machine becomes no more than a theoretical fiction with regard to organico-technical milieu. One that is, moreover, irrelevant to the alteration of categories that milieu effects. It does not characterise the actuality of prostheses, nor does it even come to explain what prostheses now do to the traditional conceptual, material and organisational barrier between the organic and the technical. While Deleuze-Guattari do surpass the conceptual-ideational register of mechanism and vitalism that posits a difference in kind between the organic and machinic orders of organisation and function, they go on to propose another similar distinction in the notion of the machine they set up in contrast. Their theory cannot explain anything of the actuality of the organico-technical as such. Instead, they redescribe it as a complex of the organic and the technical in each of their respective 'molar' characteristics of organisation. Deleuze-Guattari do not actually remobilise the standard categorial distinctions between the organic and technical orders of organisation, but restipulate and redescribe the traditional distinction between the organic and the technical, even to the point of opposing them, as molecular production is opposed to molar production. To that extent, their theoretical move contrasts with that which the prosthetic proposes as an organico-technical complex. In its actuality and in its correlative categorial instability, and even if it is the 'machinic phylum' that is commonly called upon in the arts and humanities to comprehend it, the prosthetic thus demands to be determined otherwise than by Deleuze-Guattari's theorisation.

Rauschenberg's Skin: Autobiography, Indexicality, Auto-eroticism

Joanne Morra

Painting relates to both art and life.
Neither can be made.
(I try to act in that gap between the two).

Robert Rauschenberg[1]

1. Quoted in Dorothy C. Miller (ed), *Sixteen Americans*, New York, Museum of Modern Art, 1959, p58.

It pulls back and forth all the time, and always has, even before I thought about it. I would work flat for a while and then I would start doing sculpture. The old thing about the internal dialectic of contradicting yourself ... the only thing that leads to something new. I have to use contradiction in my work not only to achieve something but to avoid something else. That sets me up for some schizophrenic tension.

Robert Rauschenberg[2]

2. *An Interview with Robert Rauschenberg by Barbara Rose*, New York, Avedon, 1997, p59.

3. On the problematic of using artists' statements see, J.J. Christie and Fred Orton, 'Writing on a Text of the Life', *Art History*, 11, 4 (1988), 545-64, and Orton's superb *Figuring Jasper Johns*, London, Reaktion Books, 1994.

4. Rauschenberg's self-portraits or autobiographic works are as varied as the painted *Self-Portrait* produced in the summer of 1948 while attending the Academie Julian in Paris, and the mixed media *Autobiography*, made twenty years later, in 1968.

As his ubiquitously quoted statement enigmatically posits, Robert Rauschenberg 'acts' - that is to say, works, paints - 'in that gap between' 'art and life', 'between the two'.[3] This oft-quoted and little analysed pronouncement forms the basis of this essay. What is this gap between art and life and how is it constituted? What exactly does it mean to work, to produce, to be active in this gap? Why can neither art nor life be made? This essay seeks to address the triumvirate - art, gap, life - through the figure of autobiography and its relationship to skin. In particular, this text considers works of art in which Rauschenberg represents himself, his skin. These self-portraits are generally referred to by the artist as works of 'autobiography'.[4] It is here, in these acts of autobiography that the most intimate traces of art and life - one's own body, skin, subjectivity and desire - are inscribed.

Beyond the actual titles of his autobiographical works, Rauschenberg often discusses himself in relation to his practice. A particularly intriguing assessment of this made by the artist, and useful for my purposes, is the one cited in the second epigraph above which refers to the formation and function of an internal dialectic within himself and his practice. The dialectic Rauschenberg speaks of can be interpreted as being manifest in various ways: in between differing parts of his practice - the flat works versus the sculptural ones, or the white versus the black paintings; as an internal contradiction within a single work of art as a means of 'avoid[ing]' something and 'achiev[ing]' 'something new'; between himself and his work; and within himself, the 'internal dialectic of contradicting yourself', leading to a 'schizophrenic tension' in oneself. Thus, the dialectic that the artist posits functions both intersubjectively and intrasubjectively: between and within practices and subjects. It is important to note that the dialectic remains unresolved. Sublimation is not achieved, as just such a resolution would put an end to the 'contradiction' and the 'tension', and therefore the practice. This type of dialectical movement has been called in very different epistemological contexts, a 'permanently unresolved dialectic', an 'aporia',[5] 'undecidability',[6] or 'divided/split subjectivity'. Each of these concepts constitutes a different discursive regime, and each undertakes a diverse kind of work. However, what each of them configures is a dialectical play without resolution. This irreducibility highlights the way in which one could conceive of the gap between art and life as an ongoing 'dialectic' of 'contradiction'. It also points to the irreducible play between art and life that constitutes autobiography: the play between the subject as author or artist, and the subject of the text or image. The graphic inscription of the autobiographical 'I' is always already a displaced and mediated representational[7] and prosthetic act. This relationship between representation and subjectivity (art and life) as a prosthesis in general, has been well theorised.[8] My own minor contribution to the issue of prosthesis concerns its specific functioning as a mediating hinge between art and life, between representation and Rauschenberg's body. Rauschenberg's skin becomes, in this autobiographical context, a privileged site from which to examine the gap between art and life.

AUTOBIOGRAPHY

The figure of autobiography has a long and formidable genealogy in the literature on Rauschenberg's art practice. From as early as 1953, in response to his exhibition at Eleanor Ward's *Stable Gallery*, both apologists and critics alike implied that autobiography had a place in the interpretation of Rauschenberg's work. Specifically, they considered it in relation to what they thought to be the Neo-Dada impulse in his work, and its engagement with Abstract Expressionism. By laying bare the autobiographical or the expressive artistic apparatus of the latter through the critical apparatus of the former, Rauschenberg's white and black paintings were considered nihilistic, anti-art, the *Erased de Kooning Drawing* a destructive act (In reference to Brandon Taylor's question, I will be considering the 'Erased de Kooning Drawing' in a forthcoming essay), and his use of found objects became a testament to the worst type of Neo-Dada - nothing more than a series of gestures. Soon, Rauschenberg's insistence on using found objects became explicitly associated with autobiography. Whether incorporated into early photographic works, such as the blueprint series, or used to form an articulated ground in the black paintings, or as 'materialized images'[9] in the red paintings and combines, this employment of found objects became a sign of the artist's autobiography. The found object came to metonymically signify the artist himself: his walks through New York City, the amalgamation of things given to him or left in his

5. See the excellent article by Gail Day, 'Persisting and Mediating: T.J. Clark and "the Pain of the Unattainable Beyond"', *Art History*, 23, 1 (March 2000), 1-18.

6. Orton, op. cit., and Fred Orton, 'On Being Bent "Blue" (Second State): An Introduction to Jacques Derrida/A Footnote on Jasper Johns', *Oxford Art Journal*, XII, 1 (1989), 35-46.

7. On autobiography see, for example, Roland Barthes, *Roland Barthes by Roland Barthes*, Richard Howard (trans), Berkeley, University of California Press, 1977 (1975); Jacques Derrida, *The Ear of the Other: Otobiography, Transference, Translation*, Christie McDonald (ed), Peggy Kamuf (trans), Lincoln and London, University of Nebraska Press, 1985 (1982); and Paul de Man, 'Autobiography as De-Facement', *The Rhetoric of Romanticism*, New York, Columbia University Press, 1984, pp67-82.

8. David Wills, *Prosthesis*, Stanford, Stanford University Press, 1995.

9. Rosalind Krauss, 'Rauschenberg and the Materialized Image', *Artforum*, 13 (December 1974), 36-43.

way by friends, the incorporation of objects at his immediate disposal in his everyday life such as magazines, clothing, furniture and utensils.

As early as 1960, William Rubin in his review of the 'Sixteen Americans' exhibition at the Museum of Modern Art, New York, summed up many of these autobiographical concerns in Rauschenberg's practice:

> In comparison with the art of the past, Abstract-Expressionism is an inherently autobiographical style. Rauschenberg has developed this dimension through the application of figurative collage elements within the framework of an abstract style of painting, rendering it even more personal, more particular, and sometimes almost embarrassingly private. Everything the eye delights in is eligible to enter into the autobiographical poem. The iconography of the Rauschenberg pictures seems to reach back through time and consciousness, memory by memory. The juxtaposed coke bottles, mirrors, snapshots, stuffed animals, and kitchen utensils do not join in the Symbolist-Surrealist manner of Lautréamont's umbrella and sewing-machine on the dissecting table. Not that they fail to evoke Freudian associations, but they are particular rather than archetypical in their interrelationships, and they never relinquish their autobiographical intimacy.[10]

10. William Rubin, 'From the Exhibition, "Sixteen Americans", at the Museum of Modern Art, New York', *Art International*, 4 (January 1960), 26.

Rubin's encapsulation highlights many of the issues which may be at play in an analysis of the autobiographical impulse of Rauschenberg's representations and practice.

PAINTING, TOUCHING, SUBJECTIVITY

In an interview with Barbara Rose, Rauschenberg is asked how he first heard about Black Mountain College which he attended, on and off, between 1948-1952. He responds:

> *Time* magazine. And Sue [Weil] heard about it too. The article in *Time* said that Josef Albers was the world's greatest disciplinarian. I could have gone on just painting with my hands, I think, and making messes forever because I really loved painting. I guess the physicality of my personality was emerging, and so I had to paint with my hands. I couldn't stand a brush coming between me and the canvas. Naturally, I cleaned my 'brushes,' which were my hands, on my clothes.[11]

11. Rauschenberg and Rose, op. cit., p23.

The need for disciplining brought him to Josef Albers. It is possible to read this desire to work with Albers as an outward enactment of the artist's 'internal dialectic'. Albers was a figure with and against whom Rauschenberg could learn how to stop painting with his 'hands', his 'physicality'. And yet, Albers would unwittingly teach him - since Rauschenberg engaged with his pedagogy through resistance - how to touch, how to enact his physicality differently.[12] This enactment would be accomplished not by applying paint with his hands, his body - since this was Rauschenberg's predilection and what he wished to counteract through Albers' disciplining - but, by applying it with a paintbrush - an object, an implement, a prosthesis - as a means of contradicting his own desire to touch. Rauschenberg was taught how to mediate his 'physicality' through the use of external objects: the camera, found objects, x-ray machines, car tires, erasers, glue. These literal prostheses became one of the means through which Rauschenberg could hold at bay his physicality, while at the same time feed his desire to touch. The mediating prostheses become metonymies through which the artist could maintain a gap between art and life, while at the same time producing intimate, autobiographical works of art: works that touch upon the artist's skin.

12. For an alternative reading of Rauschenberg's statement see Helen Molesworth, 'Before Bed', October, 63 (Winter 1993), 68-82; and, Yve-Alain Bois, 'Base Materialism', in Bois and R. Krauss, Formless: A User's Guide, New York, Zone, 1997, pp51-62.

INDEXICALITY, NARCISSISM, MEDIATION

I am interested in a kind of limbo state of identity.

Robert Rauschenberg[13]

13. Quoted in Nigel Gosling, 'A Jackdaw of Genius', The Observer Weekend Review, 9 February 1964, p23.

In 1952, while in Italy with Cy Twombly, Rauschenberg produced a series of *Untitled* objects, known as *Scatole Personali*. These small portable containers, mainly wooden boxes, held 'personal' found objects. One of these scatole consists of a stained wooden box and lid containing dirt, pins, mica, and a

Robert Rauschenberg, Untitled (Scatole Personali) *(c. 1952), Copyright, Robert Rauschenberg/DACS, London, VAGA, New York, 2002*

14. Barthes, Derrida, de Man, op. cit.

15. Charles Sanders Peirce, '[from] On the Algebra of Logic: A Contribution to the Philosophy of Notation', in C. Hartshorne and P. Weiss (eds), *Writings of Charles Sanders Peirce: A Chronological Edition, Volume I (1857-1866)*, Bloomington, Indiana University Press, 1982, pp225-28, p226.

16. Rosalind Krauss, 'Notes on the Index: Seventies Art in America' (1977), in A. Michelson, et al (eds), *October: The First Decade, 1976-1986*, Cambridge, MA, MIT, 1987, pp2-15.

17. There is work to be done, but this is not the place for it, on the dialectic at play in Peirce's theory of indexicality and Rauschenberg's practice, reading Peirce against the grain of his insistent critique of Hegelian dialectics.

18. Quoted in Barbaralee Diamonstein, 'Robert Rauschenberg and Leo Castelli', *Inside New York's Art World*, New York, Rizzoli, 1979, p311.

photograph of the artist upon which is placed a small magnifying glass. The torn and partial photograph shows us Rauschenberg's eyes and nose. As an iconic and indexical sign, this photograph registers its existence through a mediating prosthetic apparatus - the camera. However, the mediated photograph having been placed under a magnifying glass is mediated once again. What we have here is a double mediation and a double displacement: two moves away from the artist and towards the 'I' of autobiography. What intrigues me about this personal box, is its literal representation of the 'personali': a photograph of Rauschenberg which is both personal and of the person. The photograph functions as a representation of the self - an auto-photograph, if you will - which connotes both the subject of the art work and its producer. Rauschenberg is both subject and other. Of course, this is one of the main theoretical suppositions of autobiography, wherein the subject writing or inscribing the representation of itself, is re-presented in the text or image.[14] The 'real connection'[15] between the absent referent (Rauschenberg as subject and producer) and the indexical sign (Rauschenberg as subject) is an intimate one - narcissistic even.

Rosalind Krauss has provided us with a psychoanalytic link between works of art in which an artist is indexically represented and narcissism, as the cohabitation of auto-eroticism and the love-object in a single subject and its indexical sign.[16] That is, for Krauss an indexical representation of an artist in a work of art - the production of a mirror image - is representative of ego formation, specifically in relation to narcissism and the intimate act of auto-eroticism. It is the intimacy of narcissism and its associative auto-eroticism that belies my interest in Rauschenberg's skin, and its indexical, autobiographical inscription in his art practice. As a representation of ego formation, the *Scatole Personali* and its torn photograph is an index of the skin of the self as other: Rauschenberg represents a subject in a state of limbo, negotiating between the one and the other. In this art work, and its use of an auto-photograph, the internal dialectic of contradiction is being played out, between and within the artist and his art work. On the one hand, what we have is a representation of the dialectic of the autobiographical inscription - the auto-photograph as an intrasubjective representation of self as other. On the other hand, it is an iconic and indexical sign, which attests to a dialectical intersubjective art practice wherein the artist's body is both subject and producer of the work of art.[17] This mediated dialectic of a psychical projection of the self - Rauschenberg - through an image of the corporeal self - Rauschenberg's skin - leads us more intimately to the matter of skin.

THE SKIN EGO

I don't like the single ego ... I just don't want to have one.

Robert Rauschenberg[18]

Any research undertaken on the matter of skin will eventually come into contact with Didier Anzieu's theory of the Skin Ego. Expanding upon the work of Sigmund Freud, what is particularly useful in relation to the internal dialectics of Rauschenberg's autobiographic practice is Anzieu's reformulation of Freud's understanding of projection in the formation of the bodily ego and the psychic apparatus. For Freud,

> The ego is first and foremost a bodily ego; it is not merely a surface entity, but is itself the projection of a surface. (i.e. the ego is ultimately derived from bodily sensations, chiefly from those springing from the surface of the body. It may thus be regarded as a mental projection of the surface of the body, besides ... representing the superficies of the mental apparatus.)[19]

Thus, in Freud, we are confronted with a dual psychical apparatus made up of bodily ego and surface - the surface being an internal projection of something else. In other words, a dialectic ensues in ego formation which recognises that the ego has a psychical surface that is produced from a relationship with an other (a bodily surface). This other is constituted by an internal representation of an external surface. It is at this point that we can turn more fully to Anzieu's extension of Freud's theorisation through the former's work on the Skin Ego. For Anzieu, 'The development of a Skin Ego is a response to the need for a narcissistic envelope and guarantees the psychical apparatus a sure and continuous sense of basic well-being'.[20] Jean Laplanche explains that this narcissistic envelope is one of the necessary requirements for ego formation in that it allows 'the individual to love himself, love life and love in order to live'.[21] It is this necessary narcissism of ego formation that requires the practice of projection and the surface upon which this is to occur. For Anzieu, the skin functions as such a 'retainer of goodness and fullness'.[22] The skin is the interface between inside and outside: a protection from penetration and from others. It is also the site of communication with others, whereupon signifying relations are established, and the 'surface' upon which the marks left by others are inscribed. In effect, Anzieu confirms Freud's affirmation of the relationship between bodily ego and surface when the former suggests that the Skin Ego is the 'mental image of which the Ego of the child makes use during the early phases of its development to represent itself as an Ego containing psychical content, on the basis of its experience of the surface of the body'.[23] Thus skin sensations are projected and recorded onto the differentiated surface of the psychical apparatus. And this projection corresponds to the moment at which psychical and bodily ego are differentiated on an operative level. Psychically, the ego sets into motion defence mechanisms against dangerous sexual drives, while the bodily ego, not recognised as belonging to oneself, attributes sexual and cutaneous sensations to a 'devious seducer or persecutor'.[24] The dialectic initiated here is one between skin sensation and the seductive powers of the other (bodily ego), and the recognised internalised psychical mechanism of

19. Sigmund Freud, 'The Ego and the Id' (1927 English trans), *On Metapsychology: The Theory of Psychoanalysis*, James Strachey (trans), London, Penguin, 1984, pp339-408, pp364-65.

20. Didier Anzieu, *The Skin Ego*, Chris Turner (trans), New Haven and London, Yale University Press, 1989, pp39-40.

21. Jean Laplanche, *New Foundations for Psychoanalysis*, David Macey (trans), London, Blackwell, 1989, p49.

22. Anzieu, op. cit., p40.

23. Ibid.

24. Ibid.

sexual defence (psychical ego). The skin is therefore the boundary through which the bodily and psychic formation of the ego are initiated and maintained.

Anzieu's theory of the Skin Ego proposes that the place of the other is both internal and external. For him, the Skin Ego is a psychical and corporeal envelope that forms a boundary between the subject and an internal other, forming an intrasubjective relationship. The Skin Ego also denotes the engagement between the subject and an external other as an intersubjective encounter. Thus, the Skin Ego takes account of an internal dialectic between self and other, while also recognising the importance of the other as outsider. In this way, Anzieu stresses that factors such as culture and history are necessary in the formation of subjectivity. These factors are inscribed upon the subject through its relationship with an other. Thus the other's skin is representative of corporeal, as well as historical, cultural, and social determinations.

But what if the other's skin is missing?

25. Laplanche, op. cit., p49.

Following Anzieu, Laplanche notes that 'anything can be used as a substitute skin; as Anzieu demonstrates, words, themselves can be used as a skin'.[25] Most importantly for this essay, Anzieu notes in *The Skin Ego* that a *canvas* can become a 'symbolic skin': 'Projection of the skin on to the object [is ...] found in painting, where the canvas (often thickened with paint or cross-hatched) provides a symbolic skin'. This relationship to the canvas functions as an 'auto-erotic cathexis of its [the subject's] own skin'.[26]

26. Anzieu, op. cit., p19. He is summarising the research undertaken by the psychoanalyst Barrie M. Biven.

SKIN TOUCHING SKIN

Rauschenberg [has a] preoccupation with evidence of the body's presence marked on the world: through its imprint, its stains, and the geometry it engenders, the body proclaims itself to be both 'in here' and 'out there.' Bodily traces thus declare the paradoxical nature of the self's doubled identity, articulating the way we live and have our being - partly inside our fleshly envelope and partly outside it. Like Marsyas in the midst of his ordeal, we find ourselves only partially contained within our skin.

James Leggio[27]

27. James Leggio, 'Robert Rauschenberg's *Bed* and the Symbolism of the Body', in J. Leggio and H.M. Franc (eds), *Essays on Assemblage: Studies in Modern Art*, 2, New York, Museum of Modern Art, 1991, pp79-117, p107.

Implicitly reading back through the interpretation of the *Scatole Personali*, I will now consider two other types of autobiographical inscriptions of Rauschenberg's skin. The first is the practice of transfer drawing, the second is body tracing. These two processes and their relation to skin will be thought through three works of art, the *Drawings of Dante's* Inferno (1958-60), *Autobiography* (1960) and *Wager* (1957-59). During another trip with Twombly in 1952, this time to Cuba, Rauschenberg experimented with solvent and printed images to produce transfer drawings. By soaking a torn or cut out magazine or newspaper image in lighter fluid, placing it face down on paper, and then rubbing the back of it with an empty ball point pen, Rauschenberg was able to 'transfer' the image onto a sheet of paper. Transfer drawing is quite obviously an indexical and iconic practice, mediated both in its prosthetic method, and through the type of popular, mass produced imagery employed. The transferred image appears in reverse. It is framed, veiled and somewhat concealed by the hatchings produced by the pen strokes, adding an element of gestural trace to the drawings. These drawings are often supplemented with splashes of gouache, watercolour, as well as pencil drawings, and later with found objects.

Rauschenberg has suggested that the culmination of this artistic practice are his transfer drawings for Dante's *Inferno* (1958-60). These thirty-four drawings - one for each Canto - span two and a half years of the artist's working career and are representative of a long term, narrative project, unlike any other during that time. By closely following John Ciardi's Americanized translation of Dante's classic text,[28] Rauschenberg was able to produce a distinctive rendition or visual translation of the Medieval narrative. Scouring through copies of *Sports Illustrated*, *Time*, *Life*, *The New York Times* and a wealth of other popular printed matter for appropriate imagery, the *Inferno* drawings come to represent the cultural and social sensibility of a wholly fifties America: Eisenhower, Nixon, Stevenson, advertisements, wrestlers, and racing cars are but a few of the many references littering the representations. In my view, the *Inferno* drawings resemble more than a slice of American life: they represent something closer to an archaeology of the American unconscious during that time. Constituted by a proliferation of popular imagery that burgeoned during the 1950s, these drawings are notable as mappings of unconscious territory: they read as inscriptions which denote cultural, historical and social formations.

Where does this leave the practice of transfer drawing in relation to Rauschenberg's skin? Can for instance, the reinscription of imagery that takes place in transfer drawing be compared to the inscription of the other, the cultural other, onto the skin of the subject? Do the framed, veiled, blurred, hatched, layered images constitute a visualisation of the transfer(ence) that occurs between skin (Ego) and its cultural or historical context? As inscriptions, as marks on the skin (of the paper), forming indelible ink stains on a subjective and cultural unconscious, the transfer drawings touch upon the skin. Is the reversal of an image through transfer drawing similar to the moment of mirroring when skin touches skin? The erotic aspect of Rauschenberg's touching, the rubbing that initiates and completes the transfer(ence) as an eroticised practice has been noted by Laura Auricchio.[29] Can the play of seduction introduced in the act of touching be aligned with the manipulation and gestural repetition of transferring drawings? Are we witnessing the traces of an erotic sensibility? Is this a moment in which Anzieu's theorisation of the canvas as a substitute Skin Ego precipitates the more specific erotic sensibility of auto-eroticism?

The possibility of mapping the graphic inscriptions of transfer drawings as dermographic signs of pleasure, sensuality, skin touching skin in the

28. Dante Alighieri, *The Inferno*, John Ciardi (trans), New York, The New American Library, Norton, 1970 (1954), p71.

29. Laura Auricchio, 'Lifting the Veil: Robert Rauschenberg's Thirty-Four Drawings for Dante's Inferno and the Commercial Homoerotic Imagery of 1950s America', in T. Foster, C. Siegel, E.E. Berry (eds), *The Gay '90s: Disciplinary and Interdisciplinary Formations in Queer Studies*, *Genders*, 26 (1997), 119-54.

quest for ego formation are certainly available. The process of transfer drawing is in some ways a visualisation of the process of ego formation - and its dialectic - with the construction of a projected surface of the other (image/history/culture) onto the drawing as skin (Ego). Because these drawings are signs of cultural difference, as well as subjective division, they are as much about Rauschenberg as the cultural moment of their production. Is it not after all the complex matter of Rauschenberg's skin that we are ultimately attempting to inscribe?

There is potential here, and the plausibility of this metaphoric reading of the *Inferno* drawings is strengthened, and to a certain extent displaced, through a somewhat anomalous literal inscription of Rauschenberg's skin. In two of the thiry-four Cantos - *Canto IX* and *Canto XIV* - Rauschenberg uses his body in an exceptional way: here he traces the outline of his fingertips and toes, respectively, onto these two separate drawings.

Robert Rauschenberg, Canto IX, Dante's Inferno, *(1958-60), Copyright, Robert Rauschenberg/ DACS, London, VAGA, New York, 2002*

These moments of body tracing, of following the border of the skin, with an implement, are acts of a mediated indexicality; this practice of autobiographical inscription ensures that a prosthetic is literally employed as a means through which the skin is inscribed.

Body tracing can also be understood as a representation of a corporeal envelope, adding another certain literality to the way in which skin functions in this essay. At some level, what we see are the perimeters of Rauschenberg's skin. And yet, we see nothing more than a two-dimensional representation of these boundaries. Body tracing defines the border of a body as indexical trace, wherein the body becomes an absent presence. This practice also indexically inscribes the inside of the body through its outlining of the body's circumference. In psychoanalytic terms, the body tracing in the two *Cantos* is representative of the self as a projection onto a screen, a phantasmatic Rauschenberg, which must at one and the same time denote the metaphoric

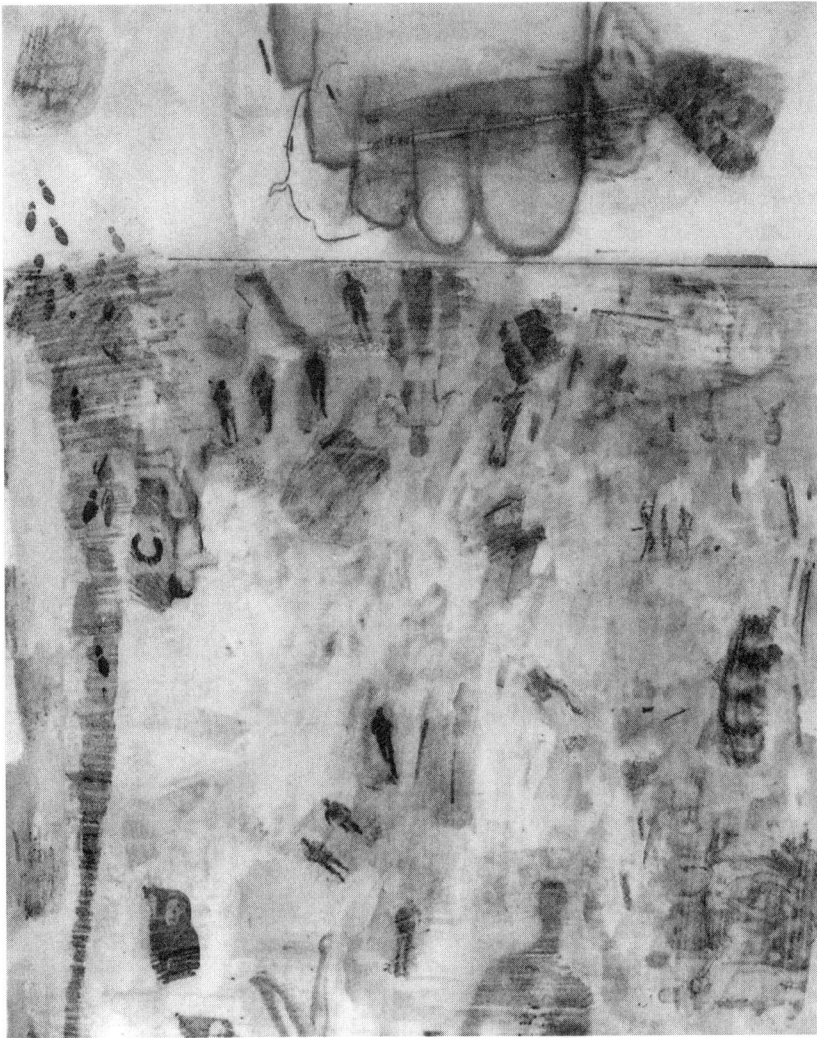

Robert Rauschenberg, Canto XIV, Dante's Inferno, *(1958-60), Copyright, Robert Rauschenberg/ DACS, London, VAGA, New York, 2002*

30. Jonathan Katz, 'The Art of Code: Jasper Johns and Robert Rauschenberg', in W. Chadwick and I. de Courtivron (eds), *Significant Others: Creativity and Intimate Partnerships*, London, Thames and Hudson, 1993, pp189-207, p201.

31. On alternative readings of feet in mid-century American painting, see for example, Rosalind Krauss, *The Optical Unconscious*, Cambridge, MA and London, MIT, 1993, pp275-89; and Benjamin H. D. Buchloh, 'Andy Warhol's One-Dimensional Art, 1956-1966', *Neo-Avantgarde and Culture Industry: Essays on European and American Art from 1955-1975*, Cambridge, MA and London, MIT, 2000, pp461-531.

32. On alternative ways in which the hand as an indexical sign signifies in mid-century American art, see for instance, on Pollock, T. J. Clark, 'Jackson Pollock's Abstraction', in S. Guilbaut (ed), *Reconstructing Modernism: Art in New York, Paris, and Montreal 1945-1964*, Cambridge, MA and London, MIT, 1992, and Bois and Krauss, op. cit., and on Johns, Orton, op. cit., and Max Kozloff, 'The division and mockery of the self', *Studio International*, 179 (Jan 1970), 9-15.

and the literal aspects of corporeality: is this then, some kind of inscription of the Skin Ego?

Canto XIV, which contains an outline of Rauschenberg's toes, represents Circle 7, Round 3 of Hell, herein reside the Violent Against God, Nature, and Art. This round of the *Inferno* is a place of sterility; the desert and rain of fire is cut through by a rill flowing with boiling red liquid. It is this redness that surrounds the gigantic toes (Rauschenberg's toes) that stamp down upon a naked male figure whose head is placed askance. The toes which belong to a right foot, represent in Dante's poem, the Roman Catholic Church, that fortress of blasphemy, sodomy and usury.

Both Jonathan Katz and, following his lead, Laura Auricchio have read this bodily tracing as a 'highly obscure' (Auricchio) inscription of Rauschenberg's homosexuality, and his relationship with Jasper Johns. The cryptic allegorical reading is for Katz 'a "coming out" legible only to those who are "in"'.[30] In terms of the Skin Ego, as an internal projection through an external skin formation, the reading of homosexual desire inscribed through a tracing of the skin is an important one.[31]

In relation to the body tracing in *Canto IX* - the 6th Circle of Hell, wherein one encounters The Heretics - neither Katz nor Auricchio refers to Rauschenberg's outlined fingertips.[32] The fingers which cover a pair of eyes represent an insistence on both Virgil and Rauschenberg's part. 'Canto IX' recounts the point at which the poet and his guide are terrorised by possibility. Unlike the guide's usual calm temperament, both Virgil and Dante wait at the Gate of Dis in dread for Medusa to appear. Rauschenberg's fingers function as an insistent shield between Dante's eyes, the potential sight of Medusa and the possibility of an ensuing petrifaction, while at the same time, making visible the younger poet's eyes through the use of body tracing, thereby acknowledging Dante's presence and vision. Perhaps there is potential here for a reading of homosexuality and vision, a '"coming out" to those who are "in"', and it is possible that this framework can be employed as a means of reading through my own interest in the relationship between skin, vision, permeability and autobiography. For now, I will pick up on this latter relationship, and suggest that these connections are made possible representationally because of the evacuated boundary that is formed through the practice of body tracing, by the indexical outlining of the skin. Hidden and yet present to the potential petrifaction instilled by the sight of Medusa[33] this fragment of body tracing connotes permeability, in a way that corresponds with Anzieu's corporeal colander: the skin, full of holes, is a fluid layering, inscribing surround and yet available for penetration. In *Canto IX* and *Canto XIV*, the fingertips and toes are cut off by the drawings and form an open and permeable boundary which indexically and synechdochally inscribes the body of the artist. The representation of the perimeter of the skin becomes an indexical sign of Rauschenberg's body, registering the corporeal envelope as a boundary between ego and other, between self and its representation, and self and cultural moment. As a

Robert Rauschenberg, Autobiography *(1960), Copyright, Robert Rauschenberg/ DACS, London, VAGA, New York, 2002*

graphic inscription of the self, body tracing denotes the skin as a formation of autobiography.

The second work of art theorised brings us back to the erotic practice of transfer drawing with which I began this section. But this time, it touches upon the artist's skin, differently. In the transfer drawing *Autobiography* (1960), Rauschenberg employs two prints of himself as the basis for two transfers. On the upper left hand corner we find an upside down transfer of the artist's portrait, and below it in the lower corner is a transferred image of the artist leaning on an object, reminiscent of his more sculptural combines. The use of self-portraits in this way, leads me to ask: what type of pleasure is elicited in the narcissistic practice of indexicality when an image of the artist is transferred onto a drawing entitled *Autobiography*?

Within the framework of this article, the erotic aspect of transfer drawing as a mediated, indexical art practice is made more complex when the image employed is of one's self and thus speaks of both the real body, and the 'I' as a sign of narcissistic ego formation (after all, this piece is entitled *Autobiography*). At this point, I will make only one comment about the erotics of this transference and Anzieu's reference to the bodily ego's projection of corporeal sensation onto a seducer and the fact of auto-eroticism. If the practice of producing a transfer drawing is in some sense an erotic, or sensual,

33. See Steven Connor, 'Fascination, skin and the screen', *Critical Quarterly*, 40,1 (Spring 1998), 9-24.

or even a corporeally stimulating experience, and if this practice of transfer drawing involves the re-representation of an already narcissistic self-image (an auto-photograph) by means of a manipulation and re-manipulation of the self through repetitive stroking, rubbing and skin excitations, then are we encountering here, not so much a homo-eroticism as an auto-eroticism. This is something similar to the auto-eroticism that Anzieu mentions in relation to art practice as a skin substitute, and Krauss proposes in relation to indexical representations of an artist's own body. In this transfer drawing of Rauschenberg's indexical self, the skin touching and rubbing the paper can be understood as the projected skin of one's self, and, this contact, forms a mediated representation of oneself by oneself. *Autobiography* elicits an understanding of autobiography and indexicality as a mediated auto-eroticism that in effect proposes a seductive practice in which the seducer is the seduced: Rauschenberg's skin rubs against itself.

The third and final inscription of Rauschenberg's skin touched upon in this essay is found in the combine *Wager* (1957-59). It is made up of four panels, its two central panels once formed the combine *Nocturnes*, which were then reworked and incorporated into the larger piece *Wager*. Very little has been written about *Wager*. However, Nicholas Calas provides some insight into the combine when he draws attention to its contrasting central and outer panels, noting that the former are filled with 'accidents' and the latter with 'the artist'.[34] These quite dark overpainted central panels are opposed to the lighter outer panels. On the left outer panel, the canvas is overlaid with a light silk gauze, four sheets of cream drawing paper placed side-by-side, two small embroidered pieces of ageing white cloth, and washes of paint, including a white streak across the centre of the panel, and small blue and black painted squares on the upper left side. On the outer right panel is, as Calas notes, a 'hardly visible' life size body tracing of a naked Rauschenberg. For Calas this body tracing is an example of Rauschenberg's 'stand against imitation exemplified by the self-portrait' and functions in opposition to the central panels so that 'the meaning of *Wager*' is 'the artist versus the accident'.[35]

Wager, a noun and verb denotes a state of affairs between persons. Historically it refers to an ancient form of trial by personal combat between the parties involved or their champions. Legally, it references a form of trial in which the defendant is required to produce witnesses who will swear to his or her innocence. The guilt or innocence of Rauschenberg's wager is up for grabs, as is the personal combat: perhaps the reference is to be read between the panels, between, following Calas, the heterogeneity of the accident and the homogeneity of the bodily tracing, between accident and artist. It is possible to read the tracing of the body as a means of counterbalancing the heterogeneity of the combine paintings in general (and by extension, the transfer drawings), and the inner panels of this combine in particular. The inclusion of a corporeal perimeter on an outer panel of *Wager* seems to suggest a homogeneous boundary in contradistinction

34. Nicolas Calas, 'Robert Rauschenberg' (1964), *Art in the Age of Risk and Other Essays*, New York, Dutton, 1968, pp169-93, p182.

35. Calas, ibid.

36. On punctured skin and schizophrenia, see Steven Connor, 'Integuments: The Scar, The Sheen, The Screen', *New Formations*, 39 (1999), 32-54.

37. Calas, op. cit., p182.

38. Rauschenberg's *Bed*, the black and red paintings have been discussed in relation to the Turin Shroud, but never *Wager*. Although the body tracing elicits just such a reading I do not have the space to undertake it now. See, Leggio, op. cit, Molesworth, op. cit., and on the Turin Shroud, Georges Didi-Huberman, 'The Index of the Absent Wound (Monograph on a Stain)' (1984), in A. Michelson, et. al., op. cit., pp39-57.

Robert Rauschenberg, Wager, 1957-59, Copyright, Robert Rauschenberg/ DACS, London, VAGA, New York, 2002

to the eclecticism of the inner panels.

And yet, when one takes a closer look at the body tracing in *Wager*, one realises that its function as an index, as evidence, mark, and trace, as a clue to Rauschenberg's skin is literally full of holes.[36] Calas suggests that 'RR traced his body faintly on the right board while standing with his back against the canvas'.[37] I would like to propose two amendments to this interpretation. The first is in relation to the canvas as the ground upon which the body tracing was inscribed. Looking closely at the body tracing, one notices that it was actually inscribed on top of a large piece of silk gauze which was secured onto the canvas. This is evidenced by the way in which the pencil's graphite inscribes the body on top of the silk and at times has marked the canvas beneath it. This leads me to believe that the silk was already secured to the canvas before the inscription took place, and thus the body tracing was not so much inscribed upon the canvas as upon the silk of the canvas. Secondly, as opposed to Calas' suggestion that Rauschenberg made the tracing while standing with his back against the canvas, it is more likely that Rauschenberg placed the canvas on the floor and lay upon it in order to make the tracing.[38] I offer this because of the way in which the feet of the body tracing echo those of *Lawn Combed* (c. 1954) and *Canto XIV* of the Dante drawings.

The feet in *Wager* have been traced around their full perimeter, and this implies that they were drawn while placed firmly and squarely on the 'flatbed picture plane'.[39] This suggests that Rauschenberg stood or sat on the canvas in order to trace his feet. These feet overlap the open ends of the traced ankles which means that Rauschenberg decided not to follow the logic of body tracing which would have produced the heels as stubs for feet. Instead of this, he chose to lay his feet flat along the picture plane and trace the feet in their entirety. The resultant inscriptions as clues speak to a continuous

39. Leo Steinberg, 'Other Criteria', *Other Criteria: Confrontations with Twentieth-Century Art*, New York, Oxford University Press, 1972, pp55-91.

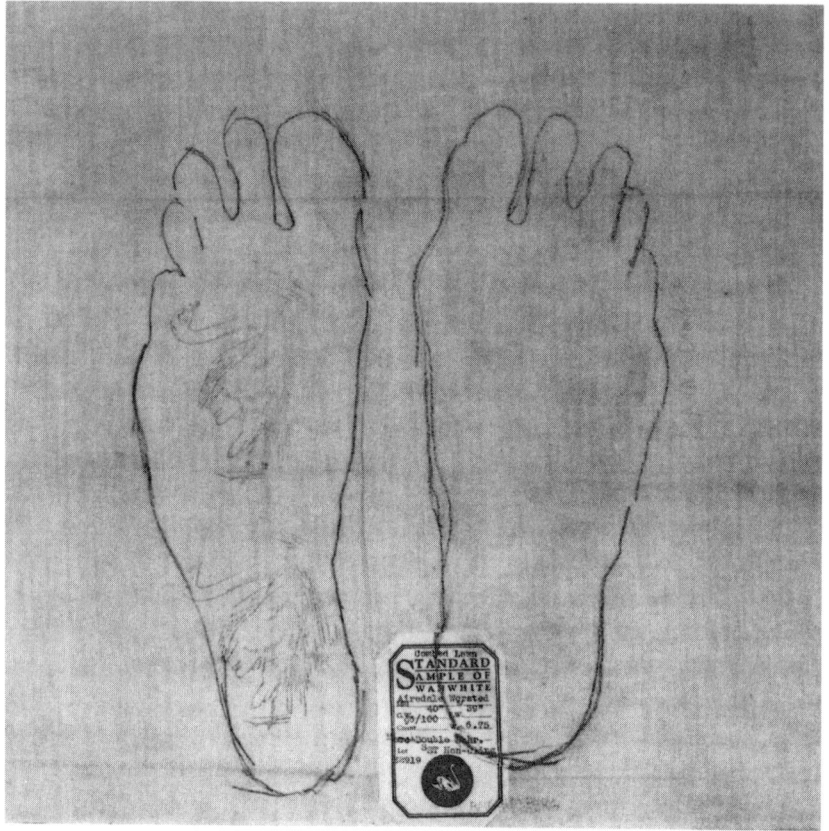

Robert Rauschenberg, Lawn Combed, *c.1954, Copyright, Robert Rauschenberg/ DACS, London, VAGA, New York, 2002*

bodily movement: Rauschenberg changed positions, lying down for some of the tracing, he also sat up or stood, rolled to one side and then the other in the making of this indexical, prosthetic sign. The resultant body tracing is made up of a series of quite short pencil marks forming a layering of inscriptions upon one another, a series of hatchings, as pencil marks go over similar ground with different strokes - this is especially the case on the body's right side; some of the traces inscribe themselves only onto the silk while others mark through to the canvas beneath it. All in all, the skin tracing in *Wager* reproduces the heterogeneity of the other artistic inscriptions in the combine. Body tracing, as a practice, forms a permeable boundary around an artist's skin; an intimate inscription; a loitering around the skin. With a pencil, a prosthesis, moving around the skin, marking its path and touching one's skin, tickling it, body tracing inscribes an (auto)-eroticism, which forms a corporeal envelope that is full of gaps, fissures and holes.

What seemed like a dialectical play between the heterogeneity of the accident and the homogeneity of the artist's bodily inscription has shown itself to be otherwise: both are heterogeneous practices. But, an internal dialectic remains within *Wager* as an anomaly is inscribed within the nude body tracing. Rather than only tracing around the extreme boundaries of the skin - which constitutes an act of body tracing - Rauschenberg cuts across the traced border by drawing an outline of the groin onto the *inside* of the body tracing - onto the interior of the traced body. That is, he closes off the top of the traced genitals. This mark transforms the tracing *around* the body into a tracing (or non-tracing) *of* a body. No longer simply a tracing of an intimate self-portrait, the figure in *Wager* also becomes a non-tracing, a drawing of this intimacy. The autobiographic inscription in *Wager* functions as an indexical sign wherein the representation of narcissism and auto-eroticism moves between the play of tracing and non-tracing.[40]

Once again, Rauschenberg's practice emerges as a representational process in which the complex matters of subject formation and art practice work through what he has named a 'dialectic' of 'contradiction'. As mediated, indexical signs, the erotics and sensual play of body tracing and transfer drawing make visible a prosthetic writing on and around the skin that is not so much an 'act' as it is a brief touching in the gap between art and life.

40. One could read this dialectical inscription as subjective violence by following Krauss on Twombly's graffitist marks as inscriptions of a différantial subjectivity. *The Optical Unconscious*, op. cit., p265.

A version of this article was presented at the Association of Art Historians Conference (2000). I would like to thank Briony Fer and Tamar Garb for this opportunity and their support; and Brandon Taylor and David Green for their insightful questions at that time. Taylor's question will be taken up in a forthcoming article. Thanks are also due to Harry Gilonis and Young Paik Chun, and especially, Fred Orton and, as always, Marq Smith.

VENUS IN FOAM

Fred Botting & Scott Wilson

PAM

SHE emerges from the waves sugar-flecked with the surf's foam, golden honeytan glistening in the California sun, scarlet swimwear clinging to her cosmetic curves and a red polymer life preserver held loosely in the hand. This is no ordinary body, even on a beach where supercorporeality is the norm: 'Pamela Anderson comes into being simultaneously with her implants, no mere enhancements of the human figure, but a total body prosthesis. She rises from the (air)waves as the televisual dream of a machinic age, her visibility and incandescence the sublime simulation of corporeal perfection'.[1] Outside the orbit of human desire and fantasy, her immaterial existence has nothing of the human about it. Indeed humanity is accessorised as little more than the life preserver: her husband, Tommy Lee, dangles as mere meat to Pam's machinic excellence.

According to the research collective called SHaH, Pam is an example of 'hyperwoman', a prototype of a new synthetic species turned on by the vision machines of a posthuman future present. Embodying the absence of a sexual relation, PAM is an acronym for 'Post-Adoration Machine': beyond masquerade, she is the sublime supplement that supplants any illusion of human mastery. For SHaH, silicone is the key to her hyperreal being: 'her silicone, for humans, marks her destiny as automaton, doll, artifice. But for the machine, the silicone is the signifier implanted on the Thing of her body, the mark of a machinic sublimation'.[2] Like the 'synthetic idol' La Cicciolina who, for Jean Baudrillard, exposes the obscenity of a pornographic gaze, PAM's perfection departs on a trajectory that voids human desire and heads towards the software stars of William Gibson's *Idoru*, Kyoto Date, or Lara Croft ... Or Irigaray's femininity when adapted for cyberspace. Sadie Plant's matrix interweaves women and computers in its fluid connectivities of simulation and self-simulation, replicating and proliferating zeroes in its 'zone of multiplicity'.[3] Out of control, cyberspace overturns masculine assumptions and privilege: 'virtual reality destroys his identity, digitisation is mapping his soul and, at the peak of his triumph, the culmination of his machinic erections, man confronts the system he built for his own protection and finds it is female and dangerous'.[4] At the crest of a wave, man is overcome by the surf. For Plant, the subversive feminisation manifested in cyberspace is coordinated with a more general feminisation evident in biochemical pollution and global economic reorganisation. The reversal and supersession of gender hierarchies enacts a practical deconstruction: the supplement that was

1. 'SHaH, 'Incorporating the Impossible: Towards a General Economy of the Future Present', *Cultural Values*, 1, 2 (1997), 180.

2. Ibid., p189.

3. Sadie Plant, 'On the Matrix: Cyberfeminist Simulations', in Rob Shields (ed), *Cultures of the Internet. Virtual Spaces, Real Histories, Living Bodies*, London, Sage, 1996, p179.

4. Ibid., p182.

once identified with toys, play, ornament, automata, dolls and artifice becomes the rule.

FOAM THEORY

To identify a rule, of course, one must first transgress it. And transgression is not liberation, as Michel Foucault points out in respect of sexuality. Far from liberating sexuality, he argues, we have carried it to the limits of consciousness, law, taboo and language: sexuality 'traces that line of foam showing just how far speech may advance upon the sands of silence'.[5] Denoting an extimate 'fissure',[6] sexuality's line of foam traces transgression's opening onto the impossible and interior limit of death and thus carries with it both the conditions of possibility and the demise of the modern philosophical subject.

Foucault, in his 'Preface to Transgression', is of course drawing on the work of Georges Bataille. In *Inner Experience*, Bataille writes of the forces of an exuberant life and an impossible reality interior to and in excess of homogenised, everyday subjectivity. It is these heterogeneous forces that are glimpsed in moments of transgression associated with eroticism, death and wasteful, general economic expenditure. Throwing humans out of isolation and into a movement 'through which they communicate among themselves, rushing with great commotion like waves one to another', the transgression which discloses the interior limit of death hollows out the subject. 'The foam which is at the crest of the wave requires this incessant slipping: the consciousness of death (and the liberation which it brings to the immensity of beings) would not be formed if one did not approach death, but it ceases to be, as soon as death has done its work'.[7] The foam that marks the interior excess of the modern subject, opening it to a movement within and beyond it, also charts the destiny that Foucault famously sketches for modernity at the end of *The Order of Things*: 'If those arrangements [of knowledge] were to disappear as they appeared ... then one certainly can wager that man would be erased, like a face drawn in the sand at the edge of the sea'.[8] Theory, then, stands on the beach as the witness to the end of man. But it is also caught up in the very foam that wipes away the human face. For Jacques Lacan, reviewing the terms that have begun to change the face of French thought, there is an Aphrodite surfing on the foam of theory and this Aphrodite has a name: différance - with an 'a'.

C'est pourquoi mon discours, si mince soit-il auprès d'une oeuvre comme celle de mon ami Claude Lévi-Strauss, fait balise autrement, dans ce flot montant de signifiant, de signifié, de 'ça parle', de trace, de gramme, de leurre, de mythe, voire and manque, de la circulation desquels je me suis maintenant dessaisi. Aphrodite de cette écume, en a surgi au dernier temps la *différance*, avec un a.[9]

5. Michel Foucault, 'Preface to Transgression', in Donald F. Bouchard (ed), *Language, Counter-Memory, Practice*, Ithaca, Cornell University Press, 1977, p30.

6. Ibid.

7. Georges Bataille, *Inner Experience*, Leslie Anne Boldt (trans), New York, Suny Press, 1988, p97.

8. Michel Foucault, *The Order of Things*, London, Routledge, 1986, p387.

9. Jacques Lacan, 'De Rome 53 à Rome 67: La psychanalyse. Raison d'un échec', *Scilicet*, 1 (1968), p47.

The little 'a' that silently signals the play of difference and deferral that precludes the closure or culmination of self-presence, self-identity, yet sustains its coming, its jouissance, displaces man from the centre of the human sciences and renders him an effect of prosthetic supplements that are at once exterior and interior to him in his existence as a speaking, desiring being.

If man succumbs to supplementarity, awash in the foam of 'a', woman (whoever she may be) does not ascend to primacy in his place: that other supplement - prosthetic, machinic - comes crashing in on the surf. Hyperwoman takes her bearings from Luce Irigaray's 'awoman'. The 'a' of Aphrodite on the waves, however, plots a different trajectory, one that emerges not from a 'mechanics of fluids' associated with the multiplicities of sexual difference, but from a noisy machinics of foam in which presence and absence, self and other no longer find solidity in opposition. The little 'a' marks, in excess of the fecundity of an absence that allies sexual and machinic non-relation, a locus of chaotic production. The spending of Chronos's seed in the formation of a figure of desire and temporality discloses flows, noise and excess in which all of the solids and structures of rationality are subjected to movement and dissolution. No longer is the absence of relation between man and woman or man and machine strictly homologous. Nor is it secure in its antithesis of solid and fluid as a point of form's recuperation. As a locus of de-formation, flows, chaotic turbulences, of course, the rich void of dissolution extends the screen of fantasy to posthuman or cyborg realms.

Woman, toys, automata, machines have been bound together throughout modernity as the fluid supplements and doubles of solid humanity (see Cixous, Dolar, Huyssen, Michelson, Penley).[10] Irigaray, too, in her discussion of the 'mechanics of fluids', notes the proximity of automata and machines to the silenced space of femininity in which the 'not-all' of sexual difference permits the universalisation of a system presided over by a phallic divinity. 'Awoman' serves as a *'projective map'* allowing fluidity to be channelled according to a law of solids.[11] But fluid femininity retains the power to disturb through diffusion, 'turbulence', a 'transgression and confusion of boundaries', and a resistance to 'adequate symbolization'.[12] Here, the 'idealism of the phallus' crumbles.[13] The traditional psychoanalytic association of the *objet petit a* with faeces is also interrogated. What of 'milk, luminous flow, acoustic waves ... gasses inhaled, emitted, variously perfumed, of urine, saliva, blood, even plasma'? What of sperm, with which the 'solidity of the penis' vanishes? For Irigaray, 'a reckoning with *sperm-fluid* as an obstacle to the generalisation of an economy restricted to solids remains in suspension'.[14] A restricted economy cannot countenance the flows, expenditures and turbulence of less than solid bodies; but nor can it generalise itself without them. An aneconomic zone, *a* becomes a locus of projection and dissolution - almost to the point of disclosing a different productivity. But Irigaray's opposition, and partial undermining, of solids

10. See Hélène Cixous, 'Fiction and its Phantoms: a Reading of Freud's *Das Unheimliche* (the "Uncanny")', *New Literary History*, 7 (1976), 525-48; Andreas Huyssen, 'The Vamp and the Machine: Technology and Sexuality in Fritz Lang's *Metropolis*', *New German Critique*, 24, 25 (1981-82), 221-37; Constance Penley, *The Future of an Illusion: Film, Feminism, and Psychoanalysis*, London, Routledge, 1989; Annette Michelson, 'On the Eve of the Future: the Reasonable Facsimile and the Philosophical Toy', *October*, 29 (Summer 1984), 3-20; Mladen Dolar, 'La Femme-machine', *New Formations*, 23 (1994), 43-54.

11. Luce Irigaray, *This Sex Which Is Not One*, Catherine Porter with Carolyn Burke (trans.), New York, Columbia University Press, 1985, p108.

12. Ibid., p106.

13. Ibid., p110.

14. Ibid., p113.

and fluids returns psychoanalysis and machines to homeostatic models of operation, governed by the '*principle of constancy*' identified by Freud in *Beyond the Pleasure Principle*:

> The avoidance of excessive inflow/outflow-excitement? Coming from the other? The search, at any price, for homestasis? For self-regulation? The reduction, then in the machine, of the effects of movements from/toward its outside? Which implies reversible transformations *in a closed circuit*, while discounting the variables of time, except in the mode of *repetition of a state of equilibrium*.[15]

15. Ibid., p115.

Returning to closure, to the circuit of pleasure's equilibrium, leaves solid systems and fluid disruptions (almost) intact in their difference, one still - strangely - defined by the other: the latter in-forms, with bursts of heterogeneous and general economic activity, the homogeneity and homeostatic rule of the former. Boundaries - disturbed, transgressed even - are re-marked.

Even Freud, however, cannot be fully contained in the restricted economy of homeostatic circulation in which solids and fluids, inside and outside are maintained. A surge of foam consumes their difference. 'Everything occurs as if Freud, who started from energy models of thermodynamics, had intuited, by a dynamics of language, the subsequent development of thermodynamics into information theory'.[16] For Michel Serres, the consequences of this displacement demand that psychoanalysis be considered in terms of an open rather than a closed, homeostatic system. Transmissions and exchanges of information operate on multiple levels in which noise, ambiguity, uncertainty intervene productively as much as disruptively in developing a system's complexity. The unconscious, no longer 'a unique black box, but a series of interlinking black boxes', is composed in the noise-information couplings of many levels: interference in a particular transmission becomes constructive on other levels as noise is rendered meaningful. Yet 'what remains unknown and unconscious', Serres concedes,

16. Michel Serres, *Hermes: Literature, Science, Philosophy*, J.V. Harari and D.F. Bell (eds), Baltimore and London, Johns Hopkins University Press, 1983, p82.

> is, at the chain's furthermost limit, the din of energy transformations: this must be so, for the din is by definition stripped of all meaning, like a set of pure signals or aleatory movements. These packages of chance are filtered, level after level, by the subtle transformer constituted by the organism, and they come crashing at our feet, like the surf at the edge of the beach, in the forms of eros and death.[17]

17. Ibid., p80.

Astride the crashing foam, of course, there comes a familiar, yet different figure.

Venus, again. Venus and foam. See one without the other and beauty's captivating form is excised from foam and frozen in an alluring figure of 'lusive (illusory/ elusive/ ludic) mastery:

Aphrodite, beautiful goddess, invisible, standing up, is born of this chaotic sea, this nautical chaos, this *noise*. Aphrodite, standing her foot upon the sea, walks upon this sea. We know only Aphrodite, if that. We turn away from the waves to admire only the wave-born.[18]

No Venus without foam; no message without noise. 'No life without heat, no matter, neither; no warmth without air, no logos without noise'. For Serres, 'background noise is the ground of our perception, absolutely uninterrupted, it is our perennial sustenance, the element of the software of all our logic. It is the residue and cesspool of all our messages'. Murmuring like the real, noise exceeds mastery as 'that incessant hubbub': 'our signals, our messages, our speech and our words are but fleeting high surf, over its perpetual swells'.[19]

The foam of *a*, of separation from and conjunction with a noise in which everything is consumed, traces the opening and closing of systems in which all final distinctions are refused. Neither outside nor inside, the foaming noise rolls on through all informational systems, be they biological or technological. In the biology of Francisco Varela, for example, 'randomness is the froth of noise from which coherent microstates evolve and to which living systems owe their capacity for fast, flexible response'.[20] The fictions and technology through which postmodernity heads towards cyberspace, too, confounds the borders of interiority with 'the frothing turbulence of the endocrine cascades bathing the synapses of our nerves, and the coaxial cables of the nerves themselves, exteriorise their constrasts onto our landscapes and civilizations'.[21] Inside and outside are infused with the noise of networked systems.

Here, of course, captivation by the figure of Venus and subsumption in the noise of the foam obscure the plane on which they are rendered homogeneous. Writing in the 1950s at the moment when US-led consumer culture began to transform capitalist economy, Roland Barthes discussed how soap-powder advertisements articulated the domestic economy and the multinational order through the play of signs and the significance of foam. In promoting the luxuriousness of foam, its apparent lack of 'any usefulness', 'its abundant, easy, almost infinite proliferation', the consumer is encouraged 'to imagine matter as something airy'. Foam becomes a 'sign of a certain spirituality, inasmuch as the spirit has the reputation of being able to make something out of nothing'.[22] All that is solid melts into foam. The 'abrasive function' of detergent is disguised. Domestic ecstasy, a transmutation, a flight beyond, outside, away from gritty matter. But it is not a flight to heterogeneity, as Barthes cautions: 'a euphoria, incidentally, which must not make us forget there is one plane on which *Persil* and *Omo* are one and the same: the plane of the Anglo-Dutch trust *Unilever*'.[23]

The pneumatic contours of PAM were first cantilevered on screen in the 1950s, the domestic goddess given a tragic gloss in the impossible shape of male fantasy - Marilyn Monroe, Jayne Mansfield, Mimie van Doren, Doris

18. Michel Serres, *Genesis*, Geneviève James and James Nielson (trans), Ann Arbor, University of Michigan Press, 1995, p25.

19. Ibid., pp6-7.

20. N. Katherine Hayles, *How We Became Posthuman: Virtual Bodies in Cybernetics, Literature and Informatics*, Chicago and London, University of Chicago Press, 1999, p286.

21. David Porush, 'Hacking the Brainstem: Postmodern Metaphysics and Stephenson's *Snow Crash*', in Robert Markley (ed), *Virtual Realities and Their Discontents*, Baltimore and London, Johns Hopkins University Press, 1996, p121.

22. Roland Barthes, *Mythologies*, Annette Lavers (trans), London, Granada Publishing, 1973, p27.

23. Ibid., p38.

Day, Diana Dors and other doubleD iconic screen clones who provided the model, the endorsements, and the locus of luxurious transcendence for the new consumers of the post-war world. In relation to their maternal-amatory gaze, radiating domestic glamour and material aspiration, the boys played with their toys, their cars, their motorbikes, their guitars, regressing, in the 1960s, to a perpetual state of adolescent boredom and rebellion. Surf's up: at the dawning of the hypermodern age, Venus rises again, swathed in the soaps suds of the 1950s, upon the crest of a wave of 'white goods' - washing machines, dishwashers, cookers, microwaves - sparkling in a foaming effervescence of washing powder, washing-up liquid, floor cleaner, showershine, bathroom mousse, toilet powerfoamer. Herself gleaming in a lather of shampoo, bubble bath, showerburst foam, hair mousse, gel depilation foam, make-up mousse and moisturiser, courtesy of the Lever Brothers and an ocean of other multinational beauty product brands. From foamy euphoria to the homogeneous plane of transnational corporations, the prostheticised figure of man glimpses his end in the silicon contours of Venus.

With the emergence of PAM, the post-adoration machine, towards the end of the twentieth century, a new figure heralds the triumph of an economy of unrestricted luxury goods, constantly multiplied and improved by technical innovation. Riding the crest of this wave, PAM manifests the absence of relation in an ironic *au revoir* to human fantasy. The goodbye is ironic because it no longer calls up a spectre of loss but quickly calls for more: overstimulated to repetitive excess, the procession of images precipitates exhaustion, evacuation, boredom. More and more. Biotechnical investment, dotcom speculation, online shopping, internet gambling and, of course, pornography. The soapy obscenity of Venus in rubber gloves gives way to a billion wetlook babes with beachball breasts applying a very different kind of facial. The latter has of course provided the spume that has lubricated the intimidating rise and power of modern technology in which bodies are informed, shaped, deployed and utilised by information; indeed they are literally reduced, shredded, to streams of genetic information. The latter is exemplary in the way that technology has developed through stimulating a transgressive desire to consume, and here again, PAM and her parodic human love toy have led the way. Apparently, virtually everyone in the US with an internet connection has a copy of that video.

Since the 1950s and 1960s, then, the primary relation between technical and social systems has been one of consumption, the consumer economy lubricating accelerating technological development. A law of consumption has replaced prohibition in the imperative for more. Furthermore, it was in the early 1960s that the origin of this law was laid down in an originary myth that suggests that humanity was always bound up in prosthesis, in an originary technicity, and a fatal imperative for innovation, speed and indeed for consumption - in both senses of the term.

24. G. Morton, P. Spector, E. Greenwich, J. Berry, © R. Mellin Music; Tender Tunes; EMI Publishing Ltd.

25. Elie Greenwich, quoted in Charlotte Greig, *Will You Still Love Me Tomorrow? Girl Groups from the 50s on ...*, London, Virago Press, 1989, p80.

26. Lacan writes, 'Le vieux papa les avait toutes pour lui, ce qui est deja fabuleux — pourquoi les aurait-il toutes de meme, elles aussi peuvent peut-etre avoir leur petit idee'. Jacques Lacan, *Le Seminaire* XVII, *L'Envers de la psychanalyse*, Paris, Editions de Seul, 1991, p24.

Produced by the legendary Shadow Morton, 'Leader of the Pack' locates Charles Darwin's dominant male in the midst of the Blackboard Jungle of an American High School in the early 1960s.[24] As Ellie Greenwich, one of the writers recalls, it is about 'that bad guy that every girl wanted to go out with ... then there was the motorbike. Back in the sixties, when you started making money, you'd buy a motorcycle'.[25] Just as, on the lawless plains of Africa according to Darwin, it is the biggest, baddest primate who hoards all the females, so it is the meanest, coolest guy on the fastest motorbike who 'every girl' wants to go out with, particularly in popular post-war high school myth. For Freud, a mythical, originary act of rebellion and murder retroactively grounds law in a guilty patricide. 'Leader of the Pack', however, rewrites Freud's myth for the post-war baby boom generation: its romantic rebellion introduces a new law of consumption in place of prohibition. Freud does not argue with Darwin's evolutionary reasoning about sexual selection in *The Descent of Man*, but does note that human societies have always involved prohibitions, notably on murder and incest. Freud speculates that these prohibitions arose out of the violent sacrifice of the tyrannical leader, his authority becoming internalised, through shared guilt, as moral law. Freud's lesson to modernity, then, is that the death of God leads not to a liberation of enjoyment, but to a redoubling of its prohibition. The Shangri-las reject this model, their myth disclosing that modernity has moved into a different phase: they sing from a different position to the murderous sons and brothers, and without the strange remorse that derives, Freud speculates, from a disappointment at discovering that no man can individually occupy the dominant place, consequently prohibiting it. Their anti-oedipal tale is told from the point of view of the women, a position neglected by Freud. But not by Lacan, who suggests that the women would have had other ideas.[26]

The Shangri-las' version of *Totem and Taboo* is, fittingly, not a macho tale of male rivalry, violence and tragedy, but a romance in which death and melodrama are, of course, key elements. Named after an imaginary earthly paradise - the hidden valley in J. Hilton's *Lost Horizon* - resonating with an all-too conventional promise of some feminine verdant cleft, the Shangri-las foreground the kind of utopian bliss, or Nirvana, that Freud associated with the death-drive. Though, on first hearing, 'The Leader of the Pack' seems to describe a tale of macho male rivalry and prohibition: the tyrannical nature of paternal law is negatively affirmed and atoned for by the sacrifice of the young biker who assumes a symbolic place in death. 'Is that Jimmie's ring you're wearing?' Jimmie reminds us of Jimmie Dean, crash dead by the time this song was a hit, and already the symbolic leader of a new rebellious generation of baby boomers. The function of the Ego-Ideal is transferred, via the crash, to the signifier in whose name rebellion is authorised, and an unspeakable jouissance promised.

But this would be to misread the song. For a start, it is clear that the romance between Betty and Jimmie has not been forbidden absolutely. In order for the paternal function to shift smoothly from father to surrogate son, the father would have had to have uttered the classic paternal prohibition: 'you will go out with that bad lad over my dead body!' Jimmie's sacrifice then guarantees the transfer of paternal authority on the father's terms. However, this is not what happens at all. While Betty's folks complain about Jimmie, are always 'putting him down', and are apparently unhappy about his background, they do not stop her riding with him on a regular basis and having a great time. All the other High School girls are jealous. She's even wearing his ring. Then, 'one day', she decides to find someone new. Her father's law is invoked, but as a law that demands novelty rather than moral judgement. He is not reported as saying 'find someone better', in a moral sense, but merely 'find someone new'. The suspicion remains, then, that Betty's invocation of paternal law is simply an alibi. While her father, no doubt slumped in front of the tube watching re-runs of 'I Love Lucy', remains vaguely disgruntled, it is Betty herself who has decided she needs a new boyfriend. As her friends say: 'what do you mean when you say you better go find somebody new?' The Leader of the Pack himself is nonplussed: 'he stood there and asked me why?' *Che vuoi?* Poor Jimmie pathetically inquires after the desire of the Other, but is met with silence: 'all I could do was cry'. Clearly, Betty is bored and is looking for someone with a better, faster bike. At least, this is how Jimmie interprets her tears, and drives off in a vain and fatal attempt to go faster, to keep up the demanding pace. The song is of course about amorous rejection. Betty knows that the Leader of the Pack is no mean, bad lad: he's just a bit sad, the cause of regret and a few tears, but no great loss and easily upgradable.

The Shangri-las' 'Leader of the Pack' re-writes Freud's originary myth according to a more arbitrary and technological law of novelty, consumption and performance. 'I met him in the Candy Store'. The initial scene of the romance is set in a conventional place of conspicuous adolescent and pre-adolescent consumption of pure luxury items: the Candy Store points towards the sumptuous spectacle of the shopping mall and an abundance of choice, an excess of sweet tempting options. The relationship is no different: Betty, wearing his ring, appears as the choicest sweetmeat of the saccharine horde that he is supposed to lord over. But it is Betty who sets the standard of performance for the male subject, Jimmie, who is precisely subject to the law of the commodity himself. Ultimately, he is no better than, and as replaceable as, his technological prosthesis, his bike. And it is of course the bike, purring and growling at significant points throughout the record, that is its real star and selling point. The Leader of the Pack, a potential Ego-ideal like Jimmie Dean, is dependent upon the technological processes that endlessly reproduce his image, to supplement and replace it with a host of Elvises, Marlons, Marilyns or whoever.

The motorbike is pre-eminently, in postwar America, the signifier of transgression, crossing thresholds and barriers. The result of technological innovation and a human desire for speed and thrills, the motorbike ideologically embodies the pioneering spirit of the lone rider of the West, the vehicle of the urban cowboy's 'rebellious' phallic narcissism. But the Shangri-las' 'Leader of the Pack' suggests that this narcissism is staged for the gaze of the Other who always demands more: be more daring, make it bigger, harder, faster. Paternal law is *secondary* to the demand or imperative that seems to drive technological innovation for its own sake: keep up with the pace of the machine that is always just that bit faster, adapt to its always new horizons ... or die in the process. By becoming the very locus of material existence, by marking its threshold, technology functions as the Other: the reservoir of an Other knowledge and, at the limit of that knowledge, an Other jouissance that exceeds the phallic imaginings of the subject. This would therefore be the meaning of the crash for the subject who crashes in this epoch of the incorporated crash: that there is no relation to the crashing machine.

If philosophers have since Hegel continually heralded the end of man, a current strand of French thought has begun to address its origin in order to claim that the human being is bound up with an originary technicity (Stiegler, Beardsworth).[27] 'Technology ... is to be regarded as constitutive of the extended phenotype of the human animal, a dangerous supplement enjoying an originary status'.[28] In an essay entitled 'Persephone, Oedipus, Epimetheus', Bernard Stiegler also takes another look at Freud's originary myth in *Totem and Taboo* and, like the Shangri-las, focuses on the issue of technological innovation.[29] Stiegler recalls Freud asking himself, 'how does the passage to the sons' murderous act take place?' Freud speculates that 'some cultural advance, perhaps, some new weapon, had given them a sense of superior strength'. Why some 'new' weapon, however, asks Stiegler? Was there an armed humanity that was not yet parricidal, or was there an unarmed, pre-cultural, pre-technical man of 'pure nature'? If the former, then the murderous history of humankind is an effect of the event of technics; technics irrupts in and as the origin of the human in the form of violence. If the latter, then the technological novelty that enabled the parricide is an effect of the determining potential of weapons technology itself, murder being just one of its consequences. Both the Shangri-las' position and Freud's are latent within the two possibilities. If there were already weapons, or at least if there were already technics - and this is indeed implied by Freud - then the law introduced by the 'parricide' is a *secondary* effect of a prior law of technological innovation, and indeed perversion (or *père version*, in the Lacanian sense, a veering towards the father). Given the *nachträglich* structure of Freud's myth, it is impossible to know who or what existed 'before the law' introduced by the parricide, but what we do know is that the impulse for technological innovation was articulated in relation to (and in a desire for) a horde of beings that were retrospectively identified as women, women belonging to a dead, symbolic father.

Stiegler does not speculate what kind of beings there might have been

27. Bernard Stiegler, *Technics and Time, 1: the Fault of Epimetheus*, Richard Beardsworth and George Collins (trans), Stanford, Stanford University Press, 1998. Richard Beardsworth, 'From a Genealogy of Matter to a Politics of Memory: Stiegler's Thinking of Technics', *Tekhnema*, 2 (Spring 1995), <http://tekhnema.free.fr/contents2.html>.

28. Keith Ansell Pearson, 'Life Becoming Body: On the "Meaning" of Post Human Evolution', *Cultural Values*, 1, 2 (1997), 223.

29. Bernard Stiegler, 'Persephone, Oedipus, Epimetheus' in *Tekhnema*, 3 (Spring 1994), <http://tekhnema.free.fr/contents3.html>.

'before the law' (also the law of gender, sexual difference and so on), and what their relationship to technicity might have been, but instead assumes that, in accordance with the structure of the myth, there must have been no prior weapons, no prior technical object so that technics, parricide and humanity come together at one and the same moment. For Stiegler, what is of interest in the Freudian myth is the suggestion that the emergence of humanity and the invention of weapons are two 'moments' that cannot be separated from each other, just as both are equally inseparable from the moment of 'parricide':

> What is at stake here? Nothing less, I wish to argue, than the question of knowing whether there was ever a state of humanity *before* the murder of the father anyway, that is to say necessarily *before technics*, and of knowing whether the murder of the father does not in fact translate the event of technics as such, an event which takes the 'form' of weaponry.[30]

30. Ibid.

For Stiegler, after Freud, the conjunction of technics and parricide introduces the tool-weapon as the signifier that incarnates the law of the father and bars access to jouissance. Humanity comes into being as the animal that can anticipate the future, and consequently, with use of prosthetic extensions like tools, weapons and language, records its history and amasses a collective memory. For the Shangri-las, on the other hand, read after Freud, the combination of an independent demand for something new, whose very expression is the independent momentum of technical development, and the crash (consumption/consummation) that it precipitates, opens up, in a flash, the lost horizon of an Other jouissance illuminating the passage from one epoch to another. As will be suggested in the next section, this can be argued through a different reading of the paleontological record.

Stiegler notes that the paleontological evidence suggests that the 'passage into humanity takes place through the invention of arms' and therefore through 'the structure of anticipation that marks the human species out from other living species'.[31] And he suggests that the Freudian myth conceptualises this epochal shift since the primordial murder inaugurates temporality, and the possibility of history, through positing an irrevocably lost pre-history, an absolute past in which the father was not yet a father, not yet the law, not yet being dead. 'The primitive weapon, the first example of technics, distances for ever the absolute past, which becomes absolute and past in this very moment'.[32] What might also be added is that the power of the primordial father, brought into being retrospectively through the 'parricide', therefore becomes associated with, even incarnated in, the weapon that killed him. To develop the Lacanian implications further, it follows that the weapon becomes the terrifying Thing that stands in for the lack, the fault, the guilt, produced by the parricide. The ghostly, retroactivated presence of paternal law (and paternal enjoyment) haunts the *tool* that he left behind, the tool that became the weapon that killed

31. Ibid.

32. Ibid.

him, undergoing the very metamorphosis that the sons now experience as their act of transgression which inaugurates Law in the form of their remorse. Undecidably both a tool, a weapon and a symbol haunted by the Thing of jouissance and castration, this signifier demarcates and determines the equivocal history of mastery and subjection that man will historically invest in his imaginary relationship with his technical things. The passage into humanity takes place by way of the 'ghost/machine' which is not just a tool, not just a weapon, it is already language, writing, law.

Of course bringing Stiegler and Lacan into conjunction lights on the problem of the inseparable separation of technics and the symbolic that concerns Stiegler in his critique, in very different respects, of Leroi-Gourhan, Heidegger and Derrida. As Richard Beardsworth writes, 'the political, the technical and the symbolic cannot be separated. This does not mean, however, that they can be *identified*' which nicely performs, rhetorically, the problematic because it is not absolutely clear whether Beardsworth means that they cannot be identified together, as one, or if he means they cannot be identified, that is, distinguished from one another.[33]

Stiegler's essay is concerned to elaborate, in relation to Freud, what he calls 'epiphylogenetic' memory, the means by which an individual unconscious is related to a collective or cultural unconscious, as it must be in order to be readable. This readability requires that, as Beardsworth writes, 'language and technics are here amalgamated in the process of exteriorization' involved in 'techno-logical memory'.[34] Speculation about an 'ancient language', said to be common to all symbolic languages, that conserves and continues to transmit the experience of 'originary wounds', runs up against the question of where and how this 'language', and the memory it structures, is conserved. Has it been biologically acquired and imprinted somewhere in the brain? Molecular biology defines two kinds of memory: (phylo)genetic, germinal or species related, and epigenetic, somatic or nerve-related. As Stiegler notes, acquired characters are a biological fiction because there can be no direct communication between these two kinds of memory. This means that when an animal dies, all that it has 'learnt' of life is lost for its species. What it 'acquires' in the course of its life is not transmitted to its descendants. However, the invention of the tool inaugurates a 'third memory' - 'epiphylogenetic' memory - for the individual experience of the toolmaker remains in the tool, beyond the life of the particular maker. The tool *is* this memory, a memory that is also a commemoration since it is predicated on the death of the toolmaker, the father, the subject presumed to know. Mythologically, the tales, upon which Freud draws, usually involve the *theft* of some weapon/fire/apple in which the murder/theft/crime is associated with the acquisition of knowledge from the gods (the father) wherein Epimetheus's fault, the lack, gives way to Prometheus's theft. But thus far, Stiegler's reading of Freud and of ancient myth merely produces a Lacanised Freud. Stiegler simply shows how the paternal function is determined and taken over by language qua technical and social system,

33. Richard Beardsworth, 'From a Genealogy of Matter to a Politics of Memory: Stiegler's Thinking of Technics', *Tekhnema*, 2 (Spring 1995), 98.

34. Ibid., p100.

the big Other. Everything here is already in Lacan.

But let us return to the Shangri-las. Let us assume that Freud meant 'some *new* weapon', as opposed to the primordial invention of technics per se, that enabled the parricide to take place. If so, that means paternal law is necessarily *secondary* to the 'universal tendency' of a technological determinism that functions 'at once according to its own rational and determinist logic'.[35] Or as Manuel De Landa argues, 'technological development may be said to possess its own momentum, for clearly it is not always guided by human needs'.[36] Technology is certainly not guided by human needs, then, but it is unquestionably accompanied by, and indeed produces, human demands, needs and desires that fund and facilitate technological innovation, thereby articulating social and technical systems in relation to consumption. But this relation of consumption clearly offers the possibility of a perversion, or rather the double swerve (and crash) of a *pére version* and a mam-a-version - a veering towards and beyond the father in a fatal amoration with, and performance for, the maternal-wife-daughter assemblage of the primal horde.

There is another element to the relationship between technics and humanity that is problematic - the degree to which the rational and determinist logic of technics' 'universal tendency' prevails and the use, misuse and abuse to which the tools and objects of a certain system of technics are put. And further, whether the evidence or memory of that misuse or abuse is inscribed in the system of technics itself therefore providing it with the ir/rational alogic usually supposed to be necessary for innovation. Is it logical, illogical or alogical for a tool to become a weapon, and therefore on that basis develop its destructive capacity and efficiency? Stiegler seems to follow Leroi-Gourhan in making the opposition 'technics qua universal tendency' … and 'the ethnic qua a factor of diversifying diffraction from which the universal tendency will nevertheless profit'. Profit, but for its own ends which, curiously, seem to be biased towards one form of social system rather than another, one gender rather than another. For Leroi-Gourhan,

> The tendency has an inevitable, predictable, rectilinear character. It drives the flint held in the hand to acquire the handle, the bundle hung on two poles to equip itself with wheels, the society founded on matriarchy to become patriarchal sooner or later.[37]

The rational and determinist logic of technics surprisingly does not limit itself to specific technical practices, but applies itself to whole social systems. Here it is not a question of a mutual interdependence between the social and the technical, but of the latter determining the former, 'the society founded on matriarchy will become patriarchal sooner or later'. But why this should be so is not at all clear.

Two points are at issue here, first the characterisation of technics itself in terms of a rational and determinist logic that is predicated upon utility

35. Stiegler, 'Persephone, Oedipus, Epimetheus', op. cit., p43.

36. Manuel de Landa, *War in the Age of Intelligent Machines*, p3.

37. Leroi-Gourhan, cited in Stiegler, 'Persephone, Oedipus, Epimetheus', op. cit., p51.

and patriarchy, and second, the primacy of this logic over any cultural or social variation that develops a number of different technical systems. On the question of these two areas, Georges Bataille, in his account of the Lascaux cave paintings, has perhaps more to say than Leroi-Gourhan in relation to the interdependency of humans and their technical things (and the technical knowledge and technical jouissance bound up with them). Following Bataille, it is possible to posit not a *relationship* between two terms 'man' and 'technics', but an interdependency that constitutes a single and singular biotechnical species that could be signified by a hyphenated or multi-hyphenated neologism. The hyphens mark the absence of a relationship that would make them whole, make them a single thing, living or nonliving. Technical artefacts are integral to the constitution of the human, but not because they exist in a complementary relationship of happy mutuality that could be said to constitute a whole: there is no relation between 'man and technics' or 'man and machine' just as, in Lacan's provocative suggestion, there is no relation between the sexes, even though there is a state of total interdependency between signifiers and fantasies of gender. The little 'a' of differance undermines and renders impossible the achievement of Imaginary union with the Other even as it supports and sustains it as an idea and a desirable end.

In the locus of little 'a', sex, death and subjectivity appear; a space of anticipation and exteriorisation, commemorating, memorialising and sustaining the human as a trace of epiphylogenetic memory. The history, perhaps even the evolution, of the human being as a bio-technical neologism, circulates around a central non-relation and forms a hole through which it has threaded a signifying chain of prosthetic substitutes and signifiers that mark its absence even as they fail to fill it. Or, to put it another way, the hyphens that punctuate the points of non-relational interdependency mark the place of death, eroticism and play; which is to say that this interdependency is generally economic, in Bataille's terms, and is the primary characteristic of a species that can only be described not as homo but as hetero: hetero-econo-techno-ludens. In this essay, then, it is not the history of a changing *relationship* between 'man and machine' that we wish to indicate, but the dynamic of a changing configuration that is predicated upon an essential absence of relation.

HETERO-ECONO-TECHNO-LUDENS

In his commentary on the prehistoric cave images, Bataille not only outlines a theory that places art at the birth of humanity, he also sketches a theory of technological originality. Tools produce more than objects of useful consumption or playful transgression. In introducing an element of durability in which products are seen to outlive their users, tools and the work they facilitate depend on the dimension of time in which alterity and anticipation come to be structuring factors:

Work anticipates, presupposes this object which does not yet really exist, which is presently being made, and which is, simply, the reason the work is being done. Two sorts of objects immediately come to exist in the worker's mind: actually present objects and objects later to come. This already dual aspect is completed by the object of the past; therewith, all the gradations of objective existence range themselves in proper order. From incoherent barkings of desire, man can advance to distinct speech now that, labelling the object with a name, he is able to make an implicit connection between the material it is made of and the work required to get it from the old state to the new in which it is ready for use. Thenceforth language firmly anchors the object in the stream of time. But man, designating the object, has been wrenched out of the world of nameless feeling - of sensibility. Though drawn back to this world, man cannot re-enter it unless, through his labour, he makes not only useful things, but creates a work of art.[38]

38. Georges Bataille, *Lascaux*, Austryn Wainhouse (trans), Geneva, Skira, 1955, p28.

The technical object, in supplementing powers yet to become human, in bringing forth humanity at a technological stroke, manifests the originary prostheticity of human being as a being constituted by a differentiation and extension in space and time. Anticipation, the deferral and direction of a desire located elsewhere, in a structured temporal stream, takes its bearings not only from the material location of the tool-object, but another - imaginary - object, the nonexistence of which is sustained by the expectation that comes from the temporal organisation of speech and language. The tool, then, is originary only insofar as it presupposes the prior origin of a system of temporal ordering given by language; its use, indeed, calls up the spectre or trace of an originary differance, with an a, associated with writing. A profound, even primordial, separation, it seems, is entailed in the scripto-technological emergence of humanity, a cut that marks its destiny with a 'principle of insufficiency' and as a chain of supplements embracing tools, language, art and ornaments.

If tools and language are originary supplements, then, an internal difference and relation of insufficiency remains a primary condition, a relation that forms and transforms all forms of alienation that flow from and elaborate that interior difference. In *Theory of Religion*, discussing the relationship of worker and tool and the manner in which the latter signifies an alienation in the world of things, Bataille underlines the reversal of conventional assumptions: 'to subordinate is not only to enter the subordinated element but to be altered oneself. The tool changes nature and man at the same time: it subjugates nature to man, who makes and uses it, but it ties man to subjugated nature'.[39] Being remains external to this nature, 'foreign to immanent immensity', so that even in the most direct human operations on nature a different order and exigency manifest itself: 'the farmer is not a man: he is the plow of the one who eats the bread'.[40] Where art playfully transgresses the daily imperatives of production, utility

39. Georges Bataille, *Theory of Religion*, Richard Hurley (trans), New York, Zone Press, 1992, p41.

40. Ibid., p42.

and servility to open festively, sacrificially and briefly onto a miraculous, sacred realm of prohibition and value, work situates humans as tools of a productive process ordered by a very different demand and economic act of consumption. With tools, with a generalised technological machine subordinating workers as its prostheses, as its ploughs, cogs and levers, humans are little more than things. The supplementary position allotted to humans, however, is masked by another supplementarity: art, play, ornament, luxury offer a glimpse of a sacred space outside work and utility where transgression and eroticism shine in the intensity of prohibition.

In the 1950s Bataille conventionally locates the miraculous birth of humanity in the cave paintings of Lascaux, a place where femininity is assigned an enigmatic and magical place beyond and at the base of nascent human being. In the act of creation, in deviating from the urgencies of material production and necessity, humanity creates itself, out of nothing and in relation to the paint blown onto the dark walls of a cave. Bataille's argument identifies 'two capital events in the course of human history': the

41. Bataille, op. cit., *Lascaux*, p28.

making of tools and the creation of art-objects.[41] Work and art both produce objects, but the former is linked to useful production while the latter performs a playful and unproductive role. Both activities - work and play - use tools, and it is in relation to the tools and the objects they produce that a crucial and determining aspect of humanity is recognised: 'regarding what they had made, these creators of objects, these users of durable tools suddenly

42. Ibid., p29.

realized that, themselves of less durable stuff, they died'.[42] An awareness of death is precipitated. It is not death alone, however, that inaugurates the human, for death works as a cause of symbolic prohibitions distinguishing human from animal and leading to what Bataille calls 'the recognition of a new value'. Fascinating, awe-ful, the faces of the dead are initially forbidden: 'in raising this barrier of prohibition round what fills him with awe and fascinated terror, man enjoins all beings and all creatures to respect it: for it

43. Ibid., p31.

is sacred'.[43] A 'fundamental categorizing of objects' occurs in which both the sacred and profane emerge to situate the human in relation to the Other, to a system of prohibitions and taboos organised chiefly around death and sexuality.

Bataille seems, like Leroi-Gourhan, to isolate two (pre-)historical moments or 'events', the tool-event and the art-event, that determine two stages of linear human development. But Bataille's distinctions between utility and nonutility, transgression and prohibition, directly imply one another. If something can be used, it can necessarily also be misused and abused. So it is not necessary to account for two 'moments' or 'events' in the pre-history of the human species. As Stiegler argues, the possibility of both moments is already there with the first flint, the first most 'primitive' deployment of technics. Since technics is constitutive of the process of anticipation it directly implies, and simultaneously, the existence of time, language, society. In his commentary on Stiegler, Beardsworth stresses this point, 'there is, then, *no opposition* between the technical and the symbolic'.

On the contrary, he writes, 'in the process of exteriorization-hominization, in the double *differantial* constitution of technics and man, there is a further differentiation of life (the human species)'.[44] The human species emerges as an effect of the differance opened out by technics and symbolisation, or indeed, by the symbolisation of technics.

But there was not just *one* further differentiation of life produced by technics that resulted in the emergence of the human species. There were many other forms of differentiation within the greater hominid genus all of whom developed their own quite different systems of technics. Technics, per se, or a view of technics possessing a 'universal tendency', is not enough to account for the origin and emergence of the only species of hominid that remains on earth. For Bataille, the technics that characterises this species is marked by a certain antagonism, an eroticism and a play that sets apart, according to recent paleontology, the technicity of the 'modern human' from the many other originally prosthetic hominid species that once inhabited the earth. The fact that the tool technology of 'homo faber' or 'homo neanderthalis' hardly changes significantly over a quarter of a million years raises questions about so-called 'technological determinism', particularly when it is understood that the mental capacity of Neanderthals was essentially the same as modern humans. This was realised when Neanderthals were discovered to have skilfully mimicked (it is supposed) the new tools, art and modes of ornamentation that they saw when they encountered the first modern humans who arrived from Africa. The proximity and difference between the two species suggests that the key distinction merely concerned a certain technical practice that in turn implied a highly singular relationship (or non-relationship) with technological artefacts; so much so that we should perhaps hesitate to apply human categories and concepts (of utility or nonutility) to other hominid species. It is not just the technological determinism that necessitates the development of a technological phylum or lineage so that the 'form-undifferentiated flint must give way to the polished knapped tool, to the brass knife, to the steel sword'.[45] The archaeological record shows that the earliest human tools were virtually always also ornamented, or painted in sacred red ochre, that is to say already bound up in a larger, excessive, somewhat perverse symbolic system that made it perfectly possible for the flint or the bone to give way to the embodied movement of the fish or a spear that could in turn give way to the phallus or to the shape of a woman in a process both metonymic and metaphorical. Bataille argues that from the earliest instances of a distinctly human evolution those forms situated as objects and instruments of production could also be transformed into objects of ornamentation and exchange (artifice, femininity, art and play) to operate as the obscure conditions, the unseen supplementary basis, of the inscription of norms and rules. Of these objects, the images, flints and stones that have been shaped into female forms remain, for Bataille, shadowy figures in and beyond representation. Indeed, in the earliest figures of Venus - the 'steatopygous

44. Beardsworth, 'From a Genealogy of Matter to a Politics of Memory: Stiegler's Thinking of Technics', op. cit., p99.

45. Leroi-Gourhan, cited in Stiegler's, 'Persephone, Oedipus, Epimetheus', op. cit., p45.

Aphrodites' of Willendorf and Lespugue - a 'deformed idealism' questions the simple rational explanation of the images as fertility symbols: 'they stray away from the realm of efficacious action and towards that obscure, profound disorder that is the heart and essence of the realm of the sexual'; as a result they 'tend away from the human'.[46] Like PAM they are prosthetic in an obscurely ornamental, yet sublime sense that hints at an Other form of jouissance.

46. Bataille, op. cit., p123.

BAYWATCH

Since Foucault evoked the disappearance of man beneath the rising tide at the sea's edge, recent paleontological discoveries have returned to the beach to redraw the face of the first 'modern human'. Confounding the long-held assumption that homo sapiens evolved in Europe 30-50,000 years ago from, or alongside, homo neaderthalis, recent discoveries place the origin of the modern human 150,000 years ago in the coastal caves of Klasies and Bombos alongside the sandy beaches of Southern Africa. The 'modern human' apparently emerged, originally prosthetic, out of the sea decked in shell beads and bone necklaces, bodies and weapons, knives and spears, smeared in red ochre.

The genetic and archaelogical record suggests that these coastal-dwelling hominids walked the coastlines of the earth, from South Africa to Southeast Asia, even to Australia, consuming, according to Marta Lahr, its resources of fish and crustaceans.[47] 'To our coast-living ancestors', a recent TV documentary announced, 'the world was one long beach, and generation by generation they moved along it'.[48] Not only did they move south and east, of course, they also moved north into Europe where they encountered an already resident Neanderthal population. The encounter with Neanderthals, and the almost identical technical abilities and mental faculties demonstrated by these two species, has led experts to identify one seemingly frivolous difference that determined their respective survival and extinction. That difference is of course 'ornamentation': objects of purely symbolic as opposed to functional value.

Apparently Neanderthals lived contentedly in Europe for about two million years before modern humans came on the scene. Their bodies and mode of existence were, it is claimed, perfectly adapted to live in a cold climate with a woodland environment. But they died out after the arrival of the 'Africans' for reasons that are obscure. One hypothesis is that the Africans used their ornaments, their chains, necklaces, earrings and so on as a means of group identification and symbolic exchange so that they could maintain links with each other; the Neanderthals, by contrast, lived in diverse groups deep in the woods: when a climate change made life more difficult, they retreated further, becoming isolated, to be easily picked off, though they were physically bigger, stronger and better adapted to life in Europe.

Curiously, in some Neanderthal sites that are contemporary with the

47. For a thorough and convincing defence of the 'out-of-Africa' thesis see Marta Mirazon Lahr, *The Evolution of Modern Human Diversity: A Study on Cranial Variation*, Cambridge Studies in Biological Anthropology, Cambridge University Press. For a less reputable, though highly suggestive theory, that argues that *homo sapiens* evolved from earlier hominids via an 'aquatic ape' species see Elaine Morgan, *The Aquatic Ape*, London, Souvenir, 1982. This theory accounts for the many characteristics - subcutaneous fat, hairlessness, perspiration, tears, inability to respond to salt deprivation, the diving reflex and so on - that are only found in other aquatic mammals. The theory is not generally supported but was first proposed by Sir Alister Hardy, a Linacre Professor of Zoology at Oxford.

48. *Ape.Man*, BBC Worldwide Publishing, 2000, BBCV6982.

human sites, there is evidence that Neanderthals started to produce their own ornaments, perhaps impressed or dazzled by the human's sacred things. Neanderthal ornaments are similar to those of the humans except that they seem to lack one crucial Thing. They were without holes. Human ornaments have perfect little holes in them, signifiers to be threaded together as signifying chains. Neanderthals noticed the chains but missed the crucial, central absence necessary for such a task. Human technology, then, circulates around a hole, a nothing or No-Thing, that nicely symbolises their European maladaption, a principle of insufficiency that necessitated their leaving Africa on the way to becoming a hyperprosthetic being.

In his comments on Lascaux in the 1950s, Lacan, drawing attention to the hole asks why it was necessary to paint in the *dark*, to climb into a hole?

> the exercise on the wall consists in fixing the invisible inhabitant of the cavern, we see the link forged between the temple, as a construction around emptiness that designates the place of the Thing, to the figuration of emptiness on the walls of this emptiness itself - to the extent that painting progressively learns to master this emptiness, to take such a tight hold of it that painting becomes dedicated to fixing it in the form of the illusion of space.[49]

At the centre, and excluded, is the extimate Thing. An odd circularity is at work, or at play, here. Techne, the technique of painting, or creating the illusion of space and movement, is an effect of the emptiness that it produces and tries to master: the emptiness that defines these humans for us as human, both in the sense of the space that we occupy and the integral insufficiency that propels us further into that empty space. Further and further into empty space. Faster and faster. Out of nothing, out of a hole that it hollows out at the heart of itself, technicity develops into a formidable emptiness machine, creating more and more space in order to collapse it through the production of faster modes of transport and quicker flows of communication. What is the law that drives this imperative for speed and for constant innovation, for the endless imperative to create and consume something new that characterises the current scene of technological development as it runs rings around the globe?

GENERAL PROSTHETIC

Vision machines, whose martial and technological history is charted by Virilio, do more than supplement powers of sight: they evacuate and reconfigure space and time according to a new imperative. The mediatisation of images is part of a wider technological mobilisation described as 'an excessive *mobilization of public space* in which moving stairways and walkways are the missing link in the chain that leads from public transport's automobilization of the domestic household in the high-rise tower of the

49. Jacques Lacan, *The Ethics of Psychoanalysis*, Jacques Alain Miller (ed), Dennis Porter (trans), London, Routledge, 1992, pp139-40.

50. Paul Virilio, *Open Sky*, Julie Rose (trans), London and New York, Verso, 1997, p90.

51. Ibid., p11.

52. Paul Virilio, *The Art of the Motor*, Julie Rose (trans), Minneapolis, University of Minnesota Press, 1995, p103.

53. Ibid., p130.

54. Virilio, *Open Sky*, op. cit., p91.

55. Ibid., p96.

wired smart building'.[50] For Virilio, teletechnologies turn the space of modernity, the city, inwards: 'the urbanization of real time is in fact first the urbanization of *one's own body* plugged into various interfaces (keyboards, cathode screen, DataGlove or DataSuit), prostheses that make the super-equipped able-bodied person almost the exact equivalent of the motorized and wired disabled person'.[51] Adding so much to the body, these technologies effectively disempower it. Interactivity is equated with passivity; overstimulation counterbalanced by inertia.

What is happening, according to Virilio, is a reconfiguration of human coordinates by the technological imperatives of speed. The pacemaker, for example, is a 'technotransplant' introducing a 'foreign heartbeat that can make the body throb in time to the machine'.[52] Bodies are reconstituted from the inside: neuroimplants form the internal prostheses electronically stimulating muscles so that 'pedestrian man thus becomes *electromobile man* in the manner of the electric car'.[53] Externally, the bombardment of vision machines induces a 'perceptual disorder': humans lose their status as '*eyewitnesses* of tangible reality once and for all, to the benefit of technical substitutes, prostheses for all seasons which will make of us the "visually challenged", living off sight handouts, afflicted with a kind of paradoxical blindness due to overexposure of the visible and of the *sightless* vision machines ... '[54] All faculties are assaulted: computers automate processes of rational decision-making, allowing no time to think, while *in vivo* implantation of 'physiology-stimulating devices' marks the 'coming insemination of *emotional prostheses* capable of adding to the pharmacological arsenal of stimulants and hallucinogens... '[55] Movement, sense and sensibility are recoded by the general prosthesis.

The pervasive colonisation and recalibration of the human body that Virilio attacks as 'technoscientific fundamentalism' is perhaps the most thoroughgoing manifestation of a technoeconomic alienation distinguished by the capacity to inscribe and realise states of being that once could only be longed for or feared in the imagination alone, in the art generated from the fissure of human insufficiency. But when, as Lyotard argues in the less cited parts of *The Postmodern Condition*, technology assumes the prerogative of determining reality according to the rules of a performative economic game, all power of legal, rational or moral judgement is suspended. Art becomes kitsch; money prevails as the only criterion of value. Aesthetics, or rather a 'general aestheticisation', comes to the fore. What distinguishes postmodern capitalism, argues Jean-Joseph Goux, is the disappearance of the sacred, general economic realm of sovereign values and unproductive expenditure along with rational and moral principles of production. There are no longer criteria available to distinguish useful activity from luxurious indulgence; demand no longer determines supply. Instead, the law of rational, moral economy is reversed: the entrepreneur becomes the giver, the generous benefactor, risking a fortune on supplying what the market may want. The metaphysical uncertainty of human desire becomes the principle of this speculative generalisation of restricted economy and its question - what does the market want? - turns the female hysterical psychoanalytical patient into the norm of consumption. At this point aesthetics and technology join the chorus of sirens, inhuman lures of desire. As Lyotard notes, 'When you *can* simulate *in vitro* the explosion of the sun or the fertilization or gestation of a living creature, you have to decide what you *want*. And we just *don't know*'.[56] The metaphysical uncertainty of desire drives the production of more and more virtual and realisable objects of creation and consumption. And the gift that is given by the generous entrepreneur is, of course, no gift at all, but an aneconomic axis of commercial circulation and capitalisation. Differance, with an a, the Aphrodite of theory's foam, once split between the restricted economy of exchange and return and the general economy of sovereign expenditure is, in Derrida's *Given Time*, no more than 'the restricted economy of differance'.[57] An excess, a remainder of paternal inheritance, it appears only in the form of surplus-value, erasing the difference between real and counterfeit money, an aestheticisation in which art and artifice are the guarantees of continued commerical circulation and a capitalisation of the difference-deferral called desire.

There is no other desire. Technoeconomic incorporation looks more and more like the utopia/dystopia of cyberpunk fiction, its accelerated future rapidly collapsing on the foaming void of the present. When art and business coalesce, when work and play occur on the same screens, a different kind of order manifests itself; a levelling of the sacred and the general economic realms gives a sub-sublime immanence to transgression, a gift that is not one, that is annulled at its very appearance. In one sense, the general prostheticisation delineated by Virilio, the alienation of the human from what has been supposed as its own powers, has been in place for a long time. According to Jean-Joseph Goux, 'only in the modern era in the West' has the economy 'been separated from all religious, political and moral ends in order to constitute a system ruled by its own laws, which are those of market exchange'.[58] The economy dissolves and reconstitutes social ties according to the dictates of a depersonalised 'regulatory mechanism'. Where a utopian and Comtean idea of society - as a unified, human arrangement - was sustained in modernity by all that it excluded (proletarians, women, artists), postmodernity radically refuses this possibility:

> what the system says (but must one believe it?) is not 'there are no more proletarians, women, or artists'. Rather, in a way that is at the same time very close and very different, it says 'we are all, structurally and ontologically, proletarians, women, or artists', since mediatization, the intermediary, the symbolic order, precede and produce what they mediatize.[59]

The new states of being expectorated by the general prosthesis of capitalised

56. Jean-François Lyotard, *The Inhuman*, Geoffrey Bennington and Rachel Bowlby (trans), Cambridge, Polity Press, 1993, p54.

57. Jacques Derrida, *Given Time*, Peggy Kamuf (trans), Chicago, University of Chicago Press, 1992, p147.

58. Jean-Joseph Goux, 'Subversion and Consensus: Proletarians, Women, Artists' in *Terror and Consensus: Vicissitudes of French Thought*, Jean-Joseph Goux and Philip R. Wood (eds), Stanford, Stanford University Press, 1998, p37.

59. Ibid., p49.

media imply something more and less than a simple reversal or levelling of older hierarchies. Foam engenders foam.

There is another myth of origins articulating the emergence of virtual reality and the birth of the universe: 'bubble physics'. Instead of a big bang, a bubble bursts scattering 'zillions of bubbles' in 'ocean foam' to collect and concentrate the chemicals necessary to the formation of complex molecules. For Arthur Kroker and Michael Weinstein, the model sits well with MUDs (multi-user domains):

> an electronic bubble, without depth or permanence, floating, simultaneous, and immediate, washing up on the shore of the virtual beach like phosphorescent (VR) foam, and then disappearing back into the data sea. MUD, then, as the evolutionary beginning of the primordial sea of life in the electronic void, a (data) ocean/ (human) atmosphere interface for the prebiotic origins of the molecular development of virtualized flesh: cybernetic foam.[60]

60. Arthur Kroker and Michael A. Weinstein, *Data Trash: the Theory of the Virtual Class*, New York, St Martin's Press, 1994, p130.

61. Ibid.

Life begins, again, in technology and is furnished with another myth, another fiction. It offers technocratic minds a fantasy-place in a single narrative as 'evolutionary foam in the evolutionary story of virtualized life'.[61] The same story flickers on, a final fantasy of digital foam erasing the face of man from the screens of a silicon beach. Forwards and backwards along an evolutionary line of originary technicity, the empirico-transcendental doublet sees its beginnings and ends, its plenitudes and dissolutions, its very own self, in eros and death. However, the fantasy of modernity's subject - a serial fantasist with his big bangs, primordial soups etc. - becomes as thin as the liquid crystal screen in which Narcissus waxes and wanes: 'The life within me, life as a local and temporary resistance to death - the universality of life is only ever local and temporary - is reflected by itself in the turbulence along the water. Narcissus dies, drowning in the reflection of the self, and Aphrodite emerges from another formation, Aphrodite the pleasure of others'.[62] The pleasure of the same, relentlessly returning in the accelerations of hypermodernity, crashes against an Other jouissance: Venus in foam.

62. Michel Serres, *The Birth of Physics*, Jack Hawkes (trans), Manchester, Clinamen Press, 2000, p155.

THE UNCERTAINTY OF PLACING: PROSTHETIC BODIES, SCULPTURAL DESIGN, AND UNHOMELY DWELLING IN MARC QUINN, JAMES GILLINGHAM, AND SIGMUND FREUD

Marquard Smith

It is no longer the case that conversations around prosthesis begin and end with the question of deficiency. But this was not always so. To stress this in a forthcoming article entitled 'Preambles: Disability as Prosthesis', David Wills points to ways in which the genealogy of prosthesis is often conceived as a discourse of deficiency.[1] Here Wills argues that the matter of identity in disability studies as well as the identity of Disability Studies itself, along with the place of prosthesis within these discourses, has previously been organised, unlike most other 'minority studies', around 'lack or deficiency'. That is, the form of the discipline of Disability Studies, the identity of its figures of articulation, and those prosthetic bodies of enunciation are always already found wanting. Prosthesis is the mark of this deficiency. As such a mark, it registers itself as a substitute for something that is no longer there, drawing attention both to what is missing and the absence remaining. Wills goes on to remark, somewhat caustically: '[d]isability cannot ever be other than deficiency, incompletion, inadequacy, terms which, within the metaphysics of presence as transcendent positivity, not only are by definition negative, but, more pertinently, explicitly connote non-integrality. The disabled are thus by definition "incapable" of identity inasmuch as identity refers to an uninterrupted-organic-sameness-present-to-itself-in-its-wholeness-and-singularity'.

But, as Wills contends, since the deconstruction of the metaphysics of presence, a deconstruction that has been ongoing arguably since the inception of metaphysics, this kind of argumentation is neither efficacious nor for that matter valid. In this instance, the dismantling or taking apart of the edifice of what he names this 'metaphysics of plenitude' is grasped through a realisation of the constructed nature of the human body, what that body is, and does, and what and how it means. Against the myths of the essentialist and organicist conceptions of the body proper, or proper body, disability studies can present a body that is a structuring principle, a lacuna, and a constituting part of this metaphysics of plenitude, ironically laying bare the deficiencies of this very metaphysics. Dismantling and assembling are inseparable. The organically integral body is itself, as Wills goes on to say, 'always already imperfect, mechanical, in relations of dependence, originarily disabled or incomplete; what I, in short, would call prosthetic'.

1. David Wills, 'Preambles: Disability as Prosthesis' in Laurence Simmons and Heather Worth (eds), *Derrida Downunder*, Palmerston North, Dunmore Press, 2001, pp35-52. Thanks to David for making this article available to me prior to its publication. See also David Wills, *Prosthesis*, Stanford, Stanford University Press, 1995, and his afterthought to this book, 'Re: Mourning', *Tekhnema*, 4 (1998), 8-25. With Wills's writing, for the most stimulating and provocative work taking place in the Humanities on the 'minority' discourse of Disability Studies see Lennard J. Davis, *Normalcy: Disability, Deafness and the Body*, London, Verso, 1995; Rosemarie Garland Thomson, *Extraordinary Bodies: Figuring Physical Disability in American Culture and Literature*, New York, Columbia University Press, 1997; David T. Mitchell and Sharon L. Snyder (eds), *The Body and Physical Difference: Discourses of Disability*, Ann Arbor, The University of Michigan Press, 1997; and David T. Mitchell and Sharon L. Snyder, *Narrative Prosthesis: Disability and the Dependence of Discourse*, Anne Arbor, The University of Michigan Press, 2000.

There are two definite and tangible consequences of how such a reconsideration of prosthesis refutes discourses of deficiency. The first is the dawning realisation that a prosthesis is never simply the addition of a foreign element, an attachment, an extension, an augmentation of the body as such - as Immanuel Kant would have it in the second part of his *Critique of Reason*.[2] Rather, to designate and define the form of the prosthetic body is to show that the organic and the artificial, meat and machinery, like the normal and the pathological and the ordinary and the monstrous, are always and already *of* one another: an originary technicity. To distinguish between the inside and the outside of the body misses the point. What matters is the continuous articulation of the ever-changing contours of these heterogeneous surfaces. This, then, is not a question of deficiency but simply a matter of how bodies as assemblages arrange themselves differently. The second consequence is to grasp not only that the human body was never whole, but that the body per se, and not just the disabled body, must be conceived of as a body that is always and already fragmented, in bits and pieces (*le corps morcelé*). Jacques Lacan has a fairly lucid account of this. For Lacan, the subject's 'coming-into-being' (*le devenir*), its desire to see itself in its totality, as a totality, is realised at the expense of a misrecognition: having previously seen and experienced itself as fragmented, constituted by disjointed limbs and jarring surfaces, the subject must assume an image of itself, identify itself, as complete. In recognising the totality of its image, this forced unification, while necessary for a de-alienation from that original fragmentary experience to take place, requires this very misrecognition - that it was, is, and will persist as the *corps morcelé*.[3] This too, then, is not a question of deficiency since the original fragmentariness of the subject's understanding of its own bodily self, never far from view, is never taken apart so much as it is always and already apart, a part, an arrangement of parts.

PROSTHESIS, SCULPTURAL DESIGN

Disability studies, and the prosthetic body, continue to work their way into the Humanities, employing and addressing not just discourses of literature, sociology, medical sociology, social policy, and empiricism but also philosophies of the visual arts from painting and architecture to photography and cinema. Strangely, the discourse of sculpture, or the point at which sculpture and design come together has been fairly unmoved by the topic of the prosthetic body. (Seldom explicit at any rate. Lennard J. Davis's article on the Venus de Milo is a rare exception.[4]) This is so strange because of its very obviousness. The prosthetic body is never not a design issue, a design matter, a matter of sculptural design. If anything, it is always already, perhaps first and foremost, a question of sculptural design. This goes beyond sculpture exhibiting itself as just a literal dramatisation of the more theoretical issues discussed above, although it is this too. More important is how sculpturing, or sculptural design instructs, renders precise, and

2. See Howard Caygill, 'Stelarc and the Chimera: Kant's Critique of Prosthetic Judgment', *art journal*, (Spring 1997), 46-51. Caygill's reading points out that Kant entertains the prospect of a radical prosthesis, but ends up pulling away from it because of his historically limited conception of the prosthetic potential of technology.

3. This is not a position put forward by Wills here, although it does appear in Lennard J. Davis's 'Nude Venus, Medusa's Body, and Phantom Limbs: Disability and Visuality', in Mitchell and Snyder (eds), *The Body and Physical Difference*, op. cit., pp51-70. Here Davis offers an astute Lacanian re-reading of Freud's (and art history's) insistence that we repress the fragmentary nature of the body - an insistence overcome by the disabled body's demand that the viewer confront, acknowledge, and overcome the fact of this primary repression.

4. Davis, ibid.

explicates these theoretical concerns anew. That is to say, the prosthetic body is always a question of crafting forms, planes, and surfaces, a figure conjured up by the will to physicality, materiality, formality, anthropomorphism, figuration, and formlessness. So too is it a matter of ingenuity and inventiveness, especially in terms of how it navigates the treacherous ground between the staging of the real and illusion, representation, and idealisation. It is also shaped by the challenge of inaction, automatism, and Pygmalion-like animation. One cannot but invoke the uncanny motifs of the puppet, the mechanical marionette, automata, and toys in the discourse of modernity, and before. The prosthetic body, as an assemblage, a partial object, as fragmented-ness personified, and as desiring machine too demands that we strive to cope with it, whether in public or private, as an intimate, shared, playful, pressing, and moveable encounter with sculptural design.[5] That all of this turns on *the uncertainty of placing* is a point to which I shall return.

For the moment I would like to stay with the far from exceptional confluence of disability, prostheses, and sculptural design, a vivid union that is perhaps most readily available in our recent cultural imaginary through the highly visible figure of Aimee Mullins. Mullins, the American double-amputee paralympian athlete, was depicted provocatively in a Nick Knight photo shoot for the fashion magazine *Dazed and Confused* in 1998. She adorned the catwalk, Barbie doll-like, on a revolving pedestal in fashion designer Alexander McQueen's 1999 Spring-Summer Collection in London; and she sprinted through the desert landscape of a television advertisement for the British internet service provider Freeserve in 2000.[6] Up until 2000, she was outfitted with leg prostheses produced by Van Phillips, the designer of the ultra-modern Flex-foot, who was also responsible for fitting her with the prototype graphite legs used in her Freeserve advertisement, modelled on the hind legs of fleet-footed cheetahs. Since then, Mullins has been using prosthetic limbs designed by Dorset Ortho-paedics, an orthopaedic prosthetic clinic based in Bournemouth, England, which, parenthetically, allow her to wear 4Din heels. (Dorset Ortho-paedics was apparently recommended to Mullins by Heather Mills, fellow model, athlete, and amputee, the then girlfriend now fiancée of Paul McCartney.)

As one would expect, the subject of design per se was never an issue for the devotional gush surrounding Mullins's appearances. Tabloid, popular magazine, and serious journalistic conversation alike concentrated on the effects of its production, on the wow-factor, on how the beautiful, sexy athlete became - although this language was rarely used - the figure of the quintessential prosthetic body, characterised perfectly in a more academic setting as a Cyborgian sex kitten.[7] Throughout, effort went into maintaining her seamless presentation - the victory of technology over deficiency. What mattered was that the seams were overlooked, the joins didn't show - even when they did. Her status as an amputee was simply an autobiographical detail, albeit a significant one, but it was never played up as an aesthetic,

5. Tracking a psychoanalytic/anti-psychoanalytic trajectory of the machinic as part-object and desiring machine, Rosalind Krauss mentions Freud, Klein, Deleuze and Guattari, and Michel Carrouges who, in 1952, named the 'Bachelor machine'. See Rosalind Krauss, *Bachelors*, Cambridge, Mass, MIT, 1999, p64.

6. In 1999 Mullins was also one of *People Magazine*'s '50 Most Beautiful People in the World'

7. Many thanks to my former students on the MA in Visual Arts at Goldsmiths College for this so suitable designation.

8. The appearances on *Oprah* and *Rosie O'Donnell* more than affirm the less than insignificant role of autobiography in Mullins's profile.

9. The celebrity face of the anti-landmine campaign in Angola, in the form of the late Princess of Wales and the footballer David Ginola, should be noted here. Thanks to Kay Dickinson for conversations about her travels in Cambodia.

10. See W. Scott and C. Eames, 'A new emergency splint of plyformed wood', *U.S. Naval Bulletin*, 41, 5 (1943), 1423-28.

11. Sander L. Gilman, 'Marks of Honor and Dishonor', in *Making the Body Beautiful: A Cultural History of Aesthetic Surgery*, Princeton, Princeton University Press, 1999, p149.

12. Oliver Wendell Holmes, 'The Human Wheel, Its Spokes and Fellows', *Atlantic Monthly* (May 1863), 567-80. See David D. Yuan, 'Disfigurement and Reconstruction in Oliver Wendell Holmes's "The Human Wheel, Its Spokes and Fellows"', in Mitchell and Snyder (eds), *The Body and Physical Difference,*, op. cit., pp71-88.

13. See Wills, *Prosthesis*, op. cit., p226. Wills says that the word 'prosthesis' appears in the

erotic, or ergonomic fact in and of itself.[8] The irony of this is most telling, etymologically at any rate, if we survey the catwalk, a showcase for *haute couture* - a term that takes us back, via Old French to *cousture*, seam, and Latin, *conseure*, to stitch together - presenting us with its first amputee model.

The celebrations surrounding the figure of Aimee Mullins are merely the most visible - because most fashionable, aesthetic, erotic, and commercially palatable - illustration of disability, prosthesis, and sculptural design coming together. There are of course numerous other instances of this confluence that, because they are either less agreeable or have fallen out of view, are publicised, exalted, or praised less often. The examples that follow briefly, while certainly not random, look to give a sense of the various patterning of this convergence. To begin, we could pinpoint Cambodia where five international organisations, active through fifteen workshops located across the country, produce and distribute prostheses made from local materials, vulcanised rubber in particular, to many of the 40,000 amputees 'disabled' by the indiscriminate use of antipersonnel mines since the beginning of the Cambodian Civil War.[9] Or we might be intrigued to discover that between 1942 and 1944, Charles Eames and Ray Eames (née Kaiser), influenced by a combination of the 'Machine Aesthetic' and 'Organic Modernism', composed their first mass produced objects out of plywood, and that these crafted pieces were not furniture but leg and arm splints made for the US Navy.[10] Further, we can seek out the German-Jewish surgeon Jacques Joseph (1865-1934), the founder of modern aesthetic rhinoplasty, whose practises in *fin-de-siècle* Berlin concentrated on so called vanity rather than real surgery. Joseph, by upholding the contemporary veneration for Albrecht Dürer and looking to Greek Ideal form in order to find models of aesthetic beauty, sought to bring 'happiness' to his patients by, say, transforming 'Jewish noses' into 'gentile contours'. He chipped away at bone, removed cartilage, and carried out exact suturing, operating tools that are still used today, thereby endorsing Sander L. Gilman's remark that for him, Joseph, 'the aesthetic surgeon is really a sculptor: he uses hammers and chisels and shapes an object - just like an artist'.[11] Oliver Wendell Holmes's article on human locomotion of May 1863 gives us a similar characterisation of the American inventor B. Frank Palmer as a 'Surgeon Artist' who shapes wooden limbs 'very much as a sculptor finishes his marble, with an eye to artistic effect'.[12] Harking back to craft production and anticipating Fordist assembly lines, Palmer saw prosthesis as part of social reconstruction after what he identified as the 'melancholic harvest' of limbs; the Civil War that was to shape 30,000 amputees between 1861 and 1865. Passaging back to the Renaissance, we might imagine the impact of Thomas Wilson's 1553 *Art of Rhetorique* which, as Wills points out, is not only the first known printed use of the term 'prosthesis' but also pictures it in such as way as for it to take a 'precise typographical form'.[13] Concomitant with Wilson is Ambroise Paré who in 1552 also brings rhetoric and medicine together by practising, as Wills remarks, 'ligature of the arteries instead of cauterization following amputation and so inaugurates modern surgery and the possibility of artificial limbs'.[14] In Book 23 of his *Oeuvres*, parts of which had already been published in 1561 and 1564, along with limbs Paré was to focus in on even more individualised prosthetic devises, all illustrated with diagrams, such as artificial eyes made from round objects or painted leather, papier-mâché noses, and so on. Which is to say nothing of the attention he lavishes on cords, pullies, threads, screws, buckles, and springs.[15] The Venus tradition from antiquity, along with ancient sculptures such as the Belvedere Torso, is self-explanatory - although I shall touch upon it later. What does need further elaboration, albeit in an abbreviated manner, is one of the earliest artificial members ever discovered, the prehistorical neolithic skull and its delicate auricular prosthesis carved from a seashell, the spondylus Graederopus to be precise, found by archaeologists in 1955 while excavating a megalithic chamber tomb at Roque d'Aille in the Var, dating from the third millennium B.C.[16]

THE UNCERTAINTY OF PLACING[17]

The historical and geographical diversity of instances from which one can draw to affirm a certain consistency in the confluence of disability, prosthesis, and sculptural design is expansive. Some of the examples given here speak of the appalling atrocities of war, others tell pleasing anecdotes, and others still are simply somewhat peculiar. In all cases, they testify that the prosthetic body - however its organic, disabled, mechanised, or otherwise disposed parts are arranged - is always and already a place of dismantling and assembling as well as one of discord and disquiet. It is this question of place, or what I am calling the uncertainty of placing, that is the logic and vitality of this confluence. And it is an etymological one. Prosthesis, from the Greek *prosthesis*, and the French *prostithemi*, as PROS-, *tithemi*, denotes 'place', or 'placing'. With this in mind, my preceding and following remarks are framed by this question of place, by the uncertainty of place, the place of prosthesis, prosthesis as uncertain placing. (Disability Studies is itself no stranger to the matter of placing, and its uncertainties, a topic that characterises the challenges of the built environment, access, locale, mobility, intimacy, and so on, as well as its very disciplinary positioning.)

In this way the matter of prosthesis as sculptural design can be invoked as a question of placing. To put this another way, prosthesis is always already organised in such a way as for it to be both in place and out of place. Placing is caught up in the circumstances of dwelling both within and extrinsic to a place as the never not shaky dilemma of an installation, a lodging, and of a displacing. It is disabling, enabling, and rarely dispassionate. Such a placing is always an occupation, an upsetting, and a misplacing too, as well as an un-building and a relocating. It is *heimlich* and *unheimlich* simultaneously. More than the feeling of unease that is brought on by the unfamiliar within the familiar, the uncertainty of place *already knows* that the homely is

margins, and in Roman type rather than the black-letter gothic of the *Rhetorique*.

14. David Wills, 'Preambles', op. cit.

15. On Paré, see David Wills, 'Cambridge, 1533', in *Prosthesis*, op. cit., pp214-49. See also Jean-Claude Beaune, 'The Classical Age of Automata: An Impressionistic Survey from the Sixteenth to the Nineteenth Century' Ian Patterson (trans), in Michel Feher, Ramona Naddaff and Nadia Tazi (eds), *Fragments for a History of the Human Body, Part One*, Zone, New York, 1989, pp430-80.

16. See Gustaf Sobin, *Luminous Debris: Reflecting on Vestige in Provence and Languedoc*, Berkeley, University of California Press, 1999, pp51-55. Thanks to Harry Gilonis for bringing the existence of this remarkable thing to my attention.

17. Many of the ideas around place, placing, dwelling, and the uncanny emerge out of an engagement with the thought of Sigmund Freud, Martin Heidegger, and Jacques Derrida, and the hugely convincing writings of Anthony Vidler and Mark Wigley. See Mark Wigley, 'Prosthetic Theory: The Disciplining of Architecture', *Assemblage 15* (1991), 7-29; Anthony

Vidler, *The Architectural Uncanny: Essays in the Modern Unhomely*, Cambridge, Mass, MIT Press, 1992; Mark Wigley, 'The Domestication of the House: Deconstruction After Architecture', in Peter Brunette and David Wills (eds), *Deconstruction and the Visual Arts: Art, Media, Architecture*, Cambridge, Cambridge University Press, 1994, pp203-27; Mark Wigley, *The Architecture of Deconstruction: Derrida's Haunt*, Cambridge, Mass, MIT Press, 1993, in particular Chapter 7 entitled 'Dislocating Space', pp177-204.

18. *GIVE & TAKE* was a collaborative exhibition between both the V&A and the Serpentine Gallery. See Leigh Markopoulous (ed), *GIVE & TAKE*, London, Serpentine Gallery, 2001.

19. On Antonio Canova see Alex Potts, *The Sculptural Imagination: Figurative, Modernist, Minimalist*, London, Yale University Press, 2000, pp38-59.

unhomely - and that the uncanny is canny too.

Having suggested that disability, prosthesis, and sculptural design are bound together, and having pointed to how sculptural design has a certain kind of place that is both defining of and dependant upon the seam between disability and prosthesis, I would like to address this place directly. Accordingly, I will attempt to ask what it means to dwell in the place of prosthesis, a prosthetic place that is in place and out of place in fractious and untimely ways because of how it *takes place*. To this end I will go on to consider three episodes, contested events, or cast studies. The first is the public curatorial placing of some of Marc Quinn's recent sculptures of amputees in London's Victoria & Albert Museum in 2001. The second is the theatrical placing of prostheses in a few photographs taken for James Gillingham of Chard, the embodiment of a Victorian surgical-machinist as artist, circa 1915. The third is the private spectral placing of a 'monstrous' oral prosthesis in Sigmund Freud as a response to his mouth cancer, first diagnosed in 1923.

CAST STUDY I: SITUATING MARC QUINN'S AMPUTEES

Between 30 January 2001 and 1 April 2001, the English sculptor Marc Quinn exhibited eight sculptures at the Victoria & Albert Museum (hereafter V&A) in London. The sculptures were on display as part of a group show entitled *GIVE & TAKE*, curated by Lisa G. Corrin, then chief curator at the Serpentine Gallery. Its aim was to bring contemporary works of visual art into dialogue with the V&A's historical collections and settings, thereby permitting us to conceive of the latter as also contemporaneous.[18] Along with this ambition, and along with an aspiration to question the shaping of history, taxonomy, and so on, Quinn's sculptures were placed in the Eighteenth Century British Sculpture Gallery already in use by Neo-Classical figurative sculptures such as Antonio Canova's *Theseus and the Minotaur* (1782) and *The Three Graces* (1814-17).[19]

Now Marc Quinn is best know specifically for his 1991 sculpture *Self*, a cast of his own head made from nine pints of his own blood, the quantity of blood carried in and by an adult human body. He is highly acclaimed for his use of his own body to provide both subject of and literal material for his work. By employing his blood, along with his own faeces, as well as marzipan, bread dough, wax, latex, rubber, polyurethane, rope, acrylic, plaster, bronze, perspex, and stainless steel, glass, silver, and ice, Quinn articulates the capacity of sculpture to cast and recast the contours of his human form. His sculpture, from *Self* and *Template for My Future Plastic Surgery Aged 80* (1992) to the *No Visible Means of Escape* series (1996-8) and *Shit Painting* (1997) offers a decidedly prosthetic aesthetic. Altogether distinct from the more explicitly prosthetic assemblages of a Cindy Sherman, a Stelarc, or an Orlan, nevertheless here too the human form, Quinn's corporeal self, is fabricated and re-fabricated, its parts are of one another,

and it is fragmentary and fragmenting ceaselessly. But in *GIVE & TAKE*, for the first time since his 1987 sculpture *Faust*, Marc Quinn exhibited sculptures of something other than himself, and of some*one* other than himself. The eight sculptures he exhibited here with their pristine surfaces unblemished by chisel marks are life-size marble portraits, made by craftsmen in Pietrasanta, Italy, of amputees who, according to the Exhibition's blurb, have been 'deprived of one or more limbs as a result of birth, illness or accident'.

Fig 2 above:
Marc Quinn,
Jamie
Gillespie,
1999. Fig 3
right: Marc
Quinn,
Catherine
Long, *2000,*
Jay Jopling/
White Cube,
London. Give
and Take, *an*
exhibition at thee
Serpentine
Gallery and
Victoria and
Albert Museum,
30 January - 1
April 2001.
Photo © Jeremy
Hardman-Jones

There are three evident purposes to the placing of Quinn's sculptures in the V&A's gallery. Firstly, they are meant to come into dialogue with the earlier neo-classical sculpture already there, thereby working towards modifying traditional models of aesthetic beauty that are premised on conceptions of the intact body. Secondly, in order to do this they draw attention to the fragmented properties of these earlier sculptures that, through either the ravages of time, iconoclasm, or by design have become or were always already fragmentary. In making the familiar strange, we come to realise, if we hadn't done so already, that some of these earlier sculptures too are born without legs, are armless, and so on - headless even. In an *acéphalic* state. Not so much sacrificial sculptural ruins as forever immaculate themselves. Grasping this distinction denies the art historian, the viewer, the possibility, as Lennard J. Davis remarks so astutely in his discussion of the Venus de Milo, of 'facing the gaze of the missing part that must be argued into existence'.[20] To use Davis's words, the art historian, the viewer, cannot 'restore the damage, bring back the limbs, through an act of imagination'; this is a phenomenon much like, as Davis points out, the experience of 'phantom limbs' for some amputees.[21] Confronted by Quinn's sculptures in dialogue with traditional neo-classical sculpture in the Eighteenth Century British Sculpture Gallery, the art historian is not permitted to ignore, avoid, or fail to see this absence in order to substitute or replace it with presence. They can no longer execute their acts of supplementary restoration to 'make good' the deficiency. It is not a question of loss, there is simply no deficiency. Thirdly, a consequence of this is that, by initiating an encounter with us, these 'deprived' amputees are displaced from the edges of discourse to the core of conversation, they become beautiful in and of themselves, and a flawless sense of self is bestowed upon them. The strange has been made familiar. In being individualised through the naming of the sculpture's titles, they can take up a singular identity - which is at once familiar and familial. The titles of Marc Quinn's sculptures, listed here in alphabetical order, are *Jamie Gillespie* (1999), *Peter Hull* (1999), *Catherine Long* (2000), *Selma Mustajbasic* (2000), *Stuart Penn* (2000), *Helen Smith* (2000), *Alexandra Westmoquette* (2000), and *Tom Yendell* (2000). Together they are known as *Group Portrait*.

Or so the arguments go. These are claims that are certainly evinced by the sculptures themselves, by the curatorial tactic, in the V&A's accompanying blurb, and in the viewer's experience of dialogue with the work itself. It is also born out, albeit in a more utopian, quixotic, if incriminating manner in an interview conducted by Germano Celant with Marc Quinn for the catalogue accompanying Celant's Milan exhibition *Marc Quinn* in which Celant asks:

> The disabled people that you have portrayed survive thanks to artificial limbs; with these prostheses they manage to run, to ride bicycles and to shoot arrows. Do you think that the new dimension is this dilatation and sublimation that comes from the machines, those in the gymnasia or those of the phantom limbs? The body with prostheses is perhaps the first and greatest vision of the future that awaits us, in which prostheses, computers and other machines will be increasingly important. Is fiction turning into reality?

Quinn replies:

> I think it's really important to acknowledge the difference between reality and symbolic function. I mean, in the collective imagination the prosthetic body is a symbol of the future and our relation to technology. But for the people who have to use prostheses, it's quite a different issue.

20. Lennard J. Davis, 'Nude Venus', op. cit., p59.

21. Ibid., p57.

They are useful but they are also not; in fact some of the sitters have stopped using their prostheses because they feel they are more about conforming with the normal body image society gives them than with making their lives better. So really fiction isn't becoming reality, what emerges is the difference between fiction and reality.[22]

22. 'Marc Quinn', curated by Germano Celant took place at the Fondazione, Prada, Milan from 5 May-10 June 2000. The catalogue for the exhibition is published by Fondazione, Prada, Milan. For a forceful critique of the 'metaphorical opportunism', of technological fetishism see Mitchell and Snyder, 'Introduction: Disability Studies and the Double Bind of Representation', in Mitchell and Snyder (eds), *The Body and Physical Difference*, op. cit., p7, fn32.

Ignoring Celant's unconditional celebration of the enabling qualities of prosthetic technology and, conversely, Quinn's talk of its debilitating character too, specifically in terms of its conforming aesthetic imperatives, I would like to question what else is going on, or failing to take place, in this exchange. For while there is evident purpose to this public placing of Quinn's sculptures - whether at the Fondazione, Milan, at the Kunstverein, Hannover, or at the V&A, London - there is also an unacknowledged prospect that elicits a question of eroticisation. In particular, it is a question of the dynamic between eroticisation and de-eroticisation. This is a question raised by Lennard J. Davis who distinguishes between our desire to eroticise the Venus de Milo while simultaneously de-eroticising people with disabilities in general - Davis employs specifically the writings of Pam Herbert, a quadriplegic with muscular dystrophy, as his counterpoint. For Davis, as I have already mentioned, the argument is that the Venus de Milo can be eroticised through the discourse of Ideal Western beauty because the art historian has learnt how to wilfully 'fill in the gaps' while people with disabilities, disabled women in his example, are consigned elsewhere. In fact they're assigned largely to a discourse of the monstrous female body which, Medusa-like, horrifies us into petrifaction. This repulsion is of course the horror of confronting deficiency, lack, absence that is so familiar to us from psychoanalysis, and, because of this, is applied to and born of the disabled body too.

But if we are to claim that there is no deficiency, no lack, that there is no absence, as I have been arguing, then we find ourselves somewhere very different altogether. If the body, and not simply the disabled body but all bodies are always and already in bits and pieces, *and that things take place because of this*, we are in no way bound by the limitations intrinsic to psychoanalytically induced anxieties. We've moved away, then, from amputation as an uncanny signifier of symbolic castration. Nor is our field of vision prevented from gazing at so supposed a grotesquery. Quite the opposite. If anything, we are drawn to gaze, without anxiety - castration anxiety or otherwise - because the Venus de Milo, Pam Herbert, and Marc Quinn's sculptures are, quite simply, part of our modified prosthetic vocabulary, and, in so being, are eroticised *because they are* amputees. It is the absences of the gaps themselves, not our efforts to disguise them, that are explicitly and knowingly eroticised by the discipline of art history and historians of visual culture. Looking to extend Davis's invaluable critique, let me propose that it is not only the case that art historians must argue missing body parts or missing limbs back into existence through acts of the imagination so that they might disavow the fact of this deficiency. Also, perhaps more so, they actually love such bodies *as* and because they *are* fragmented. And that this love is of a sexual, or at least erotic nature. Perhaps the art historian of Greek sculpture is an apotemnophile, someone interested in the desire to have a limb removed which, as Alphonso Lingis has argued, has a very real connection to the dynamics of sex and art.[23] Perhaps - and this is my preferred option simply because of its moderate character - viewers of the visual arts are acrotomophiles: that is, sexually excited by the stump(s) of others. Perhaps they're just 'wannabees'. Or simply 'devotees'. If any or all of these prospects seem likely, then there is an explicit and explicitly erotic quality to our encounter with Marc Quinn's sculptures of amputees, extended into the realm of the gallery in order that this private fondness might take place in public. Attending to the sculptural design of these prosthetic bodies, made possible through questions raised by Disability Studies, exposes us as members of the public, in a moment of mutual exhibitionism, to a flirtatious dialogue in this unpredictable sphere.

23. See Alphonso Lingis, 'The Physiology of Art', forthcoming in Joanne Morra and Marquard Smith (eds), *Prosthetics: Carnal. Assembling. Extant.*

CAST STUDY II: THE THEATRICAL STAGING OF GILLINGHAMS OF CHARD'S SUSPENDED ANIMATION

At least in part, eroticisation may well also be a motive behind a group of photographs taken of Gillinghams of Chard's products - the company made artificial limbs and body armature beginning in 1866. The photographs were taken for a Gillinghams advertising catalogue circa 1915. Above and beyond this purely commercial purpose, these photographs, housed in the archives of the Science Museum's Osteogenesis Collection, exhibit portraits of female amputees displaying their wares. Some of these women have been invited to lift up their shirts, others to remove their over-garments, in order that a potential customer might see more precisely the quality of the products crafted by Gillinghams. In giving in to this request, the amputees assist in the selling of the callipers, body supports with underarm stirrups, leather bodices, corsetry, and artificial limbs that are Gillinghams's speciality. In so doing, they expose their arms, the napes of their neck, the tops of their thighs, the shadow effected by the point at which the tops of their thighs and buttocks meet, revealing skin that has been trussed up by the confines of straps, (garter) belts, and buckles. Skin is squeezed and moulded by the bondaged taughtness of its restricted lacing, the back-straightening contraptions have a sadistic edge, and the hints of undergarment betray a less than prudent photographer inviting our voyeuristic gaze. With a twist of the hips, the women turn away from the camera, to obscure their faces, to remain anonymous, disguised, to keep their modesty intact, their identity a secret. By averting their gazes, they also endeavour to frustrate the attention we might lavish upon them, which could, in turn, distract our eye from more properly consumerist desires.

This is, then, a dual seduction, at once commercial and erotic. Another group of the same collection of photographs related to Gillinghams of Chard were taken for the same commercial purpose as those previously mentioned, in the same interior setting, the studio, with matching lighting, scenery of painted backcloths, props, and drapery. They are staged in the same way. But unlike those other portraits, or populated photographs, these are all either occupied by body parts, parts of bodies, or no bodies at all. This is certainly the case for the two photographs reproduced here. They have been vacated of humanness, or, they are about to become populated. They drift away from and toward the ghost of an inhabitation. There is a hallucinogenic quality, a dream-like character to the theatrical arrangement of these prosthetic limbs and body armature, as I have suggested elsewhere.[24] This is the case because, instead of the familiar arrested movement of human animation we have come to know as portrait photography, here we are offered a stranger morphological animation of an un-human sort in which, through narrative, display, and humour, autonomous limbs act out the scene that takes place. Ornamental, luxurious, arranged, posing, they occupy centre stage. And they do so in a way that is not so much human as it is *of* the assemblage's human-ness. Like personality traits, the limbs, joins, and seams are sutured, stitched together, surface to surface, akin to some comic Frankenstein's Monster in the making. Suspended, hanging, they incarnate the machinations of a contemplative puppet-master. They are almost animating.

Not only under the sway of another's will, they are also, in themselves, performative. Such is their uncanniness. For even as still-lives and as subject-less objects, they are nonetheless still portraits - both portraits of objects

24. Marquard Smith, 'Prosthetic Nightmares', in Joanne Morra and Marquard Smith (eds), 'the reInterpretation of dreams', *parallax*, 6, 3, (2000), 93-104.

Figs 4 and 5: Photographs from Gillinghams of Chard c1915. Reprinted with the permission of the Science Museum/Science & Society Plc Lib.

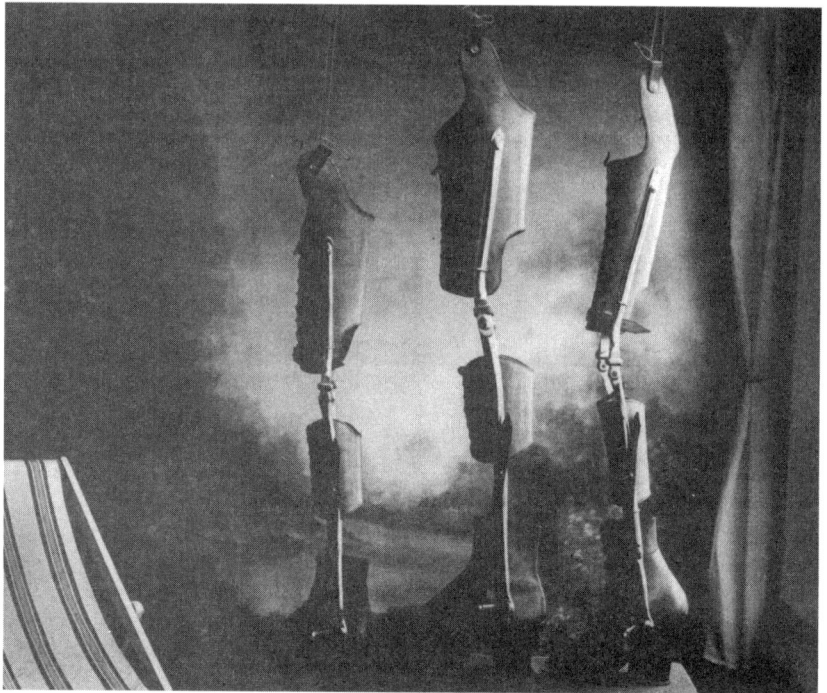

and portraits that are still. In this way, these prostheses are not deficient, none the worse for having misplaced their bodies of enunciation. They articulate without the need for support from the human forms that - through modelling, wearing, and a will to verisimilitude - previously inhabited or were attached to them. (Such is also the predicament for those bodies that may go on to occupy or affix themselves to these arrangements.) They can model and sell themselves. Within the frame of the photograph it is the human body, then, that is uncanny. It is both familiar in its spectral absence and, drawing on the definitions of the uncanny that Freud looks to supplant, also new and alien to the assemblages themselves. In a reversal of Kant's position on prosthesis, it is the foreign or alien presence of the human that would be the addition to, the augmentation of the prostheses as such.

These photographs, taken for and as illustrations of Gillinghams of

Chard's prostheses, come about just a couple of years before Freud completed writing his paper on the uncanny. As we will recall from it, '[d]ismembered limbs, a severed head, a hand cut off at the wrist ... feet which dance by themselves ... all of these have something peculiarly uncanny about them, especially when ... they prove capable of *independent activity in addition* [my italics]'.[25] Freud of course does not believe in the veracity of such independent activity, tied, as it always is, to dreams and phantasies of the recurrence of repressed infantile complexes - for Freud there is little that does not go back to intra-uterine dwelling. As such, Freud shows why it is that, within a psychoanalytic comprehension of neurosis, this kind of uncanniness takes place because of its proximity to the castration complex. The fear of losing an eye and the consequent fear of going blind, for instance, is, metaphorically, a substitute, or what Freud calls a 'substitutive relation' between the eye and the male organ. But, as we shall go on to see, metaphors aside, perhaps Freud could have been more attentive to the potential of such 'independent activity in addition'.

CAST STUDY III: SIGMUND FREUD'S 'MONSTER'

On 25 April 1923, Sigmund Freud wrote to Ernst Jones that he had 'detected 2 months ago a leukoplastic growth on my jaw and palate right side, which I had removed on the 28th. I am still out of work and cannot swallow'.[26] In *The Life and Work of Sigmund Freud*, Jones recounts that Freud had been in touch with the rhinologist Marcus Hajek who diagnosed his condition as leucopolakia brought on by smoking.[27] Hajek recommended an operation, the first of thirty-three efforts made over the next sixteen years to salvage Freud's life by brutally redefining the contours of his mouth. Following a botched operation at Hajek's clinic, and after huge blood loss, further incompetence resulted in the failure to carry out the usual precautions that prevent the shrinkage of post-operative scars. From then on it became more and more difficult for Freud to open his mouth, thereby further obscuring the unfamiliar composition of this interior shelter.

Growing ever more distrustful of Hajek, Freud turned to Felix Deutsch who, spotting a recurrence of the original growth, the return of an uncanny harbinger of death, recommended more radical operations. It was Deutsch who persuaded Professor Hans Pichler, the oral surgeon, to take on the case. As Jones reported, on 26 September Pichler and Hajek examined Freud together and found 'a malignant ulcer in the hard palate which invaded the neighbouring tissues, including the upper part of the lower jaw and even the cheek'.[28] Pichler operated on 4 and 11 October. In the first of these two operations, remarked Jones, 'the external carotid artery was ligatured and the submaxillary glands, some of which were already suspiciously enlarged, removed. In the second operation', he goes on to say, 'after slitting the lip and cheek wide open, the surgeon removed the whole upper jaw and palate on the affected side, a very extensive operation

25. Sigmund Freud, 'The Uncanny' in *The Pelican Freud Library, Volume 14: Art and Literature*, James Strachey (trans), Harmondsworth, Penguin Books, 1985, p366.

26. See R. Andrew Paskauskas (ed), *The Complete Correspondence of Sigmund Freud and Ernest Jones 1908-1939*, London, The Belknap Press of Harvard University Press, 1995, p521.

27. Ernst Jones, *The Life and Work of Sigmund Freud*, London, Pelican Books, 1974. The historical and biographical details reproduced here are culled largely from Jones's account.

28. Ibid., p552.

which of course threw the nasal cavity and mouth into one'.[29] Sigmund Freud was then fitted with his first oral prosthesis:

> The huge prosthesis, a sort of magnified denture or obturator, designed to shut off the mouth from the nasal cavity, was a horror; it was labelled 'the monster'. In the first place it was very difficult to take out or replace because it was impossible for him to open his mouth at all widely … Then for the instrument to fulfil its purpose of shutting off the yawning cavity above, and so making speaking and eating possible, it had to fit fairly tightly. This, however, produced constant irritation and sore places until its presence was unbearable. But if it were left out for more than a few hours the tissues would shrink, and the denture could no longer be replaced without being altered.[30]

Ernst Jones writes that Freud's oral prosthesis, 'the monster', caused constant trouble. It could not be taken out or replaced easily, having to be modified every few days, it lead to defective smoking, eating, and breathing, a change in his appearance, and, because it was ill-fitting, it caused unbearable irritation and sore places. It also made it difficult for him to speak, a change in the sound of his voice was noted, and not just in his native tongue.[31] (One can only imagine the impact all this was to have on his working practices and thus the analytic situation.)

The incessant craving for comfort lead to daily visits from Pichler for a period in 1923, to the styling of a second oral prosthesis in February 1924, and a third in October of the same year. In 1931, Professor Varaztad Kazanjian of Harvard University, another founding father of plastic surgery, was pressured into working on Freud's prosthesis for twenty days, but, as Jones comments, the results were 'very far from satisfactory'.[32] In 1936, following painful treatment with Röntgen rays and radium, it was discovered, says Jones, that 'the metal in the prosthesis was producing secondary radiation' as a consequence of which 'another apparatus was built to obviate this'.[33] During Christmas 1938, Max Schur removed a further segment of dead bone from Freud's mouth, which offered relief for a while. In early 1939 Freud informed Jones that Dr Harmer has told him that the recent treatment has had 'an unmistakable influence on the appearance of the sore place'.[34] But by July, Freud, attacked by a cancerous ulceration, was apathetic and unable to sleep. By August, the odour from the wound was such that his favourite dog is seen to shrink away from him in disgust. On 21 September, Freud and Schur engage in by no means their first conversation on euthanasia. On 22 September, Schur administered a small dose of morphine to Freud. On 23 September 1939 Freud is dead.

By way of Freud's troublesome and somehow autonomous oral prosthesis as a harbinger of his imminent death, from the 23 of September 1939 right back to that fateful day in February 1923 we begin to picture him from the inside out. As the evidence of his war with the mutable conditions of his

29. Ibid., p553

30. Ibid, pp553-54. On Freud's oral prosthesis see Scott Wilson, 'Dying for a Smoke: Freud, Addiction and the Management of Life', in Roger Starling (ed), *Angelaki*, 7.2 (2002). Thanks to Scott Wilson for supplying me with an earlier version of this article. Mark Wigley also mentions Freud's prosthesis in his 'Prosthetic Theory', op. cit., p8. The most extended philosophical and psychoanalytical speculations on Freud's prosthesis take place in 'Berchtesgaden, 1929', chapter 4 of David Wills's *Prosthesis*, op. cit., pp92-129. See also Ernst Jones, *The Life and Work of Sigmund Freud*, 'BOOK THREE: *The Last Phase (1919-39)*', pp483-657, passim.

31. Jones recalls an anecdote in which Freud, visiting Yvette Guilbert, 'turned to her husband with the pathetic humorous remark, "my prosthesis doesn't speak French"', p559

32. Ibid., p605.

33. Ibid., p621.

34. Ibid., p652.

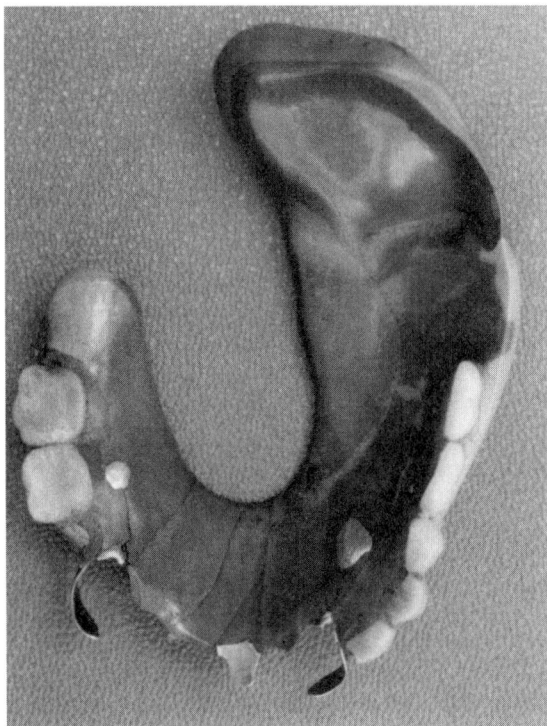

Figs 6 and 7:
Sigmund Freud's
oral prosthesis,
© The Freud
Museum,
London.

35. Freud's letter to
Lou Andreas-Salomé
appears in Ernest
Pfeiffer (ed),
*Sigmund Freud and
Lou Andreas-Salomé
Letters*, William and
Elaine Robson-Scott
(trans), London, The
Hogarth Press and
the Institute of
Psycho-analysis,
1972, p137. They
continue to discuss
Freud's prosthesis in
letter exchanges
throughout the rest
of 1924. Mark
Wigley mentions the
first of these
exchanges, see op.
cit., 'Prosthetic
Theory', p8, fn6.

corporeal self, the sculptural design and re-design of his prosthesis scores itself into the matter of his very body which is stripped away and reconstituted, taken apart and reassembled, the effects of which are both enabling and dis-abling. In the cavernous dwelling of his mouth, Freud's oral prosthesis was in place, sometimes, and out of place at other times. It was at once placed and displaced, located and dislocated, lodged and dislodged, situated, erring, misplaced, replaced, and unsuccessfully effaced. It could not be a secret - Freud often had to keep it in place with his thumb, although he managed to disguise this to some extent by turning the action into an intellectual affectation. In this way, the disclosure of the enclosure is the disclosure of its secret. This inhabitation is a secret that is not a secret, a hiding that is betrayed by the man himself. Or let us put this upside-down, back to front. Perhaps Freud was betrayed by the prosthesis itself. This prospect is noteworthy. Freud possesses a haunted mouth. Like a phantom limb, his oral prosthesis, occupying a proper place and also being located in a non-place, takes place in the uncertainty of this invocation. Attaching and detaching, it haunts him and he haunts it. Sigmund Freud was not buried with his prosthesis. He gives up the ghost. Abandons it. It gives him up too.

Freud's oral prosthesis is certainly an instance of uncanny dwelling. For it is not the case that this foreign element, the unhomely is extraneous to the home, that the unfamiliar is extrinsic to the familiar. Rather, the unhomely is already always of the home, belongs in the home, and the unfamiliar is forever already a structuring part of the familiar. Freud already knew this, theoretically at least, when, in 1919, he published his essay on 'The Uncanny'. But it seems he didn't know it personally until 1924. In this year he was compelled to know that his oral prosthesis was more than simply foreign to himself, an extension of his own body. And he knew this from Lou Andreas-Salomé. In a letter dated 11 August 1924, Freud, writing about his small-scale war waged with his 'refractory piece of equipment', asked Andreas-Salomé what she thought of 'the analogous relationship to a substitute such as this, which tries to be and yet cannot be the self'.[35] In her reply, dated 3 September, she made it clear she understood - as he would go on to understand - that his prosthesis was not so much a departure *from* as it was a necessary component *of* the condition of the human body: 'For that is after all the most quintessentially human thing in man, that he both is and is not his own body - that his body despite everything is a piece of external reality like any other, which can be identified by him with the help of his sense organs from outside himself'.[36]

Such is the uncertainty of placing: a body is by no means wholly owned by the body inhabiting it. It is not proper to, the property of, itself. To some extent, this is the most significant question to which this essay has hoped to attend: the certainty that things, bodies for instance, are, in a host of ways, always separate from and imminent to arrangements of other things and also themselves. This was the reason for beginning the essay by emphasising how prostheses are never simply additions to the body as such, that the body is itself always and already in bits and pieces that fit together awkwardly, and that the figure of the prosthetic body is really the only way to make sense of these intricacies. As I proposed from the outset, dismantling and assembling are inseparable. The organic and the machinic are always and already of one another. The prosthetic body, in its many manifestations, is testament to this. And this is the case, in this instance at any rate, because of the extent to which it is a matter of sculptural design. Hence the need to foreground the task of sculptural design in the discourses of the body in general and the prosthetic body in

36. Pfeiffer, ibid., pp138-39.

particular. For surely the question of the body is and has never not been a question of design, and re-design - whether in the discourses of atomism, cosmology, anatomy, organicist or evolutionary theory, feminism, identity politics, queer theory, and so on. This painstaking, necessarily uneven prospect of re-design is very much the reason for having begun from the premise that the question of deficiency needs to be drawn out, exposed, and held accountable. For the prosthetic body, however differently-abled it might be, along with the discourses appearing from the emerging discipline of Disability Studies and elsewhere, can not be bound to, further debilitated by, and endlessly forced to return again and again to this question of deficiency. No longer reiterating this question of deficiency, of lack, instead the challenge to the prosthetic body becomes one of modifications to the production of re-design.

Such is the need to be attuned to how

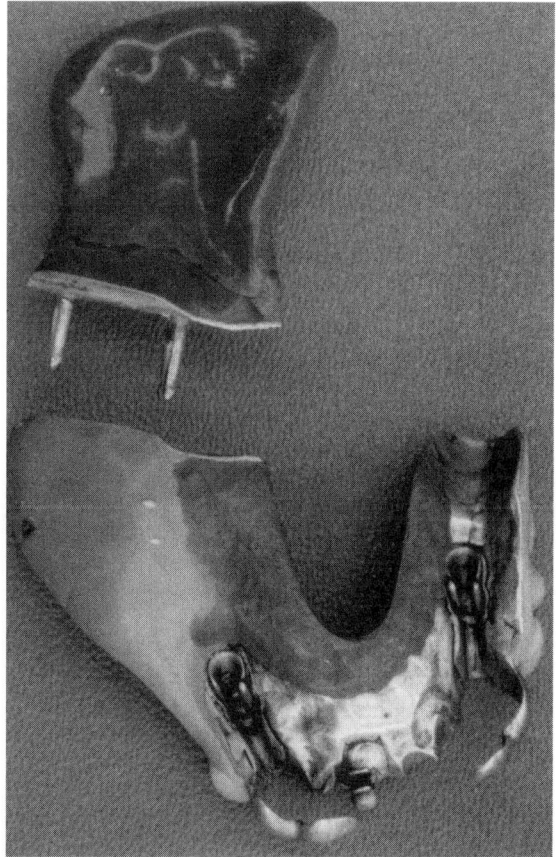

something is worn, inhabited, dwelt in, how it is in place, and how it can find itself out of place. As we have seen, this is certainly the case whether we are addressing the interior contours of Freud's oral cavity, the exterior armature and appendage of Gillinghams of Chard's prostheses and their missing bodies, or the interaction between the body of the spectator and Quinn's sculptural form. Having said this, it is no longer simply only a case of being sympathetic to the sensation of things being either in place or out of place. Rather, it is this, and it is also a need to be sensitive to the experience of things, bodies for example, coming into contact with one another, how different surfaces, some familiar, others unfamiliar, some both familiar and unfamiliar at one and the same time, touch one another. Sometimes things are bolted onto one another, other times one responds to the slightest hint of a caress. Such contact is founded upon intense pressure or an unmistakable ghosting. Either way, what matters is the attention one pays to the points of contact between things, between the human and the machinic for example, and how these points of contact indicate, demarcate, and circumvent our sense of the shifting extremities between and within things. This is not then just a matter of things being either in place or out of place. For things do not stay in place, nor do they remain out of place. Rather, they take place. As contested events, things take place, and the uncertainty of their placing is at the heart of their unhomely dwelling. Taking place drives the possibility of animation, the rhythms of thinking, the intensity of practice. It offers the prospect of being capable of 'independent activity in addition'.

It obstructs it too.[37]

For making it possible to secure images for this article, gratitude is extended to Susan McCormack (GIVE & TAKE), Tim Boon and Craig Brierly (The Science Museum, London), and Michael Molnar, (The Freud Museum, London). Thanks to Scott McCracken for his careful editing and as always to Joanne Morra for her sharp mind and keen eye.

37. This article was completed before the events of Tuesday 11 September and their aftermath.

Puppets and Prosthesis

Aura Satz

A frantic figure moves on stage, syncopating between the regularity of gesture and the moments at which gesture breaks free. The *rhythm of this body confesses another rhythm*, collapses out of itself, moving as though it didn't 'belong within itself'. A limb suddenly dies, and the disparity becomes transparent, all I can see is the asymmetry of the dancer's body, its un-oneness. It is as though the body has broken in two, and one part lives on whilst the other succumbs to being dragged, thrown, limp and lifeless. This is not about the surrogate limb that offers to empower whilst threatening to contagion the whole body and replace it. Nor is it simply a tale of mastery and slavery, although subjection and control are central facets, particularly in terms of choreography. It is a more subtle narrative, one that touches upon the strange rhythm that a body can take on when it is simultaneously a step ahead and a step behind of itself, both dictating and dictated, a body that is carried and carrying, within and without, at once phantom and wholly present. In this body the de-animation of the *tableau-vivant* takes place only partially, in segmented limbs which are then re-animated, brought back to life whilst retaining something of their previous inertia.

An almost breathless memory of a child bouncing up and down on the piece of inanimate wood, the peg-leg that is his father's prosthetic limb:

> ... this 'I' that speaks henceforth out of the caesura of a broken rhythm, punctuating the citation whereby a father fends off his ghosts of pain, thrown into a space above him, the waiting space where I share the anticipation of an unwelcome spasm, it is I who floats in the air inches or miles above him, a rudimentary orbital contraption flying high over a father who could no longer ever jump free of himself and of his mechanical attachment but who wants me to come down with all the certainty of a dependable surrogate, the sensation landing where and when he knows how to prepare for it ... [1]

The bouncing-knee game marks a rhythm of separation and unity, of rising and falling, of breaks and continuity. In this memory it serves to amplify a connection of both belonging and autonomy between father and son, a son who is both light enough to bounce and old enough to fall, eventually. For now he floats above in a kind of weightless suspension, awaiting the spasm that will jerk him down, off the knee. He floats, the force pulling him upwards being - for an instant - greater than the one that pulls him downwards. I am touched as in this moment it suddenly becomes apparent

1. David Wills, *Prosthesis*, California, Stanford University Press, 1995, p6. I refer to the sections of Wills' book which touch more directly on the autobiographical, which he skilfully intersperses with the more 'theoretical' sections on prosthesis as essential to language, in relation to cyborg literature, Derrida, etc.

that the son is parallel to the prosthesis, as though it were his reflection, painfully occupying a similar space, similar height and perhaps inverse weight. The child hovers above, the symmetrical mirror image of the father's anchor to gravity.

The unpredictability expected of a surrogate limb is reversed, it is the child who is undependable, having too much will of his own, too much autonomy, therefore not responding to the predictability of weight, of inert matter. The leg is still at the mercy of sudden convulsions of pain and impulses of nerves, but nonetheless anticipatable. The spasm grieves the loss of the leg, the nerves animated as if by some external force, external that was once internal. The passivity, the limplimbedness that the real leg would have had it not been amputated, and the prosthetic leg does have in replacing the lost leg, become reliably dependable: it falls and despite the infinite variations of the fall it always falls consistently, there is something mathematical about it. The father bounces it just as much as he bounces his son, and yet the one is more attached to him than the other, it has an axis of belonging that is more geometrical. The leg falls with a limited number of articulations and less variables in its movements. In contrast, the body of the son is almost too much of a body, too complex in its articulation and weight-distribution, too autonomous and self-standing. The child is not a crutch to lean on but a 'rudimentary orbital contraption', defying gravity thanks to the gravity-bound piece of leg.

In a multiplicity of languages, David Wills describes his guilt and compassion, his phantom pain for his father's phantom limb. The father's movement animates the leg whilst evidencing its lifelessness; his footfalls fall as he limps between carrying it and letting it go. In the more literal moments of release, of in between-ness, the child would often hold the leg (when the father went for a swim, for example), observe it, watch over it, lie in its place at night (for he is about the same length), make silent pacts with it, regard it with a respect that almost implies it is alive. So long as it is 'on' the father, it is more animate than inanimate. But even when detached it has a secret life of its own, 'It begins at night standing in a corner of the bedroom, holding taut one trouser leg and letting the other fall, while he sleeps, dreaming who knows what dreams of walking straight ...'[2] The leg remains in its function of verticality, of support and uprightness, it never sleeps, for it is constantly asleep, inert matter that it is. The leg leans, paused between animation and de-animation. Even propped up against the wall, immobile, it limps, conveying the possibility of walking, letting the other trouser leg fall. Suspended in a vigilant uselessness, the leg now has a phantom body, sleeping in bed. Still, the 'stand-in' stands, which is the basic function of a leg.

In another place and time, in another text, a different tale of fatherhood and son-hood and a piece of wood. Consider the legs of the puppet

2. Ibid., p29.

Pinocchio, equally stumbling between the rhythms of being wood and becoming real.

At the very beginning of the famous story, written between 1881-3, the piece of wood, the future Pinocchio, shows up at the workshop of the Carpenter Master Cherry, who gleefully announces 'I think I'll use it to make a table-leg'.[3] He is about to strike the wood when a little voice cries out for mercy. Already the wood refuses to be a 'leg' or supportive crutch of any kind, as his later adventures will reveal. In comes Geppetto, asking for a piece of wood with which to make himself 'a fine wooden puppet ... who can dance, and fence, and make daredevil leaps'.[4] Hyper-mobility will undoubtedly characterise this lively puppet. Master Cherry is delighted to rid himself of the piece of wood that gave him such a frightful scare, but just as he was handing it over 'the piece of wood gave a strong jolt and, bolting suddenly out of his hands, banged against the thin and shrivelled shins of poor Geppetto ... "You've almost crippled me", cries Geppetto'.[5] The precariousness of the poverty-stricken father's ability to stand runs throughout the story (Geppetto then 'hobbles' home), as does Pinocchio's scurrying and his unsupportive, wounding woodenness. Once at home, Geppetto sets out to sculpt this surrogate son. Gradual insolence animates the puppet at the carving of each feature: the eyes stare unashamedly, the nose grows unstoppably, the mouth laughs, the tongue pokes out, the hands snatch his wig, and, as soon as Geppetto finishes limbering the legs and feet, the puppet dashes out and runs away clattering his wooden feet against the pavement. Several times during Pinocchio's adventures we hear the rattling sound of his wooden body scampering about or dangling in the air. It is Pinocchio's incapacity to stay still that gets him into trouble time and time again, as though a return to the silence of the 'pedestal' were the ultimate threat. His father jailed overnight and hunger caving in, he runs around looking for food, until finally, worn out, he returns home and falls asleep with his legs on top of a brazier full of burning embers. His wooden feet catch fire and turn to ashes, but the inanimate wooden puppet continues in a state of slumber and inanimatedness, 'snoring as though his feet belonged to someone else',[6] inert matter that he is. Hearing his father knocking at the door, he jumps down from the stool 'but after two or three lurches all at once he fell flat on the floor ... "I can't stand up, believe me. Oh poor me, poor me. I'll have to walk on my knees all my life"'.[7] The puppet pleas with Geppetto to make him new feet, prostheses, promising that in turn he will be 'the comfort and staff of your old age': *about to remain a cripple, he promises to become a crutch.* After a series of adventures all threatening to still him - including being hung from a tree, getting his feet caught in a snare, being chained by a heavy dog collar, getting his foot stuck in a door - finally he is rejoined with his father Geppetto and becomes his crutch: 'Just lean on my arm, dear Father, and let's go on'.[8]

In comparison, Wills relates of his desire to be carried, not carrying: 'My only regret here is possibly his greatest, the fact that he cannot carry

3. Carlo Collodi, *The Adventures of Pinocchio: The Complete Text in a Bilingual Edition with the Original Illustrations*, Nicolas. J. Perella (trans), Berkeley and Los Angeles, University of California Press, [1881-3] 1986, p83.

4. Ibid., p89.

5. Ibid, p93.

6. Ibid., p121.

7. Ibid., p123.

8. Ibid., p443.

me when he is relying on his crutch, and so as we retrace steps holding hands across the house I am in a sense carrying him, walking for him, translating his failure to walk right, standing in for the leg he lacks, he robbed of his strength and I of my weakness. Once I am in bed I make a pact with the leg in the corner - if it will let me sleep as I am letting it sleep, I shall agree to return to it the function I have usurped, and neither of us will say a thing when he emerges from his room dressed the next morning in his suit ... '[9] The crutch and the son alternate, rather than become one another.

9. Wills, *Prosthesis*, op. cit., p29.

As he is on the road to becoming good, in other words, real, Pinocchio even makes his father a wheelchair out of wicker. Mobility and immobility are the alternating themes around which this family drama articulates itself. Pinocchio thus becomes real when he is most supportive, most crutch-like, enabling his father to walk or wheel. Only from his wood-like solidity and support, his vertical angular leg-likeness, only from this can he soften to become a true boy of supple flesh.

> 'And the old Pinocchio of wood, where could he have gone to hide?'
> 'There he is over there' answered Geppetto; and he pointed to a large puppet propped against a chair, its head turned to one side, its arms dangling, and its legs crossed and folded in the middle so that it was a wonder that it stood up at all.[10]

10. Collodi, *The Adventure of Pinocchio*, op. cit., p461.

The strings are cut, and the useless piece of wood, as Pinocchio is often referred throughout the story, turns back to limplimbed puppet. He should be sprawled out on the floor, with nothing to hold him upright now, but somehow, almost miraculously, he stands, though transparently revealing his non-resistance to gravity. Like the prosthetic leg of the father, the piece of wood rests propped up against something else, standing whilst falling, limping though stationary, communicating both uprightness and horizontal yearning, lying on the threshold of being 'real' and being 'of wood', inhabiting this dilated pause between animation and de-animation. Pinocchio the wooden puppet, his body now a pile of limbs, becomes the phantom body of Pinocchio the real boy.

Without delving into the psychological aspect, the father/son relationship in these two discussions of puppets and prosthesis is undoubtedly due to the implied notions of making, begetting, belonging, and ownership. It is easy to see how the strings between puppet and puppeteer become the umbilical cords through which the latter gives life to the former. Likewise, the prosthesis participates in aliveness inasmuch as it is connected to the living body, and mobilised into functioning in place of the absent limb. Autonomy does not yet seem to be an aspiration, or a necessity. Both belong to the figure that animates them, both are visibly engrafted onto the living body, both are projections, protrusions, surrogates, *hanging from the body like an object that has not yet freed itself from its maker*.

11. Heinrich von Kleist, 'The Puppet Theatre', in *Selected Writings*, David Constantine (ed and trans), London, J.M. Dent, [1810] 1997, pp411-16. There's a vast amount of critical essays attempting to resolve the riddle of this text. To name just a few of the most interesting and useful in this context: Helene Cixous, 'Grace and Innocence: Heinrich von Kleist', in *Readings: The Poetics of Blanchot, Joyce, Kafka, Kleist, Lispector, and Tsvetayeva*, V.A. Conley (trans), Minneapolis, University of Minnesota Press, 1991, pp28-73; 'Les Marionettes: Lecture de Kleist, Le dernier

Taken a step further, the father/son relation stretches to the diametric opposition between the God and the Puppet, between infinite consciousness or the body which has none. This is the enigmatic conclusion of Heinrich von Kleist in his short essay from 1810, 'The Puppet Theatre',[11] which reflects on the superiority of the inanimate puppet over the live dancer. A text as slippery as it is rich, it can be read at a very basic level as a wonderfully articulate description of the patterns of weight-shifting and the dance aesthetics that emerge from the agitating of an inanimate object.

Until now we have focused on the mirroring of the puppet/prosthesis with a real counterpart, the intersections or exchanges between them, the instant of crutch-like stability that the leaning-on enables towards locomotion. In Kleist's essay a different perspective unravels through the description of the reverberation of movement through the inanimate. The dialogue between dancer and narrator serves as the frame for the discussion on the mechanics of control and lack of it. How does the puppeteer translate movement to his puppet? How is it 'possible to govern [the puppet's] separate limbs and particular points'?[12] How can a minimal gesture dilate into a myriad of movements, an animate hand contract lightly to produce a shuddering expansion? If the limbs simply respond to gravity, does the puppeteer not require any choreographic knowledge in order to produce dance? The answer according to Kleist is a combination of straight lines, curves, ellipses. The minor twitches of the hand trickle down and the puppet is torn to movement in the conflict between vertical pull and push, the relation of the fingers to the puppet being 'rather like that of numbers to their logarithms or the asymptotes to the hyperbola'. Some form of freedom, of autonomy, could eventually be attained, 'the last remnant of intelligence ... taken out of the marionettes', although in truth this would simply mean that the strings be replaced by the mechanical gesture of 'turning a handle'.[13] Until that mindless eventuality, movement takes place through the projection of the operator into his marionette, who must dance (not 'wholly without feeling') through the object, though hovering over it quite motionless in observation.

> Each movement, he said, has a centre of gravity; it sufficed if this, inside the figure, were controlled; the limbs, which were nothing but pendula, followed without further interference, mechanically, of their own accord. He added that this movement was a very simple one; that whenever the centre of gravity was moved *in a straight line*, the limbs described a *curve*; and that often, if shaken by accident, the whole thing was brought into a kind of rhythmical activity similar to dancing.[14]

Like some anthropomorphic mobile or kinetic sculpture, a gust of wind or a shake is enough to set the thing in motion. Limbs are pendulums, or rather, the entire object is a series of jointed pendula of which the torso, we imagine, is the heavier centre. Gravity dictates the choreography, which is

chapitre de l'histoire du monde', in *Prénoms de Personne*, Paris, Editions de Seuil, 1974, pp127-52; William Ray, 'Suspended in the Mirror: Language and the Self in Kleist's *Über das Marionettentheater*', *Studies in Romanticism* 18 (1979), 521-46 (contains a useful summary of scholarship previous to 1979). Several scholars have taken up from de Man (cf. note 7) analysing the essay in terms of its form being self-reflective on its content: Brittain Smith, 'Pas de Deux; Doing the Dialogic Dance in Kleist's fictitious Conversation *About the Puppet Theatre*', in K. L. Cope (ed), *Compendious Conversations: The Method of Dialogue in the Early Enlightenment*, Frankfurt am Main, Bern, New York, Paris, Peter Lang, 1992, pp368-381; Jena Osman, 'The Line and the Arc: An Analogical Discussion of Kleist's "On the Marionette Theatre"', in J. Spahr et al (ed), *A Poetics of Criticism*, Buffalo, New York, Leave Books, 1994, pp223-36; Bernard Franco, 'From Popular Genre to Aesthetic Model; The Marionette Theatre according to Kleist', *Études Germaniques*, 54, 3 (1999), 391-413.

12. Kleist, 'The Puppet Theatre', op. cit., p411.

13. Ibid., p412.

14. Ibid., p411-12.

at once mathematically predictable and subject to chance. But the essence of puppets is a precise tension between the 'force lifting them into the air' and the anchor of weight 'attaching them to the earth'.[15] The upwards tug must be the stronger (contrary to the grounding of the prosthesis), but ultimately it is the delicate balance between the two forces that lies at the foundations of the puppet's existence and gives it its charm. The pull from above that enables it to sway to and fro is also what can give it the dead and inert appearance of a lynched corpse or, if let go, of a limp fallen figure at the bottom of a staircase. The limbs of the marionette are, according to the dancer, 'what they should be: dead, mere pendula, and simply obey the law of gravity'.[16] This suspension is what positions the puppet at a fascinating conjunction between stillness and mobility.

15. Ibid., p414.

16. Ibid., p413.

The novelty of Kleist's reading of the marionette figure is in his shift away from the traditional focus on metaphorical mastery and slavery, to the ways in which control and lack of it are physically embodied, giving the choreography of the jointed puppet an unprecedented conspicuousness. Like the Pinocchio story, which decelerates through the trapping or stilling of the puppet on the run, Kleist's essay follows a curious pattern of acceleration and fossilisation, concentrating for the most part on the lower half of the body and its connection to the floor. The movement that he so eloquently describes is often on the verge of quietening itself, and at times it is precisely this economy of stillness that aligns itself with a marked instance of grace, or non-grace. In the short anecdotes that follow throughout the dialogue, each reaches a punctuation mark, a moment of immobility centred on an impetus or an off-balance. Thus, in the first encounter between the dancer and the narrator, the former asks the latter if he hadn't found 'the dance movement of the puppet (particularly the smaller ones) very graceful ... A group of four peasants dancing the rondo in quick time couldn't have been painted more delicately by Teniers'.[17] The playful diminutive status of the puppet is emphasised in relation to its human original, as, being lighter, they are less subject to gravity and to all appearances swifter in their movements. Nonetheless, their firefly velocity introduces the first stilling, as the quickness of their miniature movements is flattened, captured into a painting by Teniers. The grace of the peasant's delicate flitting and darting is expressed through a comparison with the static image.

17. Ibid., p411.

This momentary fixity takes a small step, looks back, and becomes imprisonment. Indeed, in the same breath as the comparison between dancers and marionettes, the dancer describes a choreography of Daphne and Apollo, a narrative of metamorphosis, her fleeing away only to become rooted and soil-bound. 'Pursued by Apollo, she turns to look at him: her soul is somewhere at the bottom of her spine, she bends as if she would snap, like a naiade a la Bernini'.[18] Passion, not gravity, is the dictating force here. In his pursuit, he draws her to him, pulling the reigns of an invisible string tied as it were to her back. Her soul is displaced, disharmonious with the centre of gravity, and her turning becomes a grotesque twist which

18. Ibid., p413.

hardens her body rather than continuing the movement, stiffened to look as though she were on the verge of snapping. She is turned into a Bernini-esque sculpture, but here the sculptural parallel evokes an instant of non-grace, of becoming inert matter that, instead of swaying, might crack.

The marionette never fossilises completely, as it uses the ground only to glance it, 'like elves, the momentary halt lends the limbs a new impetus'.[19] The pause, always looming, is fleeting, a mere brushing. The heavy weight of inert matter that human dancers experience lasts longer than that of the marionette, becoming instead a moment of rest and recovery from the 'exertion' of movement. So much so that it is on the oncoming of a stillness which Kleist calls non-dance. Leaning is here not a propelling force into motion, but a threat of immobilisation, an incorporation into the pedestal.

The next anecdote, this time offered by the narrator, relates the loss of grace of a youth. The narrator is with him at the baths when the youth catches a glimpse of his reflection in the mirror whilst drying a leg, and is reminded of the classical statue of the *Dornauszieher*, the Spinario or thorn-puller, who removes the painful spine that would otherwise force him to limp. Again, this is an impulse of movement towards instability, for the youth stands precariously on one leg. And again, the flash of grace is caught through the resemblance with a static image recently seen in Paris, 'The cast of the statue is well-known; most German collections have it'.[20] The youth comments on his discovery, but the narrator denies it, though he too had noticed it at the same instant. The youth is incapable of reproducing the pose, of being yet another cast of the proliferated sculpture. Gradually, his repeated attempts make him lose his poise, and paralysis sets in: 'An invisible and incomprehensible power seemed to settle like an iron net over the free play of his manners'.[21] His fleeting likeness to a statue representing not a pedestal-bound stance but a moment of quasi one-leggedness, recalls the mid-air steps of the Teniers dancers or of Daphne's attempted escape. Ensnared in a web of self-consciousness, his attractions 'slip' away from him, as though each pulsating movement has led inevitably to his winding down, a coagulation that ends in solidification.

The last story describes a fencing match between the dancer and a tamed bear. The dancer wins a match with a young student, who in turn dares him to fight with the bear his father had been rearing in a shed. The bear's fighting posture was 'reared up on his hind legs, and leaning back against a post to which he was fastened, his right paw lifted in readiness and his eye fixing mine'.[22] The quadruped animal is taught to stand like a biped, a classic lesson of domestication to which even Pinocchio was subject during his incarnation as a donkey. It implies using the body against its natural distribution of balance, lifting two feet of four, as opposed to one of two. The bear barely moves, parrying the dancer's accelerated thrusts and feints with an economy of movements that border on stillness: 'The bear did not move'.[23] Like the puppet, he remains anchored to his post, as though this were the pivot that secures his uprightness, without which he would collapse

19. Ibid., p414.

20. Ibid., p415.

21. Ibid., p415.

22. Ibid., p415.

23. Ibid., p416.

back into the four-footed animal kingdom.

A tense intersection of both immobility and contained dynamic of motion emerge from these stories of standing on one leg (or hind legs). After all, legs are the stipulation for verticality and locomotion. It as though with the one leg the swaying of the pendulum were to stop and hang still, ready for the next propulsion. The prosthetic leg of the father, awaiting the next walking spree, propped against the wall, fallen yet standing, is a perfect embodiment of this split sense of movement. The puppet, the prosthesis, and the manoeuvring body itself, oscillate between hardened erectness and collapsed pliability.

The figure of the puppet itself hangs suspended between these two states of precipitation and retention. It falls while it stands, this is its basic condition. Perhaps Kleist's fascination with the figure of the marionette stems from the very fact that whilst the figure asserts itself as limplimbed inert dead matter, subject to the heavy laws of gravity, it creates an effect of resurrection, of animation, of life. Kleist was deeply moved by this vital image of rising amidst the fall, indeed whilst falling. In a letter dated 16 November 1800, he wrote to his fiancée describing a powerful caving in of two walls, collapsing at precisely the same time and thus forming an arch: 'Why, I asked myself, does this arch not collapse, since after all it has *no support*? It remains standing, I answered, *because all the stones tend to collapse at the same time* - from this thought I derived an indescribably heartening consolation, which stayed by me right up to the decisive moment: I too would not collapse, even if all my support were removed!'[24] This image of architectural, almost choreographic cohesion gave him undescribable consolation in a moment of existential crisis, and the two-way movement of falling/standing runs throughout his entire oeuvre.[25] True standing seems to occur only in those fleeting moments when a posture takes shape amidst the chaos of falling.

In these accounts of one-leggedness, Kleist's almost shameful introduction of the theme of cripples and prosthesis seems inevitable. Paul de Man brings up the recurring theme of violence throughout the essay, a procession of mutilated bodies, to which he then adds 'one should avoid the pathos of an imagery of bodily mutilation and not forget that we are dealing with textual models, not with the historical and political systems that are their correlate'.[26] On the contrary, like Stefani Engelstein, I think that the emphasis is Kleist's own.[27] The speakers lower their gaze as earlier on the dancer asks the narrator if he has heard of the mechanical limbs craftsmen make for those unfortunates who lose their limbs. Not having heard of them, the dancer answers:

'A pity ... for if I tell you that those poor people can dance with them I am almost afraid you will not believe me. - Dance? What am I saying? The range of movements is limited, I grant you; but those they are capable of they execute with an ease, grace and poise that every thinking person must be astonished by'.

24. Kleist, *An Abyss Deep Enough: Letters of Heinrich von Kleist with a Selection of Essays and Anecdotes*, P.B Miller (ed and trans), New York, Dutton, 1982, p76.

25. A useful, if generic, survey of this imagery in the rest of his works can be found in Helmut J. Schneider, 'Standing and Falling in Heinrich von Kleist', *MLN*, 115, 3 (2000), 502-18.

26. Paul de Man, 'Aesthetic Formalization: Kleist's *Über das Marionettentheater*', *The Rhetoric of Romanticism*, New York, University of Colombia Press, 1984, p289.

27. Stefani Engelstein, 'Out on a Limb: Military Medicine, Heinrich von Kleist, and the disarticulated body', *German Studies Review*, 23, 2 (2000), 225-44.

I remarked, in jest, that there he had found the man he was looking for. For a craftsman capable of making such a remarkable leg would no doubt be able to construct him a whole marionette to his requirements.[28]

28. Kleist, 'The Puppet Theatre', op. cit., p413.

The step from prosthesis to marionette is a small one, a simple dilatation of the limb into the body. Throughout the dialogue a series of reversals of mimesis are suggested, from the attempt of the viewer to replicate the cast of the Spinario, for example, to the puppet, the delightful miniature of its operator. The object's imitation of life changes direction, and it is now life that attempts to imitate the object seeming to yearn for the advantages of the inanimate. However, this aspiration is virtually unreachable, as demonstrated by the failure of the youth. Indeed, elsewhere the dancer asserts that it would be almost impossible for a human body to even equal the marionette. The prosthetic limb is introduced almost as some kind of compromise yielding to the human body's incapacity, a concession that relies precisely on incapacity, on the body's lack as a starting point. Prostheses in Kleist are merely visible signs of the hidden fractures inherent to the human body and human understanding. (See Marquard Smith, this volume for the same conclusion. The body is always already 'apart, a part, an arrangement of parts'.) This maimed body is the possible human equivalent of the marionette, where puppet-ness has already developed in a limb, and might gradually advance into the rest of the body, replaced bit by bit by the same craftsman who made the first limb. The one-leggedness of all the figures populating the dialogue tend towards this mimesis in the direction of object-hood, an imbalance quavering between motion and stillness, one foot mid-air, the other fossilised into the pedestal of gravity.

Why this preference of the marionette over the living dancer, we ask together with the narrator, almost taken aback by the audacity of such a statement by a dancer seemingly expressing a death wish of his art, of his body. The advantage is, in the first place, 'a negative one ... that it would be incapable of *affectation*'.[29] The inanimate body, simplified in its movements, responding only to the vertical axis of up and downward pulls, would not be subject to sideways longings, would not express magnetism, attraction, affinity towards another object of desire. The prosthetic limb cannot reach out, implies Kleist pitilessly. It cannot suffer from the adornment of affectation (for the German term 'Ziererai' evokes 'Zier', ornament). The prosthesis is not an ornament, it is a replacement that responds to the needs of the kinetic body (or the aesthetic one, aspiring to visible wholeness), not to the emotional or conscious one, that freezes in yearning, falling outside itself in falling for the other. The gestures of the puppet, like those of the prosthetic limb, are absorbed in mechanics, not longing. The acting of desire expressed by inner tension in the magnetism between Daphne and Apollo (or Paris and Venus) is eviscerated in the relation of the puppet and the puppeteer. 'The arm and hand do not reach over to the role and the partner in a gesture of seductive representation, but they are reduced to their operating function', writes Schneider.[30] The 'soul (*vis motrix*)' is not displaced

29. Ibid., p413.

30. Helmut J. Schneider, 'Deconstruction of the Hermeneutical Body: Kleist and the Discourse of Classical Aesthetics', in V. Kelly and D. von Mücke (eds), *Body and Text in the Eighteenth Century*, California, Stanford University Press, 1994, p219.

into the back or elbow as with humans; in the puppet it remains centred, subject to gravity. Nor can such displacement take place with the prosthetic limb.

A cripple dance? 'What am I saying?' The cruelty of the dancer's unsaying clarifies that, all the same, the human equivalent is in Kleist's view a failed one. These are but small tasters of dance, of puppetry, object manipulation, interspersed with moments of non-dance, of rest, of weight-shifting. This is a 'balancing act performed by the body, a shift or transfer between the body and its exteriority'.[31] If the puppet is a duplicate projection, relatively autonomous from the body of the puppeteer, the prosthesis is a smaller projection, a replacement stemming from the desire for wholeness and ease of movement. It is in a sense less exterior than the puppet, more incarnated in the flesh. Kleist's main emphasis is on the upwardly pull from above, rendered visible in the way in which the feet merely glance the ground. It is only here that he hints at the downwardly stabilising socket as a secondary option. Although the prosthesis hangs down from the body, the pendular movement works not from above but from below.

When the children whisper at bed-time, they hear the rhythm of the father's angry 'prosthetic gallop' coming towards their room:

> they listen to the amplifying iambic beat as he advances with his remarkable sprint, the wooden leg serving as a pivot while the other does all the energetic work, he propels himself rather than runs, always veering slightly off centre then correcting just in time, dealing with the sideways as well as the forward momentum, the instinctive compensation that flesh makes for the rebound that comes when rigid steel strikes the unyielding ground, it *is that opposition of soft and hard that sets the metre*, except that it does not quite have the regularity of iambic feet, there is a slight syncopation, a pause between the strong and weak beats as the shift occurs from one to the other, such that the shift itself almost has a beat of its own, shifting rhythm slightly towards the epic dactylic mode as he bounds toward the bedroom ... [32]

The leg is a pivot, the step of propulsion, the anchor around which the ground is effectively skimmed. To recall Kleist, 'the momentary halt lends the limbs a new impetus'. The rhythm of this body is one that must be constantly corrected, where the soft flesh goes at one pace and the hard steel at another. Each step rectifies the other, compensates directionality and motion. One movement shudders into the next, reciprocating different tempos, revealing a negotiation between two consistencies, two responses to movement and gravity, two ways of stepping. One hears the split very clearly. Even though visually the prosthesis aims at imperceptible fusion, acoustics render it visible. The alternating sounds of carrying and being carried create a rhythmic tap dance of sorts: the lifting and dropping of the hard matter onto the unyielding drum that is the floor, and the propelling

31. Wills, *Prosthesis*, op. cit., p20.

32. Ibid., p25.

bounce of the live leg. Even when not galloping, when standing almost still, simply swaying slightly, the father 'builds up to a mechanical twitch, whereby the apparent fluidity of movement enacted by the human body is revealed as something more like the jerk of a cog or a piston'.[33] The father experiences joy when cycling, perhaps freed from the sounds of percussion and intervals, translated into the continuous whiz of wheels.

33. Ibid., p22.

The prosthesis' bodily movement is often called mechanical, but it is so in the Kleistian sense, not yet the cyborg one. The leg is not robotic, replacing the tedium of repetitive and strenuous operations. It is more humble, it lives with the body's weariness, sleeps with it (albeit propped against the wall), does not exceed it but accompanies it through movement. Although they are leashed to their owners, *the prosthesis and the puppet are not slaves*. The sounds they make are not the industrial sounds of mechanisation, but rather the sounds of gravity affecting an inanimate object, the clanking of matter one might hear when a puppet is shaken, interspersed with the sound of human footfalls.

Kleist's essay touches upon the mutual interaction of the living body and the inanimate object, a reciprocal yearning come absorption: by nature the puppet, looking upwards to its maker, aspires like Pinocchio to become (or at least appear) real, whilst the live dancer looks down and mourns for a state of puppet-hood. An object is painted, sculpted, made to imitate the live pulsation of flesh; in turn, the body looks back at its image and yearns itself object. Maybe Kleist wanted to rid the human body of its painful sentiency. Perhaps, to follow Elaine Scarry, the prosthetic leg absorbs the pain of the father's body, and likewise the father absorbs something of the immunity of the prosthetic leg.

> Thus, the reversal of inside and outside surfaces ultimately suggests that by transporting the external object world into the sentient interior, that interior gains some small share of blissful immunity of inert inanimate objecthood; and conversely, by transporting pain out onto the external world, that external environment is deprived of its immunity to, unmindfulness of, and indifference toward the problem of sentience… it is part of the work of creating to deprive the external world of the privilege of being inanimate.[34]

34. Elaine Scarry, *The Body in Pain; The Making and Unmaking of the World*, Oxford, Oxford University Press, 1985, p285.

The prosthetic leg implies the violence done to it, it knows of its phantom 'other', hurts with it, for it, protects the memory of it like a hard and unbreakable shell. The same projection might explain the violence inflicted on so many puppet characters, which seem to suffer the violent bashings that only inanimate matter can withstand (think of the cruel bodily punishments of Pinocchio, or the domestic violence implied in Punch and Judy). They too seem to readily absorb the hardships of having 'a body'. Their articulation gives them just enough mobility to disperse the blows without cracking, without breaking as would do the solid statue or the frail human body.

The body that unites with or extends itself through the inanimate object longs for this reciprocation, this exchange of vulnerability and immunity, soft and hard, conscious and unconscious. These reciprocations, not entirely consummated, create the sounds of carrying and being carried, the broken rhythms of the body that is at once host and parasite, thrusting ahead and lingering behind itself.

We have moved through the two-ness of the puppet/puppeteer and the split one-ness of the body with a prosthesis, both professing an estranged rhythm in their reactions to gravity. There are bodies that interiorise both these states without such a visible divide. Barely discernable, still, like the father's prosthetic walk, this state seeps through in rhythm. The effect it produces in the observer can swerve into the territory of either the 'comic' or the 'uncanny', according to Henri Bergson and Ernest Jentsch, both writing around the same early decade of the 1900s.

The youth who lost his grace repeats the ghost of the Spinario pose in desperate over-activity: 'In confusion he raised his foot a third time, a fourth, again and again, a dozen times: in vain'. The narrator finds this failed repetition is 'so comical I could scarcely refrain from laughing at him'. What appears to cause laughter is the ridiculous futility of such replication, the gesture that circulates over and over upon itself, flailing towards a stiffening and winding down, as opposed to some sense of progression. The same can be said of the flustered fencers, first the student, then the dancer, who become enervated in their hyper-kinetic attempt to re-stabilise themselves.

In his essay on 'Laughter' from 1900, Bergson explains this effect as due to a 'lack of elasticity … absentmindedness … a kind of physical obstinacy, *as a result, in fact, of rigidity or of momentum*'.[35] Bergson's notion of laughter articulates itself around a web of tension and elasticity, and laughter is in his view a social correction that aims at softening rigidity, whilst in itself creating a relaxing effect on the laugher. The human body should be in a constant state of 'wideawake adaptability' and 'living pliableness', yet it often slips into a state of absentminded mechanical inelasticity, automatism and involuntary movement. Fundamentally, this unsociability is ridiculed and corrected by laughter, whose humiliation is intended to soften the social body from its distraction and solidification. It is as though in Bergson the body is constantly on the verge of slipping outside of itself and coagulating, curdling towards a stand-still, losing vital mobility and jointed articulation. Unfortunately for the youth, the narrator's laughter fails to soften his body, as instead a steel net immobilises and rigidifies his body. Indeed, if in Bergson the corrective aims at recuperating consciousness, regaining a forgotten awareness, in Kleist the hypothetical return to grace would involve precisely the opposite: a loss of consciousness, a state of regained innocence and lack of self-awareness.[36] The laughter of the narrator could be said to be directed at the youth's self-consciousness, not his lack of it.

35. Henri Bergson, 'Laughter', in *Comedy*, W. Sypher (intro. and appen.), Baltimore & London, The John Hopkins University Press, [1900] 1980, p66.

36. The famous finale of Kleist's essay reads: 'grace will be most purely present in the human frame that has either no consciousness or an infinite amount of it, which is to say either in a marionette or in a god … we have to eat again of the Tree of Knowledge to fall back into the state of innocence' (p416).

Regardless of this difference, Bergson's theory of laughter is also a useful measure of the body that splits within itself, that confesses another rhythm. Puppetry inevitably comes up, as it is par excellence a body that is stiff despite its mobility. Anything that makes one view the living body as a marionette creates a laughable impression. When we see man as a 'jointed puppet' we try and rid him of his stiffness; educate him, as the adventures of Pinocchio illustrate at length, into a state of pliable realness. This stiffness must expose itself whilst remaining dormant.

> The suggestion must be a clear one, for inside the person we must distinctly perceive, as through a glass, a set-up mechanism. But the suggestion must also be a subtle one, for the general appearance of the person, whose every limb has been made as rigid as a machine, must continue to give us the impression of a living being. The more exact these two images, that of a person and that of a machine, fit into each other, the more striking is the comic effect ... [37]

37. Bergson, 'Laughter', op. cit., p80.

The body must be at once transparent and opaque, still alive yet on the brink of object-hood. The perception of strings or springs working behind/within the figure conveys a twofold movement quality, negotiating simultaneously autonomy and lack of agency. The seemingly strings-free person seems to be controlled by something subtly external to it, laced with invisible threads that enable some other force and rhythm to overtake it, thus revealing both the downward pull of inert matter and the upward tug of the operator. Movement becomes somewhat automatic, predictable, lifeless, though still moving and to all appearances alive - the inanimate establishes itself in life and imitates it. It is as though parts of the body have been numbed, have fallen asleep and no longer express the pulsation of animation. If only we were always attentive, wide-awake, body alert, 'nothing within us would ever appear as due to the workings of strings or springs. The comic is that side of a person which reveals his likeness to a thing'.[38] It would appear as though the comic is this slipping into inanimatedness.

38. Ibid., p117.

Yet it is not so much the stilling of the entire body as much as the hardening of the articulations, the obtrusive jointed-ness of the body. Rather than motionless inertia setting in, the asperity of the body reveals itself precisely through movement and through breakages in the flows of mobility. The limbs might be rigid but they remain pliable. Again, it is a question of rhythm. For 'gestures can only be imitated in their mechanical uniformity, and therefore in what is alien to our living personality'.[39] With the exception of stillness, humans can only imitate the inanimate through gestures that communicate a beat estranged from their own pulsations. Rhythm is what conveys this split body: the interspersion (or even dissimulation) of an erratic, irregular, impulsive pattern, with the reliable, regular, and uniform correction of a piece of wood. Where we perceive something mechanical encrusted onto the living, we perceive a limp.

39. Ibid., p81.

The comical is produced by the human body that leans towards object-hood and mechanisation. It steps out of synch with the ebb and flow of the social body, and starts to lack resilience. Its movement becomes more regular, broken, full of paced intervals. When an arrhythmia slips through, it appears to limp. The same body confesses a different pace, a second body, coinciding with the first one, fitting in with it as perfectly as possible, so that the parallel vision of the puppet and the puppeteer juxtapose into one single image, and the prosthesis and the body are seemingly one. The implied automatism is not of the mechanical machine kind, but a combination of involuntary movements dictated by the sheer force of weight and gravity. This is Kleist's definition of the mechanical: not functional, perfunctory, preset, robotic, but choreographic, responding to the laws of gravity. Bergson too seems here to refer to the mechanical as something that is still in the realm of aesthetics, of shapes, sequences and rhythms. In both authors, the descriptions serve as potential guidelines for actors, dancers, comedians. Thus, the difference between the marionette and the automaton becomes not so much human agency but human rhythm. In the marionette the choreography of the human body is echoed, it runs through the strings like blood through a vein, albeit translated into a different configuration. In the automaton it is more discontinuous, it hitches, awaiting the next cranking. As Cixous points out in her writing on Kleist, the automaton is distinct from the puppet in its rhythm: in the former 'a coarse interruption of movement pervades. But with the marionette, motion is continuous'.[40] The comical effect theorised by Bergson is not limited to one or the other. It is more simply a discernment of inelasticity, the tight fit of a second body encrusting itself onto the first one, which causes laughter.

40. Cixous, 'Grace and Innocence', op. cit., p34.

Not so in the writings of Jentsch on the *Unheimlich*. Jentsch was the first to tackle the aesthetic implications of the Uncanny, and Freud is greatly indebted to him in his seminal essay on the subject written a decade later.[41] Indeed, Freud starts by following Jentsch's idea that the uncanny appears in the confusion between animate and inanimate, such as waxwork figures, automata, dismembered limbs, but eventually he discards this idea to oscillate instead between the familiar and the unfamiliar (or rather the resurfacing of repressed beliefs). Jentsch, on the other hands, views the uncanny as a 'lack of orientation', an uncertainty and doubt as to whether an apparently living being is inanimate, and conversely, whether a lifeless object may not in fact be animate. Unfortunately, the success of Freud's essay has lead to a great deal of misinterpretation and misuse of the term, most of which is more akin to Jentsch's uncanny than to Freud's (that is to say, the confusion between animate/inanimate, rather than familiar/unfamiliar). In the first instance, Jentsch seems to imply that an internal physical uncertainty leads to the perception of uncertainty in the outside world. The effect of the uncanny is therefore greater in those of a nervous disposition, experiencing 'deadening of all kinds', such as 'light sleep ... forms of depression and after-effects of terrible experiences, fears ... severe cases of exhaustion or

41. Sigmund Freud, 'The Uncanny', in *The Standard Edition of the Complete Psychological Works of Sigmund Freud*, Vol. 17, J. Strachey (ed and trans), London, Hogarth Press, [1919] 1955, pp219-52.

general illness'.[42] It as though the perceiving body itself partakes in the effect it observes in or projects onto the outside world. The body that doubts as to the animate or inanimate character of something external to it, is itself experiencing this hazy numbness and indistinction.

Though using a similar set of juxtaposed elements to those employed by Bergson, here doubt rules in the relation of the inanimate to the animate. If in the 'Laughter' essay the suggestion must be at once 'clear' and 'subtle', here, so long as doubt remains, the effect lingers. When knowledge dissipates doubt, Jentsch's uncanny evaporates into clarity and intellectual mastery. But what instigates this doubt, what is the actual visual experience? Again, it would appear to be through the rhythm of movement that the animate exposes itself as inanimate, and vice versa. In his example of a tree that suddenly moves, showing itself to be a giant snake, he writes that the mass that at first seemed lifeless suddenly reveals 'an inherent energy because of its movement', which might eventually show its origin to be an organic body through 'its methodical quality' and thus dispel doubt.[43] Likewise, a person experiencing the view of a locomotion or steamboat for the first time will find 'the enigmatic autonomous movement and the regular noises of the machine' similar to the sounds of 'human breath'.[44] In these illustrations the objects appear to come alive in their kinetic rhythms, recalling the throbs of living flesh. The sounds are 'methodical' and 'regular', simulating life, though not quite. Jentsch's most intriguing example refers to the human body that shakes and quavers like a machine. Lay people, he writes, are generally affected by the sight of the articulations of mental and nervous illness, which disrupts the relative physical harmony that tends to characterise normal bodies. When this disruption occurs,

> and if the situation does not seem trivial or *comic*, the consequence of an unimportant incident, or if it is not quite familiar (like alcoholic intoxication, for example), then the dark knowledge dawns on the unschooled observer that *mechanical* processes are taking place ... the epileptic attack of spasms reveals the human body to the viewer - the body that under normal conditions is so meaningful, expedient, and unitary, functioning according to the directions of his consciousness - *as an immensely complicated and delicate mechanism.*[45]

Jentsch distinguishes this from the effect created by the sight of hysterical people, as in those cases consciousness still remains visible. For the expert such a view will not appear uncanny for he is familiar with such sights and therefore does not experience uncertainty and doubt. Freud too briefly refers to the uncanny effect of epilepsy and madness as implying 'the working of forces hitherto unsuspected'.[46] Jentsch recognises in line with Bergson that such an effect can easily cause laughter, not unease, the body can however slip into an area of uncertainty whereby it appears to be manipulated by a source external to and greater than itself. This epileptic movement recalls

42. Ernst Jentsch, 'On the Psychology of The Uncanny', *Angelaki*, 2, 1 (1995), pp7-16, p10. The essay was first published as 'Zur Psychologie des Unheimlich' in *Psychiatrisch-Neurologische Wochenschrift*, 8.22-23 (1906), pp195-98, 203-05. This is the first and only (way overdue) English translation, which nonetheless has been taken for granted as obsolete and redundant in relation to the Freud essay.

43. Ibid., p11.

44. Ibid.

45. Ibid., p14. My italics.

46. Freud, 'The Uncanny', op. cit., p243.

the puppet Kleist describes as 'shaken in a purely haphazard way', falling 'into a kind of rhythmic movement which resembles dance'. Strings seem to dominate its movements, and the body is no longer 'unitary' but split into two bodies, the one absorbed by the other, acting against and despite the 'directions of his consciousness'. It is perhaps an overstatement to say that this unconscious dancer complies with Kleist's ideal choreography, but it is nonetheless an interesting comparison. The body tenses, hardens into spasms and is rearranged according to a different set of movements, of rhythms. Although the epileptic body is apparently one, it confesses some other presence inhabiting it, manoeuvring it, as the long-established accusation of possession impeaches. The affinity of the movements of an epileptic and those of a puppet can be traced back to the etymology of the ancient Greek term for marionette, *neurospasma*, meaning violent and involuntary nerve contraction or convulsion.[47] The strings are envisioned as the raw externalisation of nerves trifled with by some greater force. Indeed, close observation will reveal that the marionette is brisk and precise in resisting weight upwards, yet any movement downwards cannot exceed the speed of the pull of gravity. One might say that descent conforms to the rhythm of collapse, whereas ascent to that of contraction. And as the marionette is a figure in which the pull upwards must be to some degree more forceful that the pull downwards, it is in fact first and foremost a creature of contractions, which are then followed by collapses. In the human body these two-way dynamics seem to tear it in two, fracture it into a pattern of more than one being. The word 'convulsion' comes from *con-vellere*, to tear apart, to pull in all directions, yet the prefix 'con' works to add the sense of pulling together. Convulsion is a 'held-together-coming-apart'.[48] It is a movement quality that emphasises the sinewed jointed-ness of an articulated body, which is perhaps why in his text on the marionette Kleist alternates the term with that of *Gliedermann*, jointed-man.

Moving away from the split convulsive body, back to the stage. Edward Gordon Craig (inspired by Kleist) wanted a prosthetic body, a symbol of man, a puppet, more than a puppet. In 'The Actor and the Über-marionette' (1908) he writes: 'The actor must go, and in his place comes the inanimate figure'.[49] Reversing Pinocchio back into inanimate matter, Craig's ideal actor would be both the sculptor and the sculpture, having total mastery over his malleable material. If only the actor could make his body into an obedient 'machine, or into a dead piece of material such as clay', who could perform without affected variation, mathematically.[50] Craig yearned for a unitary body in which there was no translation from animate to inanimate, a body that could *die and manipulate its own corpse*, interiorising the rhythm of the puppet whilst ridding itself of the confessional pulse of man.

47. Maurizio Bettini, *Il Ritratto dell'Amante*, Torino, Einaudi, 1992, p249.

48. Steven Connor, 'The Shakes: Conditions of Tremor', paper given at the Roehampton Institute Department of Drama, 30 March 2000, <http://www.bbk.ac.uk/eh/eng/skc/shakes/>

49. Edward Gordon Craig, 'The Actor and the Über-marionette', in *On the Art of Theatre*, London, The Seven Arts Book Club, [1908] 1958, pp54-94, p70

50. Ibid., p70.

A Phantom Limb: Feeling the gap between invisibility and touch in recent British art

Andrew Patrizio

By way of introduction, it is worth recounting how this essay began its life. It was first sketched out as a proposal for a contemporary art exhibition. The proposal drew serious interest from an internationally recognised venue. The Exhibition Gallery's Director and Board agreed to my suggestion that, to fit the theme, the gallery would include *no* objects at all, while, at the same time, the exhibition should be as carefully curated and promoted as any other show. The phantom-as-bodily-catastrophe would be converted into the spatial trauma of an empty gallery. The expression of that idea has still 'not to happen'.

A number of international artists have explicitly used versions of the phantom limb phenomenon in their work, but they differ widely in intention and it was never my purpose to bring such objects together in an exhibition. As a medical enigma the phenomenon presents intriguing problems in the areas of neurology, psychology and physiology, and as such it had become something far more suggestive. Through the phantom limb phenomenon we can identify a kind of fault-line in the models we have built between self and the world: or what we might term between coherent and incoherent self knowledge (each of which is a kind of error in how we conceive and construct the world). We might recall American sculptor Carl Andre's seductive observation that, 'a thing is a hole in a thing it is not'.[1] Phantom limbs blur our distinctions between what is internal and what is external, and between the spaces that an object does and does not inhabit. They warn us against defining too firmly 'the thing' and 'the thing it is not'.

As it is often the job of artists to tease out cultural fault-lines maybe it is natural or understandable that a number of quite unrelated artists have created works which can be positioned in relation to the phantom limb as both idea and reality. I concentrate here on three British artists - Alexa Wright, Caroline Rye, and Douglas Gordon. But the sheer complexity and controversy surrounding the subject in medical and psychological circles forms part of my attraction to it and this also merits detailed explication. Bringing the phenomenon out from its containment within medical circles produces, or allows for the possibility of producing, another kind of cultural meaning, which the basic phenomenon itself does not have. The key elements - trauma and pain, memory (including body memory), the presence/absence axis - have been regular concepts appearing in recent art, although not specifically through the phantom limb phenomenon. The juxtaposition of two distinct types of discussion - a 'factual' history of the phantom limb

1. Lucy Lippard, *Six Years: the dematerialisation of the art object from 1966-1972*, London, Studio Vista, 1973, p40.

phenomenon and a critique of three artists' works - stages the possibility of translation between medical enigma and artistic representation, with only a speculative awareness of how others may make sense of such an approach. It is worth restating that this project started life as an exhibition idea: that is, a corporeal event, rather than a textual thesis that would make itself available only to weightless theoretical speculation.

It is a commonplace that visual art has become less political or, more accurately, less concerned with overtly political and programmatic ideologies. That is not to say artists working in the areas under discussion here do not inform the body politic, at least in the broadest way. In this context, and with increasing regularity over the twentieth century, we can find examples of artistic practice that have been explicitly attracted by subjects that are enigmatic, curious and resistant to explanation. Those imprecise, doubtful and undecidable parts of the world are often a focus for visual art, not least as a positive alternative to textual and verbal explanation as the prime means of explaining and translating the world. As the Enlightenment paradigm represented by 'hard science' subjects broke apart long ago, visual artists have been energetically prising open the gaps further. Art embodies another kind of knowledge and often attends the birth of new paradigmatic shifts. When ostensibly hard subjects like medicine and neurology attempt to deal with 'soft' phenomena such as phantom limbs, a kind of epistemological vibration can be felt in the struggle, a movement which is picked up by artists and others outside of the specialist domain.

So the physical rather than the social body has increasingly been the site of embodied ideas in art. As we will see, all these artists stage or make reference to a complex physical interaction of some kind, in which deep memory in particular is an evident presence. Alexa Wright's work centres on collaboration between amputees and herself as photographic artist. Caroline Rye undertakes an extended and near private performance that has only ghostly evidence. Douglas Gordon presents us with a three-way textual confrontation between a victim, experimenter and ourselves. Put more simply we see towards the end of this discussion three bodies in relation to the phantom limb phenomenon: the disabled, the gendered and the criminal.

DOLOR MEMBRI AMPUTATI
THE PAIN THAT REMAINS ...

A phantom limb is among the most bizarre conditions that hover between the medical and the psychological. When a limb is lost, through accident or amputation, patients at some time experience the sensations of an invisible limb. Around sixty per cent of patients get phantom limb sensations or pain in the months following amputation, and after two years at least five to ten per cent continue to feel sensations or pain.

Various myths, fables and anecdotes illustrating what we would now recognise as the phantom limb phenomenon were observed in antiquity and throughout the Middle Ages. This is most thoroughly presented in Price and Twombly's *The Phantom Limb Phenomenon: A Medical, Folkloric, and Historical Study*.[2] The authors' interest was in publishing early texts - whose content was invariably coloured by belief systems that valued superstition, dreams and miracles - where missing limbs were fantastically reinstated on the body. The sources they drew together, from Old Norse, German, Italian, Catalan, Middle and Early Modern English, are too wide-spread and simultaneous to suggest one root fable from which the phenomenon springs. They identified six basic legends, the earliest of which, 'The German's Hand', was first committed to paper by the Saxon chronicler and Benedictine monk Widukint in 941 AD. Widukint writes: 'A certain man's left hand, which had been amputated by an iron instrument [sword], was restored to him after almost an / entire year as he slept; and he was marked, as a sign [proof] of the miracle, with a bloody line at the place of the joining'.[3] Only one of their basic legends post-dates the first true medical, rather than superstitious, reference to the phantom limb phenomenon, and that was by the French surgeon Ambrose Paré, writing a treatise on gunshot wounds in 1551. Paré wrote: 'Verily it is a thing wondrous strange and prodigious, which will scarce be credited, unless by such as have seen with their eyes and heard with their ears, the patients who have, many months after the cutting away of the leg, complain that they yet felt great pain of that leg so cut off'.[4]

The occurrence of a phantom limb almost always follows some kind of trauma - sometimes violent (an accident which removes a limb directly) or a more measured disaster (such as amputation following a serious infection or wound). The American neurologist Silas Weir Mitchell first wrote up the subject in 1866 during the Civil War, when many case studies were available. He focused on one individual, George Dedlow, who had lost all four limbs and it was Mitchell who coined the now-familiar term 'phantom limb' shortly after in 1871. As Hillel Schwartz has noted, Mitchell marks the beginning of the modern manifestation of phantom limbs: 'amputations ... could henceforth never be considered perfectly clean cuts. Willy-nilly, the body extended its lines of force towards the lost extremities ... In addition to the tender youth of many of the recent amputees, the cultural image of the phantom limb undergirded, 1 suspect, the revival of interest in machining prosthetics that accommodated a wider variety and greater fluidity of movement'.[5] The phantom thus is a virtual prototype, sketching out the ambition of the modern prosthetic.

Since Mitchell, the literature on the phantom limb phenomenon has grown considerably, but has not provided any great enlightenment. Phantom limbs manifest themselves as mundane and reassuring (in that they help maintain some kind of coherent body-image) or else deliriously disturbing (a pathological affliction which itself requires medical attention). Forms and feelings of considerable variety spring from the area of the missing limb: tingling or shooting pains; feelings of hot and cold; phantoms foreshortened,

2. Douglas B Price and Neil J Twombly, *The Phantom Limb Phenomenon: A Medical, Folkloric, and Historical Study. Texts and Translations of 10th to 20th Century Accounts of the Miraculous Restoration of Lost Body Parts*, Washington DC, Georgetown University Press, 1978.

3. Ibid., pp1-2.

4. *La maniere de traicter les playes faictes tât par hacquebutes, que par fleches ...*, Paris, Par la refue Iean de Brie, 1551.

5. Hillel Schwartz, 'Torque: The New Kinaesthetic of the Twentieth Century', in J. Crary and S. Kwinter (eds), *Incorporations: Zone #6*, New York, Zone, 1992, p102.

telescoped or rigid. The most common locations for phantoms are the arms and legs, but there are also recorded sensations by those who have lost a nose, genitalia (both male and female), breasts and even an appendix. It is largely true, as neurologists Siegfried and Zimmerman found, that the greater sensitivity of the body part, the more forcefully the phantom is felt: 'The phantom ... appears to consist predominantly of those parts which have the most extensive representation in the thalamus and in the cerebral cortex'.[6]

Even more bizarre strains of this phenomenon can occur - people born with only a stump can suffer from phantom limb pain after *injuring* their stump. They begin to suffer from a limb they never had. Walking in water can produce a feeling of wetness against the phantom leg. Touching the face of an amputee can stimulate parallel sensations in the area of the lost limb - this phenomenon has been described by the best known populariser of the phantom limb phenomenon, neurologist V.S. Ramachandran.[7] Amputees can experience a twinge in their phantom hand that 'holds' an object when that object is pulled away. Phantoms can merge and fuse with part of a prosthetic limb. Seeing a mirror image of a lost arm can reduce the pain; and, most extraordinary, using virtual reality simulations some phantom limbs have been successfully 'amputated'. After undergoing a digital removal of the phantom limb, amputees report the loss their phantom sensations.

Oliver Sacks devotes an entire book *A Leg to Stand On* (1984) and a chapter in *The Man Who Mistook his Wife for a Hat* (1985) to phantom limbs. Sacks himself has suffered from a version of the phenomenon, not through actual loss of a limb, but through a walking accident which resulted in a dislocated knee-joint and the complete rupture of his quadriceps tendon. He writes: 'I was now an amputee ... for the leg, objectively, externally, was still there; it had disappeared subjectively, internally. I was therefore, so to speak, an "internal" amputee ... I had lost the inner image, or representation, of the leg ... Part of the "inner photograph" of me was missing'.[8] His personal experience of phantom limb sensation was also unusually dynamic, almost filmic:

> I was infinitely unsteady, and had to gaze down. There and then I perceived the source of the commotion. The source was my leg - or, rather, that thing, that featureless cylinder of chalk which served as my leg - that chalky-white abstraction of a leg. Now the cylinder was a thousand feet long, now a matter of two millimetres; now it was fat, now it was thin; now it was tilted this way, now tilted that. It was constantly changing in size and shape, in position and angle, the changes occurring four or five times a second. The extent of transformation and change was immense - there could be a thousandfold switch between successive 'frames'.[9]

Sacks' book is a masterpiece of biographical self-diagnosis and discovery.

6. J. Siegfried and M. Zimmerman (eds), *Phantom and Stump Pain*, Berlin / Heidelberg, Springer-Verlag, 1981, pv.

7. See V.S. Ramachandran and Sandra Blakeslee, *Phantoms in the Brain: Human Nature and the Architecture of the Mind*, London, Fourth Estate, 1998, pp28-30.

8. Oliver Sacks, *A Leg to Stand On*, London, Picador, 1991 (1984), p50.

9. Ibid., pp104-5.

His detailed self-exploration illustrates an important point - that phantom limbs are hallucinations of the body. But not just anyone's body: only one's own. The sufferer is the sole repository of evidence as, of course, no signs of the phantom are visible and available to anyone else. Medicine uses the term 'subjective sensation' for phantom limbs, and all theories of the sensation arise *from case studies* and *first hand description*, that is, they could not and cannot be discussed as *a priori* theories about the world. Phantom limbs therefore exist in a space outside theory, or at least do not arise *from* theory. Practice infiltrates theory, whilst theory likewise infiltrates practice in an appropriately ghostly and indeterminate way.

Around the large anecdotal clinical history indicated here has arisen a complex neurological debate which itself has involved very many different and competing branches of medicine. There are currently no less than sixty-eight methods of treatment proposed across the literature and whole areas of pain management and drug use have been developed around the condition. The disputes over these well-documented experiences revolve around fundamental issues of identity, memory, sensation and pain. Do our sensory perceptions exist in a relatively federalised way, close to the part of the body in which they reside, or do they exist in the somatosensory cortex, in the neuromatrix, in our brain or spinal cord alone? This is still very much a live issue in medical circles, though V.S. Ramachandran, working at the Center for Brain and Cognition in San Diego, has been among the first to experiment incisively in this area to produce new thinking. Whilst some experimenters have seen the peripheral nervous system and the spinal cord as important, over the last twenty years neurologists have favoured the idea of pain existing in deep cerebral structures; pain that has imprinted itself on the brain so it continues for months or years after.

Over the last two centuries, the medical profession has suggested four broad areas within which possible answers may lay, in increasing likelihood:

a) The so-called, hard-wire explanation that we genetically inherit a biological map that plots exactly where our body parts should be. The nerves send out information roughly mapping onto this map regardless of the physical reality, with impulses indicating the body is intact.

b) Neurons in the spinal chord continue to send information to the brain, although they are receiving no signals from the peripheral nervous system.

c) Remaining nerves in the stump grow into nodules, or neuromas, at the end of the stump and continue to fire signals to the brain - the memory of the hand exists in the wrist.

d) Signals in the somatosensory circuits of the brain change when the limb is lost; the brain compensates for the loss by creating a phantom of its own. Ramachandran proposes specific ways the brain maps changes, each indicating a remarkable plasticity of the neuro-matrix: 'new, highly precise and functionally effective pathways can emerge in the adult brain as early as four weeks after injury'.[10]

10. Ramachandran and Blakeslee, *Phantoms in the Brain*, op. cit, p31.

There are even more poetic, part medical, part psychological proposals; one for instance is that endorphins are released into the victims bloodstream at a time of trauma that serve to tranquillise the effect of trauma. Over time people become addicted to their endorphins and the memories which triggered the release of the chemicals. Cycles occur which repeat and re-expose bodily memory from the past to the present. Pain, in this model, is internally re-experienced rather than cognitively recalled. The pain that often accompanies phantoms is a very distinct strain. It occurs not as a warning of potential or increasing injury, which is the standard function of bodily pain, but as an example, if you like, of pure pain in that no 'ulterior motives' or prophylactic mechanisms operate.

Whilst now largely discredited, some surgeons have doubted the authenticity of phantom limbs completely. They suspect a psychological basis and therefore do not discuss it with future amputees. Pöllmann found fourteen out of 6,600 young men experienced a phantom following removal of a tooth, and that all fourteen registered as 'introvert' in the Eysenck Personality Inventory test. Phantom limbs have been found to be more prevalent in 'sensitive, intelligent and neurotic individuals' and less prevalent in people who are deemed less bright and more emotionally balanced.[11] Some sources have said that phantom limbs have never been documented in children under four, yet one authority, Ronald Melzack, states that: 'A substantial number of children who are born without a limb feel a phantom of the missing part, suggesting that the neural network, or "neuromatrix", that subserves body sensation has a genetically determined substrate that is modified by sensory experience'.[12]

Despite the controversies amongst specialists, it is clear that the body after the trauma of losing a part of itself is undergoing remarkable post-injury re-organisational changes - cortical remapping - in order to adapt to a new relationship with the outside world. The means to reduce amputee suffering will be found, no doubt, within the domains of neurology and psychology. For someone outside the field, it is enough to marvel at the mystery and create phantasmal propositions about the world. One such field might be the interconnections between time and body memory. The body and the brain it contains develop over years to establish the neurological foundations of the self. We undergo a process of learning to fit our own bodies, and so develop deep memory and instinctual awareness of its behaviour in relation to our brain functions and the immediate outside world. An accident that results in the loss of a limb disrupts, very quickly and severely, this long-established neural architecture. Identity proves itself to be a profoundly unstable concept. The particularities of our body form a deep matrix of habits based on our self-image, muscle patterns and sensations stimulated by the external world around us. When this is disrupted forever - as in the case of amputation - our relationship with the world needs to be established afresh. And establishing new co-ordinates that determine our relationship

11. L. Pöllmann, 'Phantom Tooth Phenomenon: Painless and Painful Sensations', in Siegfried and Zimmerman (eds), *Phantom and Stump Pain*, op. cit., p77.

12. Ronald Melzack, 'Phantom Limbs and the Concept of a Neuromatrix', *TINS*, 13/3 (1990), 88.

with the world can be proposed as one of the higher functions of cultural practice, including art.

SPEAKING THE PHANTOM INTO THE WORLD
ALEXA WRIGHT

Alexa Wright, unlike many artists one might discuss here, has actually produced a body of work specifically on the phantom limb phenomenon. In 1997 the Wellcome Trust commissioned a collaborative project between Wright, a neurologist and a neuro-psychologist. The project investigated amputees' real experiences by attempting to visualise the presence of phantom limbs using digital photography. Wright wanted to represent the subjective experience of people with conditions which alter the perception or manifestation of the self. She was especially interested in the morphological gap that exists between a person's sentient perception of their own body and that same body as seen by others. Her series of twenty-four c-type prints was called *After Image* and focused on eight individuals. One of these, identified as 'GN' (Fig. 1), and an amputee for over 30 years, has experienced a gradual telescoping in and reducing of his arm. If he is not wearing his prosthesis he experiences a thumb on his stump. This patient's phantom thumb also moves down to the end of his hand when he wears his false arm. One might characterise this as a caustic counterpart to the Pinocchio fable, where the act of lying produced telescoping outward. For Wright contraction and telescoping is demonstrably a consequence of telling the truth.

Fig 1: After Image: GN2, *digitally manipulated c-type print,* © *Alexa Wright*

It would seem to me that Wright's work represents an innovative extension of the established tradition of medical illustration, particularly the genre where maladies and deformities are depicted in order to make pathology visible. There are numerous examples of pathological illustrations which reveal how the body should *not* look (Fig. 2). In terms of visibility, a woodcut from 1562-3 by an artist referred to as Monogrammist RS illustrates the point (Fig. 3). This type of work is termed a 'flap anatomy': a mechanical trope, where by lifting the hinged piece of paper representing the stomach surface one is able to see into the otherwise invisible stomach interior. Interestingly, lifting the flap enacts an accidental decapitation - amputation of

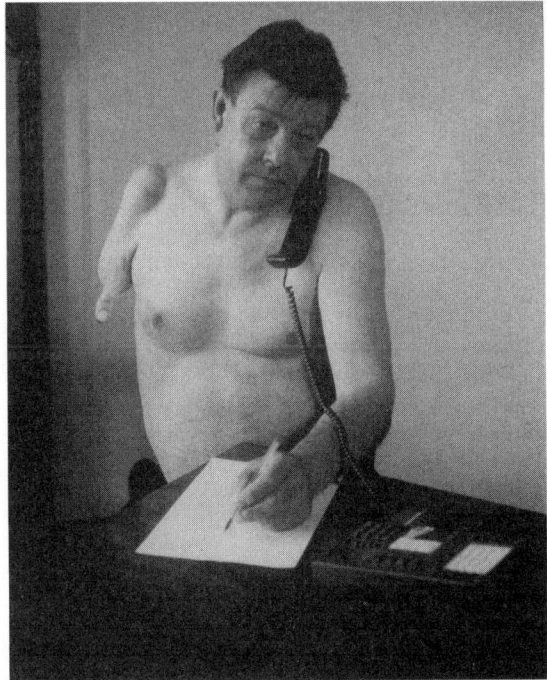

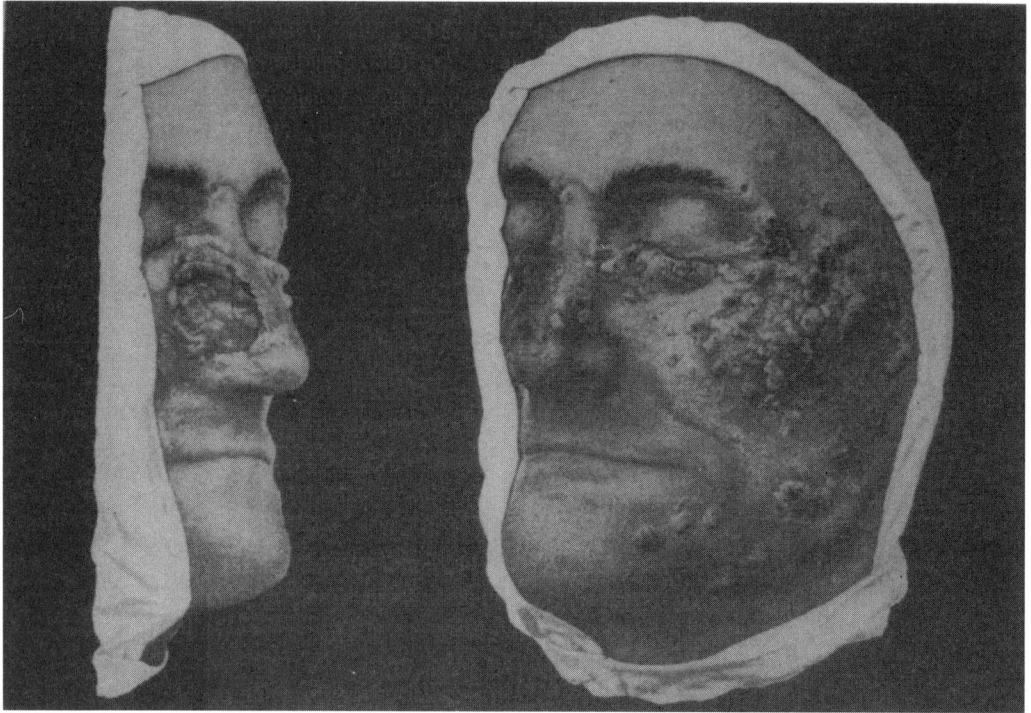

Fig 2: Colour photo-lithograph of wax model, from John Pringle's Pictorial Atlas of the Skin Diseases, *London 1897*

the head is something to which I will return. Wright is extending a tradition of medical illustration, by way of digital photography, into virtual and psychological territory. The internal projections of individuals can be summoned into convincing visibility through digitally manipulated imagery.

Yet digitally manipulated photographic imagery is convincing enough to be not only shocking and absurd - and to this extent worthy of Surrealism - but also, conversely, very real. The realism is important as it offers a source of empowerment to Wright's subjects - not always an intention of artistic practice, even within the genre of portraiture. She explicitly sought to raise awareness of the amplified feelings of difference experienced by disabled people. Wright and her medical collaborators worked largely at the service of the sufferers, by making their very real (though entirely subjective) sensation as visibly clear to us as it is neurologically clear to them. Wright's photographs create a territory, by way of art, in which those with impairments can share their distressing subjective selves with a public. As Wright comments: 'The new challenge of representation in virtual reality seems to be that of representing the self to itself ... Investigation of [the] experience of a split between the physical and visual boundaries of the self provides a point at which medical and virtual bodies may begin to intersect'.[13]

Wright is among a number of artists in Britain and elsewhere who have tried to find ways of exploring the relationships between the physical self, the external world, and the interior, non-material self. Wright's work sustains multiple readings, one of which explores human limbs as marking obvious

13. Alexa Wright, 'Partial Bodies: re-establishing boundaries, medical and virtual', in Cutting Edge The Women's Research Group (ed), *Desire by Design: Body Territories and New Technologies*, London, I.B. Tauris, 1998.

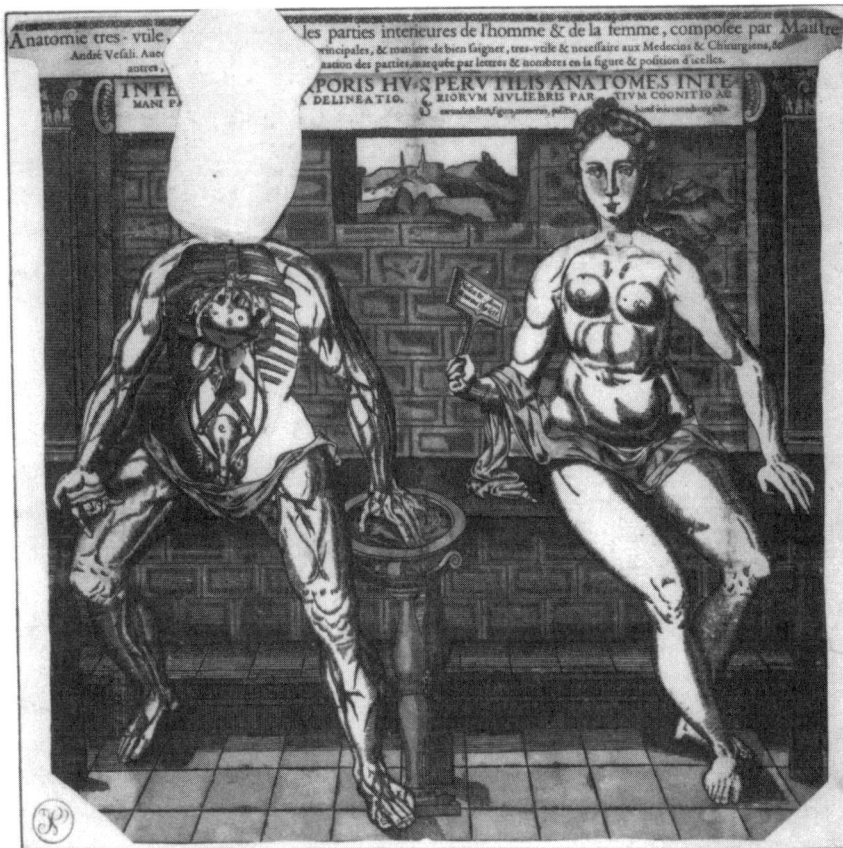

Fig 3: Monogrammist RS, untitled woodcut, 1562-3

Fig 4: After Image: RD1, *1997, digitally manipulated c-type print,* © Alexa Wright

and important territorial limits of the body. The un-injured limb, of course, operates as a tool: a physical extension to enable working within the world. Viewed in this light, loss of limbs means both a removal of tool attributes as well as an erasure of territory. In some of her series, Wright has explored the co-existence of the phantom with the prosthetic device (Fig. 4). This introduces a complex yet suggestive double image of the insubstantial body and the non-human prosthetic device as tool. Although Wright's work does not directly address the issue, developments in organ transplantation, and genetic intervention and commercialisation are blurring the parameters of selfhood to such an extent that traditional prosthetic devices seem, by comparison, to hark back to the dark ages; although that would have to be the subject of another essay.

THE PHANTOM IN THE MACHINE
CAROLINE RYE

Fig 5: from The Turin Machine, *1996, © Caroline Rye*

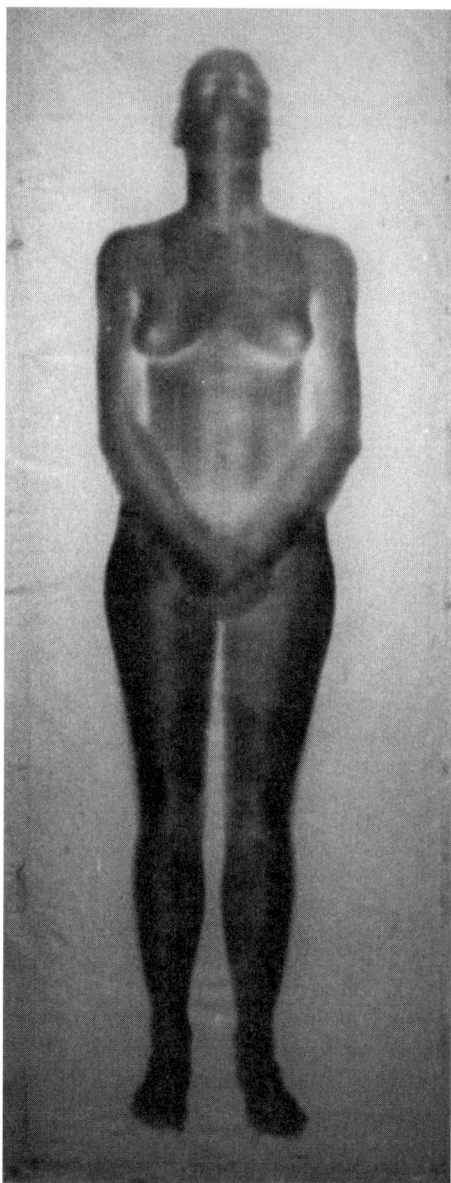

One of the most powerful creations by a British artist of any generation made over the last ten years is Caroline Rye's *The Turin Machine* (1996). Positioned precisely between performance and photography, the piece is difficult to describe to anyone who has not seen it. The work is a room-sized pinhole camera, built in three distinct sections. One part is big enough for the artist, who stands in it, unclothed, under a bright light. The second chamber is dark, but light from the first chamber travels through a pinhole and is caught on a large screen where it forms a faint image. The third chamber is no bigger than a photo-booth and members of the public may enter, one at a time, to look through an aperture at the screen. It is difficult to see anything at first and it takes several minutes for the inverted image of the artist to achieve a ghostly visibility. After a six-hour performance, the screen, which has already been primed with photo-emulsion, is developed. It looks like a photographic negative, and is displayed on the gallery wall (Figs. 5 & 6). This is very much a residue. The magical event is the one that slowly but surely etches the pinhole image of the artist on your eye in such a way as to defeat photographic reproduction.

The chosen title for the work evokes a clear connection with the shroud at Turin, with its complex mesh of meanings, around authenticity, iconism, mystical magic and technical possibility. The idea that Rye has invented a machine to produce semi-industrial versions of the iconic body is one of the more immediate concepts put out by the work and its title. But at least two further readings of this work are possible. One is suggested by the artist herself, quoting Kaja Silverman's *The Threshold of the Visible World*: 'The relation between the camera and the human optical organ might now seem less analogous than prosthetic: the camera promises to make good the deficiencies of the eye and to shore up a distinction which the eye alone cannot sustain - the distinction between vision and spectacle'.[14] The camera might also be read as prosthetic in another, related way: as a device for shoring up human memory and filling its gaps. That is, after

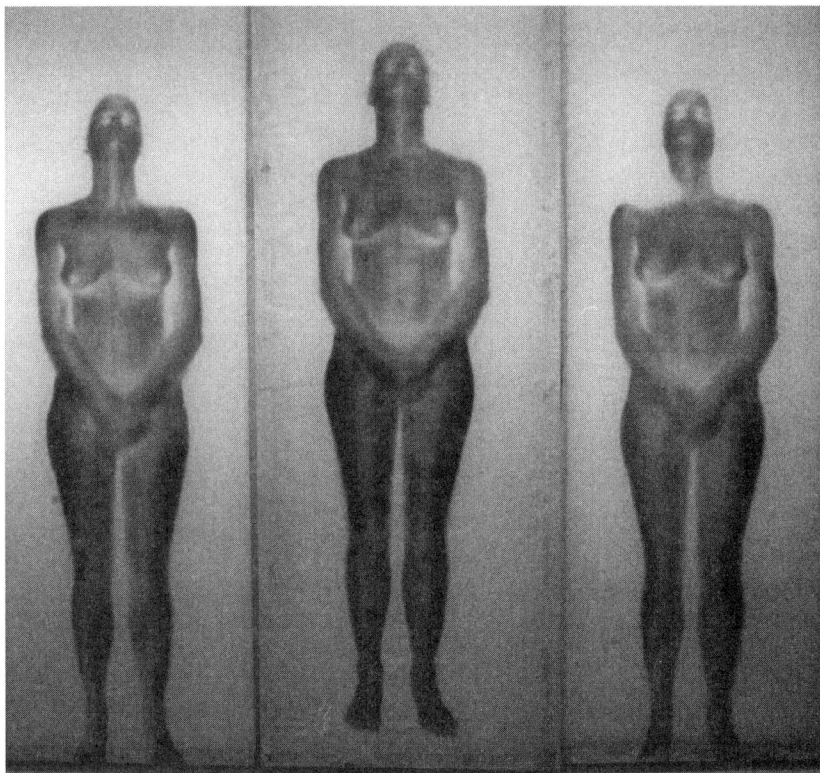

Fig 6: from The Turin Machine, *1996, © Caroline Rye*

all, one of the reasons why the camera, and indeed other lens-based media, have become so ubiquitous in our culture. The six-hour soaking up of light which is itself reflected off a standing, but very slightly moving, body articulates the gap between photography (a static event) and film (a sequential event), but without ever becoming either. The large prints that result are like a sequence of film frames superimposed seamlessly on one another. Rye's *The Turin Machine* is a large yet simple prosthetic, using only the most rudimentary technology; a move which asserts its distance from digital and media art. Her work not only blurs the distinction between live performance and archival record, but also, true to the theme of the phantom limb, produces, under the initial alarm of being trapped in almost total darkness, something fantastical and mysterious - deeply embedded in both vision and memory.

One of the chief issues raised by phantom limbs is the way they problematise the relationship between the perceived subject and its sensation of self. This connects with some of the intentions described by the artist in the following terms: '*The Turin Machine* acknowledges the futility of language to capture the real and in doing so stages the consequences of this failure for the definition of the subject'.[15] The work thus stages an enquiry into what might be termed 'hierarchies of presence' between the body and its image in culture. Her focus is the inability to fix the notion of 'being' and

14. Kaja Silverman, *The Threshold of the Visible World*, New York and London, Routledge, 1996, p130

15. Caroline Rye, unpublished typescript of paper delivered at research seminar, Napier University, Edinburgh, 5 March 1998.

its ostensible subject (whether in textual or visual language) and even though the initial intentions of the artists are various, Rye nevertheless creates a poetic abstraction arising from the phantom limb phenomenon.

THE HALF-MINUTE PHANTOM
DOUGLAS GORDON

The sixteenth-century medical flap anatomy, mentioned above, raised the question of decapitation. We now come to a beheading that explores the limits of selfhood and self-knowledge. Deliberate amputation of the head - as one might pedantically call decapitation - has a distinguished history both in politics and in art, from the French Revolution to its recurrence as a subject in the sculpture of Ian Hamilton Finlay. But there is only one work I know of which suggests that decapitation, despite its deadly impact on the body, produces a phantom experience. The work is *30 seconds text* (1996) by Douglas Gordon. It is usually presented in a small room, which becomes illuminated only at the moment the viewer enters. The viewer has thirty seconds to read a few paragraphs after which the light goes out and the trauma begins. A graphic and troubling event is etched on our mind more graphically because of its removal from the viewer's gaze. The enforced darkness that follows our actual reading of the work re-enacts a decapitation. The absolute line that is drawn between what is considered peripheral - such as an arm and a leg - and what is considered central - such as a head - is made faint, at least for half a minute. The work, which, in a sense, is being performed now through publication - should last precisely 30 seconds; but after reading, another kind of phantom remains - the reader's memory of the work as you have experienced it:

30 seconds text

In 1905 an experiment was performed in France where a doctor tried to communicate with a condemned man's severed head immediately after the guillotine execution.

Immediately after the decapitation, the condemned man's eyelids and lips contracted for 5 or 6 seconds … I waited a few seconds and the contractions ceased, the face relaxed, the eyelids closed half-way over the eyeballs so that only the whites of the eyes were visible, exactly like dying or newly deceased people.

At that moment I shouted 'Languille' in a loud voice, and I saw that his eye opened slowly and without twitching, the movements were distinct and clear, the look was not dull and empty, the eyes which were fully alive were indisputably looking at me. After a few seconds, the eyelids closed again, slowly and steadily.

I addressed him again. Once more, the eyelids were raised slowly, without contractions, and two undoubtedly alive eyes looked at me attentively with an expression even more piercing than the first time. Then the eyes shut once again. I made a third attempt. No reaction. The whole episode lasted between twenty-five and thirty seconds.

… on average, it should take between twenty-five and thirty seconds to read the above text.

Notes on the experiment between Dr Baurieux and the criminal Languille (Montpellier, 1905) taken from the Archives d'Anthropologie Criminelle

Gordon's work is relevant here for a number of reasons. He chooses to put before us, in a very straightforward and lightly mediated way, a description of a scientific experiment where the evidence suggests that consciousness and self-awareness can exist without a body, albeit briefly. Considered in the context of the phantom limb discussion, it becomes unclear whether the head or the body of the victim is the phantom, the part of the body that acts out a life after death. As the head reacts to a name call, then the body from which it has been separated becomes for a moment the 'lost limb', the unnecessary or discarded other. But it is more usual for the smaller proportion of the body - the hand, arm, leg - to be the source of the phantom. The double vision this sets up is consistent with other obsessions in Gordon's work, in particular with the careful juxtaposition of opposites, such as good and evil, dark and light, neurosis and mental health. *30 seconds text* is a little different in that it fingers a brief moment that lies between two opposites - life and death - and suggests there is an identifiable hiatus in between. The gate between the world and the hereafter has a distinct thickness and weight. Finally the staging of the piece, in a room whose light is timed to allow only thirty seconds in which to read the work, sets up an unsettling parallel between the consciousness of Languille the criminal and our own experience. We thereafter have to rely on our own memory of the story, but at least for us that is still possible.

SILENCING THE PHANTOM

If, as Paul Antze and Michael Lembeck observe, 'the past is a treacherous burden, which would crush us if we did not continuously divest ourselves of its weight',[16] then one might say that a phantom limb is a part of the self, poorly or incompletely forgotten; an obliteration not yet registered in the corporeal world. Once the physical form has changed, the memory of a prior self becomes indistinct over time as the body reconciles itself to its new body shape. The body is suspended between a long acquired memory and a newly acquired need to forget. The dysfunctional conversation that the body is having with its absent limb gives rise to fanciful forms, distortions,

16. Paul Antze and Michael Lembeck, *Tense Past: Cultural Essays in Trauma and Memory*, London, Routledge, 1996, pxxix.

enigmatic sensations and eventually, the patient hopes, silence.

The move from incoherence to silence presents us with a fantastically generative metaphor. For Alexa Wright it takes the form of a collaborative opportunity between subject and artist, in which the vision and technical facility offered by art can work with patient accounts of malfunctioning neurological networks. The higher aims are to achieve an embodiment of invisible symptoms by the patients and to explore troublesome ideas around identity for the artist and the viewers. For Rye, the staging of a near invisible performance by herself encased within a simple and enlarged technology is a way of exploring the linkages between perception, memory and time as 'duration' - each being key concepts underpinning the existence of phantom limbs. Gordon's work underlines a problematic issue illustrated by phantom limbs, which is the difficulty of delineating the borders of identity, chiefly through the powerful resistance of human bodies ever to forget themselves, and so remain whole - not to die.

Despite suggestive theories discussed earlier, the lack of a precise medical explanation for phantom limbs allows, as we can see in these three works, a translation to take place into culture, through which cultural practices can in turn be explored. A wider view of knowledge is opened up; one in which problems are embraced not only as enigmas to be solved but as ambiguous signs which help us generate, negotiate and propose new views of the world. Finally, the translation of the phantom into culture becomes also a way of reflecting on artistic practice itself - a practice which is never as simple as being the visual expression of a textually available concept. Phantom limbs are generated out of deep structures that exist within our neurological substrata, and yet they have no utilitarian function. They hurt or at best confuse the sufferer and so can never be as useful as a prosthetic device. (We recall Alexa Wright's fusing of the insubstantial body and the non-human, machined prosthetic tool. The phantom is real, as is the metal device, but both cannot be fused together, except in the unreal space of digital photography or in the mind of the victim.) Art, like the phantom, springs from a deep, sometimes troubled necessity, yet shares with the phantom no (universally agreed) utilitarian function. But whilst phantoms may be useless as prosthetics, they may be said to have some use in giving form to the 'kinaesthetics' of our inner world.

Prosthetic Gestation: Shulamith Firestone and Sexual Difference

Mandy Merck

Sexual difference, according to Jean Baudrillard, disappeared by the 1980s, supplanted by 'a new game of sexual indifference'. The sexual revolution had left behind an agnosticism of identity and desire whose emblematic figure was the transsexual, neither masculine nor feminine and invulnerable to *jouissance*. This avatar of artifice was said to embody the destiny of our mutant species, whose anatomy and imago are endlessly subjected to technological and symbolic augmentation, diffraction, hybridisation: 'to become a prosthesis'.[1] But if the transsexual was the postmodernist's sequel to the symbolic order of sexual difference, poststructuralism conjured a prosthetic emblem of its own, not as Baudrillard had in the name of trans (or post) politics, but in an explicitly political challenge to 'the law ... which installs gender and kinship'.[2] Plastic, transferable, expropriable, the lesbian phallus was wielded by Judith Butler to challenge the heterosexist hegemony of sexual difference itself. Theorised as the logical consequence of the Lacanian scheme it undermines, it was held to displace the masculine signification of the phallus and deprivilege anatomy as the site of power.

Neither Butler nor Baudrillard were being entirely literal. As the former points out, the lesbian phallus (like any other) is a theoretical fiction, if one that derives a good deal of its notoriety from its resemblance to the plastic and transferable strap-ons previously unmentioned in academic discourse. As for Baudrillard, he is writing from his usual standpoint of avowed delirium, declaring the disappearance of art, politics and economics, as well as sexual difference, in terms more hyperbolic than hyperreal. Yet it is difficult to see past these two exponents of the *post-prosthetic* to an earlier, less ironic, age. And perhaps we shouldn't try, since what will we discover there is no less inflected by the ontological conundra with which we now so deftly engage. If anything, the story of Shulamith Firestone can be said to intensify the complexities of reproduction and representation both produced and signified by the prosthesis: reality and artifice, the original and the copy, the subject and her uncanny double. As she warned in *The Dialectic of Sex*, 'No matter how many levels of consciousness one reaches, the problem always goes deeper'.[3] Returning to Firestone's polemic more than thirty years after its original publication, these remarks are an exercise in the deferred revision now familiarly known by the Freudian term *Nachträglichkeit*. Written as science announces the imminence of the cybernetic pregnancy so scandalously predicted by Firestone, they will re-examine her writing and the context of its emergence, as well as the twice-made film portrait of

1. Jean Baudrillard, 'Transpolitics, Transsexuality, Transaesthetics', in William Stearns and William Chaloupka (eds), *Jean Baudrillard: The Disappearance of Art and Politics*, New York, St Martin's, 1992, pp19-20.

2. Judith Butler, 'The Lesbian Phallus and the Morphological Imaginary', *Bodies That Matter*, New York and London, Routledge, 1993, p72.

3. Shulamith Firestone, *The Dialectic of Sex*, New York, Bantam, 1970, p168.

its author which suggests a time, and indeed a sexual order, 'that hasn't necessarily passed'.

The author's note to *The Dialectic of Sex* declares that Shulamith Firestone was born in Canada 'toward the end of World War II' and grew up in the midwestern United States. At the age of twelve, she later recalled, she experienced doubts about the existence of God which made her feel so guilty that she welcomed being sent away to an orthodox Jewish school. Later she attended Washington University in St Louis and the Art Institute of Chicago, majoring in painting and drawing. In her graduation year, 1967, the 22-year-old was chosen as the subject of a half-hour film documentary, one of a series on the 'Now Generation' shot by four male students from Northwestern University. In it she was filmed around Chicago, photographing people in the street, taking in Warhol's *Chelsea Girls* with a woman friend, working part-time in the Post Office. She is also shown enduring a fairly brutal critique of her painting by four male instructors from the Art Institute, who call her canvasses 'dreary', dismiss her attempt to explain why she paints male nudes, accuse her of evading their questions, and finally inform her that she should switch from painting to another medium, possibly film, to better express the only merit they note in her work, her 'feeling for people'. In the filmed interview which comprises much of this portrait, Firestone complains that four years at the Art Institute has made her 'completely inarticulate' and observes that any intellectual or artistic woman is 'going to have problems with men'. She also declares her identification with minority groups and outsiders, and discusses the subordination of the 'Negroes' she works with at the Post Office.

By that summer Firestone was one of the 2000 attending the radical National Convention for a New Politics held in Chicago. There she co-drafted a resolution condemning the media 'for perpetuating the stereotype of women as always in an auxiliary position to men [and as] sex objects', calling for 'the revamping of marriage, divorce, and property laws' and demanding 'complete control by women of their own bodies, the dissemination of birth control information to all women regardless of their age and marital status, and the removal of all prohibitions against abortion'. But when it came time to debate this resolution, the chairman refused to call on its authors, despite protests in the hall. As one witness remembered, the chair 'patted Shulie on the head and said, "Move on little girl; we have more important issues to talk about here than women's liberation"'.[4] In the following week the first Chicago women's group was formed.

To understand the founding politics of Second Wave feminism in the US, it's important to grasp its roots in the Movement, as the loose coalition of anti-Vietnam War, anti-racist, anti-capitalist 'radicals' was described at the time. Several of the original Chicago women's group had also been members of Students for a Democratic Society, where the term 'women's liberation' was first employed to label a conference workshop, and many founding feminists had come from the civil rights movement. The Chicago

4. Alice Echols, *Daring To Be Bad: Radical Feminism in America 1967-1975*, Minneapolis, University of Minnesota Press, p49.

group's first manifesto, advising women to avoid making 'the same mistake the blacks did at first of allowing others (whites in their case, men in ours) to define our issues, methods, goals', was addressed 'To the Women of the Left'.[5] And, although the early American women's movement (1967-69) would divide between those who regarded it as a wing of the struggle against the 'military-industrial complex' and those who increasingly targeted male supremacy (including that on the left), both factions identified with the radical politics of the period.

Indeed, when Firestone moved to New York that autumn and co-founded (with Pam Allen) its first women's liberation group, it was called New York Radical Women. Not until spring 1968 did 'women's liberation' achieve wide currency. And 'feminism' - doubly disadvantaged by its association with the bourgeois reformists of the suffrage movement as well as their paradoxically 'unfeminine' image (which Firestone later parodied as 'George Sand in cigar and bloomers'[6]) - was an even more problematic term for a group of young women as avowedly feminine (and heterosexual) as they were leftwing. It is in this context that 'radical feminism' and Firestone's unique theorisation of this tendency, was to develop - highly conscious of economic and racial inequality, but concerned to oppose those forces which most oppressed women as women.

The evolution of this theory can be traced from the June 1968 publication of New York Radical Women's *Notes from the First Year* ('$.50 to women, $1.00 to men'), which includes an early version of Anne Koedt's 'The Myth of the Vaginal Orgasm' as well as three articles by Firestone. Reporting on the January 1968 women's march on Congress to oppose the Vietnam War, Firestone explains her group's disagreement with the 'traditional female role' adopted by the other marchers: 'They came as wives, mothers and mourners; that is, tearful and passive reactors to the actions of men rather than organizing as women to change that definition of femininity to something other than a synonym for weakness, political impotence, and tears'.[7] And, in a piece reflecting on the history of feminism, she challenges the caricature of the 'granite-faced spinster obsessed with the vote' to argue that the then widespread demeaning of the early women's movement neglects the 'revolutionary potential' of its attempt to organise women workers, oppose slavery and expose 'the white male power structure in all its hypocrisy'. The movement died, she argues, not because it won its objectives with the suffrage, but because it was defeated on the terrain of legal rights, economic equality and sex: 'For though women may strive for a "natural" look, they do indeed strive. Girls today are as concerned about "image" as ever … As for sex itself, I would argue that any changes were as a result of male interests and not female. Any benefits for women were accidental'.[8]

Initially these were the views of a minority, even inside New York Radical Women. But as they gained acceptance in successor groups (New York Radical Feminists and Redstockings, co-founded again by Firestone and others in 1969), Firestone remained stubbornly non-conformist, particularly

5. Ibid.

6. Shulamith Firestone, 'The Women's Rights Movement in the U.S.: A New View', in *Notes from the First Year,* New York Radical Women, June 1968, p2 <http://scriptorium.lib.duke.edu/wlm/notes/>.

7. Firestone, 'The Jeanette Rankin Brigade: Woman Power?', in ibid., p17.

8. Firestone, 'The Women's Rights Movement in the U.S.', op. cit., pp2-7.

9. Ann Snitow,
'Feminism and
Motherhood: An
American Reading',
Feminist Review, 40
(Spring 1992), 37.

10. Alice Echols,
Daring To Be Bad, op.
cit., p112.

in her attitude to maternity. Although early Women's Liberation expressed what her New York feminist contemporary Ann Snitow has called 'a harsh self-questioning about motherhood', in demands that 'women go beyond justifying themselves in terms of their wombs and breasts and housekeeping',[9] there were many mothers and no anti-natalist consensus in its ranks. The report of a conference held in Illinois in 1968 to commemorate the 120th anniversary of the first Women's Rights Convention at Seneca Falls records '"heated reactions" to the suggestion - probably Firestone's - that pregnancy is physically debilitating and inevitably oppressive'.[10] One mother of several children replied to Firestone's description of pregnancy as 'barbaric' with the claim that many women thrived on it. But Firestone was adamant, reportedly arguing that such conferences should not provide childcare but instead require mothers to leave their offspring at home.

Such remarks were consistent with her public stance in the movement, which was as provocative as it was innovative. Although Firestone supported the internal democracy of women's liberation, contrasting it with the failures of other revolutionary movements 'to practice among themselves what they preach', she would later write that its anti-leadership line put its members in the 'peculiar position of having to eradicate, at the same time, not only their submissive natures, but their dominant natures as well, thus burning the candle at both ends'.[11] And although she would stress her opposition to making 'women ... become like men, crippled in the identical way', the masculine identification implicit in her later description of the pre-pubescent girl's 'body ... as limber and functional as her brother's'[12] was evident in her accusation that those feminists who criticised her domineering style were 'trying to castrate me'.[13]

11. Shulamith
Firestone, *The
Dialectic of Sex*, op.
cit., p39.

12. Ibid., p54.

13. Alice Echols,
Daring To Be Bad, op.
cit., p151.

Meanwhile, the rapidly growing movement was increasingly torn between commitments to consciousness-raising and public activism, between small affinity groups and mass participation, between the radicalism of its founders and the mainstreaming impetus of its dissemination. And when theorists like Firestone, Ann Snitow and Ellen Willis gained increasing public prominence, the result was criticism from other feminists for monopolising the creative role. By October 1970, when *The Dialectic of Sex* was published, its frustrated author had left the movement she had helped to found.

Firestone's retirement from public politics is one reason why her polemic is read less today than contemporary works like Greer's *The Female Eunuch* and Millett's *Sexual Politics* (both also published in 1970, a remarkable year which also saw the launch of Eva Figes' *Patriarchal Attitudes*). Another is its status as what Snitow calls a 'demon text' of women's liberation, which she defines as books 'apologized for, endlessly quoted out of context, to prove that the feminism of the early seventies was, in [Betty] Friedan's words of recantation, "strangely blind"'.[14] And while defending *The Dialectic*'s utopian ambitions, Snitow herself apologises both for its abjection of the pregnant body and its 'undertheorized' advocacy of a cybernetic solution to female oppression. Subsequently, my own attempt to assign it for a graduate seminar

14. Ann Snitow,
'Feminism and
Motherhood', op.
cit., p35.

on theories of sexual difference from de Beauvoir to Butler evoked antagonism and bewilderment, eventually leading one former student to request this essay. Perhaps this was because, unlike other works assigned in that seminar, *The Dialectic* takes a very simple position on the question of sexual difference: abolish it. Or perhaps it was because Firestone's polemic, reaching for the anthropological scope of Bachofen and Morgan, the nineteenth century scholars who influenced Engels, never eschews the grand narrative students are now taught to abhor. To take only one example, the 21-page chapter on 'The Dialectic within Cultural History' attempts to supersede C.P. Snow's two cultures and their gendered division of technology and aesthetics in a meta-history complete with charts labelled 'Merging of Art and Reality' and 'Realization of the Conceivable in the Actual'. And that was how *The Dialectic of Sex* was marketed, as 'the missing link between Marx and Freud'. Thirty years after I first read it, in a Bantam mass paperback blurbed 'Chapter 6 Might Change Your Life', it seems absurdly grandiose, deeply contradictory, dubiously dialectical and still urgently relevant to sexual politics.

Subtitled 'The Case for Feminist Revolution', *The Dialectic of Sex* opens with a dedication to Simone de Beauvoir 'who kept her integrity' and a Heraclitean epigraph from Engels concluding 'everything is and is not, for everything is fluid, is constantly changing, constantly coming into being and passing away'. It is my contention that sexual difference remains, for feminism and psychoanalysis, the test of this proposition. Although the problematic itself - anatomical dimorphism? social division? symbolic difference? social construction? performative materialisation? or - in the most recent Lacanian position - sexuation? - has certainly mutated in the past thirty years, it is arguable that the problem has not. And that problem, as articulated in *The Dialectic of Sex*, is that 'genital differences between human beings … matter culturally'.[15] It's worth noting here that Firestone's formulation, 'the sexual distinction', is neither quite the biological reduction so often described, since her concern is how bodies matter culturally, yet nor is it an early anticipation of Butler, who emphasises how culture materialises bodies. What one could say is that, like most ambitious theory of early women's liberation, Firestone's is a highly eclectic formulation, concerned at once with the biological, the social and - if not the psychoanalytic - the psychological. And, as the opening of her book suggests, the main sources for this synthesis are Engels and de Beauvoir.

In common with many of her radical feminist contemporaries and the 'social reproduction' feminists who followed them - indeed like Butler in her recent debate with Nancy Fraser[16] - Firestone seizes on Engels' *The Origin of the Family, Private Property and the State*, and its argument that the first division of labour is that constituted by reproductive differences between the sexes. But critiquing the limits of a purely 'economic diagnosis traced to ownership of the means of production, even of the means of reproduction',[17] Firestone moves on to de Beauvoir's observations on the gendering of the distinction between Same and Other in *The Second Sex*.

15. Shulamith Firestone, *The Dialectic of Sex*, op. cit., p11.

16. Judith Butler, 'Merely Cultural', *New Left Review*, 227 (January/February 1998), 33-44; and Nancy Fraser, 'Heterosexism, Misrecognition and Capitalism: A Reply to Judith Butler', *New Left Review*, 228, (March/April 1998), 140-150.

17. Shulamith Firestone, op. cit., p5.

18. Ibid., p8.

Challenging the Hegelian abstraction of this dualism into *a priori* categories, she argues instead for its origin in procreation. Human biology, according to Firestone, is responsible for an 'inherently unequal power distribution'[18] between the sexes. Pregnancy, painful childbirth, lactation and the consequent responsibilities of infant care enforce female dependency as well as mother/child interdependency. But this situation, although 'material', is not inevitable. Citing de Beauvoir on human society's refusal to submit to nature, as well as the Communist admonition to seize the means of production, Firestone declares that women must take control of reproduction, from their own fertility to the social institutions of childbearing and childrearing.

Spurred by late-1960s developments in oral contraception, artificial insemination and, incipiently, *in vitro* fertilisation and artificial placentas, as well as industrial automation - technologies whose oppressive as well as beneficial capacities she acknowledges - Firestone sketches a quasi-dialectical sequence in which automated service-sector employment (for instance computer programming) is initially offered to working-class women, eroding the dominance of male heads of households and upsetting familial hierarchies. Meanwhile, related developments in reproductive technology offer the possibility of 'cybernating' reproduction as well as production. But with the rapid obsolescence of industrial technologies, unemployment becomes endemic, control is consolidated by an engineering elite and social unrest increases. Although the transformation of that unrest into revolution, and the means by which it might succeed, are not specified (undermining any claim to a 'dialectic' of sex), the polemic concludes with an evocation of a future in which not only the class system, but sexual distinction would be eliminated: 'genital differences between human beings would no longer matter culturally'. This utopia is projected to provide for (optional) extra-uterine gestation, the consequent withdrawal of ego investments from reproduction, the socialisation of childrearing in collective households, an end to the incest taboo, and the practice of a polymorphously perverse sexuality.

It is typical of the eccentric character of Firestone's polemic that it invokes Freud as an important ally in this project without mentioning any of his writings on sexual difference. Neither his observations on the impossibility of establishing a psychological meaning for 'maleness' and 'femaleness' in the *Three Essays on the Theory of Sexuality* nor the complaint (in 'A Case of Homosexuality in a Woman') that our understanding of masculinity and femininity inevitably 'vanishes' into activity and passivity, nor the statement (in *Civilization and Its Discontents*) of the 'fact that each individual seeks to satisfy both male and female wishes in his sexual life'[19] are cited against the sexual distinction. And while we know that Freud was inconsistent in these views, returning periodically to the assumption of a more stable sexual dichotomy, that too Firestone ignores. Instead, she appropriates 'Freudianism' not as psychoanalysis, but as social critique. As late Victorian

19. Sigmund Freud, 'Civilization and Its Discontents' [1930], in *Civilization, Society and Religion*, Pelican Freud Library Vol. 12, Harmondsworth, Penguin, 1985, p296.

contemporaries, Freudianism and feminism are said to be 'responses to centuries of increasing privatization of family life, its extreme subjugation of women, and the sex repressions and subsequent neuroses this causes'.[20] And one by one, she works through the central tenets of psychoanalysis - oedipality, fetishism, penis envy, etc - to ascribe them to social forces. Thus, the male oedipus complex, to cite her most extensive example, is entirely about social power: the father's ideological influence, physical dominance and access to law, culture and adventure versus the mother's confinement by pregnancy, child care and the father's bullying; and the consequent transformation of the little boy's initial love and sympathy for his primary care-giver into identification with her oppressor.

20. Shulamith Firestone, op. cit., p61.

This sort of social reductionism was widespread in the women's movement at the time of *The Dialectic*'s publication, and it is the main target of Juliet Mitchell's 1974 *Psychoanalysis and Feminism*. Like Millett and Greer, Firestone is accused by Mitchell of denying infantile sexuality and replacing the unconscious with the subject's rational negotiation of the familial realities. (As Mitchell points out, Firestone's claim that 'most children aren't fools' requires an updating of the Oedipus complex to about age 6). As for *The Dialectic*'s call to eliminate 'the sex distinction itself', this is consigned to a millennarian fantasy 'that differences can be annihilated in the interests of harmony',[21] that (as in Reich's dialectic precursor to Firestone) the contradictions of unconscious desire and social repression will be reconciled under socialism. Arguing from the Lacanian standpoint which her study did so much to propagate, Mitchell insists instead on the foundational importance of difference (difference as separation, absence, lack) to the constitution of human subjectivity. And, in the argument of the period, Freud's phylogenetic myth of origins in *Totem and Taboo* is linked to Levi-Strauss's structuralist account of the incest prohibition and female exchange between kin groups to make a gender system organised by paternal interdiction co-extensive with human culture. It is patriarchy, not procreation, and indeed not men's economic and political power, that Mitchell's psychoanalytic feminism targets for 'overthrow'.

21. Juliet Mitchell, *Psychoanalysis and Feminism*, London, Allen Lane, 1974, p398.

That the latter term could even be used in 1974 seems striking from the perspective of contemporary Lacanian accounts of sexual difference, which have withdrawn it from a historicised symbolic order to insist instead on its liminal situation 'neither as biological fact nor as a specific cultural formation, but as the articulation of a certain deadlock that pertains to the most elementary relationship between the human animal and the symbolic order'.[22] As developed in Lacan's formulas of sexuation, this deadlock is one of signification, which offers speaking beings two points of orientation in regard to castration - submission and accession to phallic jouissance, or not. While Lacanians stress the non-physicality of the two categories, the autonomy of our official and erogenous identifications, and the historical contingency of their symbolisation, there are nonetheless only two positions available and they are mutually exclusive. In this logic of non-contradiction,

22. Renata Salecl, 'Introduction', in Renata Salecl (ed), *Sexuation*, Durham and London, Duke University Press, 2000, p9.

23. Colette Soler,
'The Curse on Sex',
in Renata Salecl (ed)
op. cit., *Sexuation*,
p42.

the choice of 'both' comes at the price of psychosis - the price, Lacanians confidently assert, paid by transsexuals, accused of claiming exemption from the bar of castration, of thinking they can have it all. Moreover, the gendering of each position (submission to castration as masculine, nonsubmission as feminine) creates, as Colette Soler observes, a 'strange homology'[23] between the binary classification of speaking beings and sexed organisms.

Within this formulation, there is no call to overthrow anything, certainly not patriarchy, since sexuation, like the (admittedly) prosthetic phallus around which it is organised, is said to be both virtual - fraudulent, failing, empty - and transcendent - founded in drives which are literally unspeakable, 'a real and not a symbolic difference'.[24] Unlike ethnic or class differences, sexual difference in this theory is the default difference, the difference that guarantees 'difference in general', that defends each subject's particularity against cultural determination.

24. Joan Copjec,
*Read My Desire:
Lacan against the
Historicists*,
Cambridge, MA. and
London, MIT Press,
1994, p207.

This was not quite the view of those who first attempted to graft Lacanian psychoanalysis onto feminism. Although that theory adopts structural anthropology to suture sexual difference into subjectivity at the dawn of culture, Mitchell herself concludes her remarks on the subject with 'Some way of establishing distinctions will always be crucial; that it should be this way is another question'.[25] And, despite her argument with Firestone, that question is - for both theorists - posed by the conflicts of contemporary kinship. For Firestone, citing Durkheim, the exogamy and incest taboos prescribed by early human societies survive in the patriarchal structure of the contemporary family, whose archaic nature is obscured by the romanticisation of marriage and the limited economic support, social intimacy and sexual satisfaction that it offers. For Mitchell (in one of the most dialectical, and least remembered, chapters of her study) the exchange of women between kin groups said to inaugurate early economic relations is rendered obsolete by capitalist exchange, even as patriarchal authority is reinforced by the capitalist family. To Mitchell, the modern family is inherently unstable, doomed to surrender its functions to social production and its gendered subjectivities to 'new structures ... in the unconscious'.[26] To Firestone, its oppressive nature, together with new technological opportunities, will result in its replacement by contractual collectivities raising their non-genetic children.

25. Juliet Mitchell,
*Psychoanalysis and
Feminism*, op. cit.,
p416.

26. Ibid., p 415.

Since this debate took place in the 1970s, there have been vast developments in reproductive technologies, but surprisingly few attempts to theorise their effect on sexual subjectivity. The most obvious exception to this silence are lesbians, for whom artificial insemination is now a long-established and widespread practice and for whom the potential to combine the chromosomal material of two different donors' eggs would offer female couples the prospect of genetic reproduction. Writing in defence of homosexual parenting, Judith Butler has recently re-examined the structuralist tradition in psychoanalysis to question whether it continues to mobilise 'the theorization of a primary sexual difference' in order to taboo new kinship relations. In particular, she notes the opposition of a number of French psychoanalysts to the recent legalisation of non-marital 'contracts of alliance' in the fear that these would eventually lead to homosexual marriage and parenting and the consequent threat of their children's psychosis, 'as if some structure, necessarily named "Mother" and necessarily named "Father" and established at the level of the symbolic, was a necessary psychic support against engorgement by the Real'.[27] (Among the opponents of this measure was Lacan's son-in-law and executor, Jacques-Alain Miller, who argued that homosexual men should not be allowed to marry, because their unions would be deprived of feminine fidelity). Against the psychoanalytic exposition of an inviolable law regulating kinship and sexual identity, Butler counterposes 'a socially alterable set of arrangements' confounding the 'normative heterosexual family structure' - not only lesbian and gay parenting, but the black urban families headed by groups of mothers, aunts and grandmothers, other parenting arrangements shared by more than two adults, or voluntary single parenting - arrangements that have attracted increasing state opposition in recent times. If these family forms constitute de facto challenges to the structuralist norm, should the same be said of the possibilities now offered by the new reproductive technologies?

Another lesbian theorist, Camilla Griggers, thinks not. Reflecting on the development of new technologies including artificial insemination, *in vitro* fertilisation, surrogate pregnancy, embryo transfer, etc., she argues that such innovations can both challenge and confirm 'biological relations to gendered social roles', since the prospect of lesbian maternity is conferred by 'a repressive straight economy of material production, body management, and a class-privileged division of labor'.[28] But neither the radical kin groups defended by Butler nor the technically-assisted lesbian pregnancy exempted by Griggers from the 'repressive straight economy' would obviate the psychopathologies which Firestone perceived in even the most 'alternative' families of her era: 'the attempted extension of ego through one's children … the "immortalizing" of name, property, class and ethnic identification … child-as-project',[29] and the consequent continuation of maternal and child dependency and subordination. The recent scandals of reproductive technology - such as the French brother and sister, aged 52 and 62, who obtained IVF treatment in the US in 2001 while posing as husband and wife, or the 47-year-old infertile woman who sought implantation with an egg from an anonymous donor fertilised by her own brother at a London clinic in August that year - have been defended on the presumptive benefit of the biological family's genetic perpetuation. As the spokesman from the London clinic involved put it, fertilisation by one's brother is no more incestuous in this context than egg donation from one's sister (thereby underlining the persistence of a sexual differentiation whereby impregnation by sibling of the opposite sex somehow requires more justification). Although such procedures may present ethical problems for Britain's Human Fertilisation and Embryology Authority, they clearly conform to traditions of

27. Judith Butler, *Antigone's Claim: Kinship between Life and Death*, New York, Columbia University Press, 2000, p70.

28. Camilla Griggers, *Becoming-Woman*, Minneapolis, University of Minnesota Press, 1997, p47.

29. Shulamith Firestone, *The Dialectic of Sex*, op. cit., p 229.

surrogacy and adoption dating back to the Old Testament, as well as contemporary norms of maternal fulfilment, familial narcissism and sexual difference.

Firestone's prosthetic womb is proposed precisely against such norms, since its artifice would be employed to distance gestation from any human parent, and therefore facilitate the infant's bonding with a group whose biological connection to the child would be irrelevant. (Interestingly, *The Dialectic* makes no stipulations about the circumstances of the child's conception, despite noting the then looming possibility of *in vitro* fertilisation. Although Firestone's conviction that a relaxation of familial taboos would encourage polymorphous sexuality leads her to speculate about a future without exclusive couples or an over-emphasis on genitality, heterosexuality is not seen as the root of gendered dominance and submission, *a la* Dworkin and MacKinnon. Firestone's polemic is not aimed at conventional intercourse, which she describes in passing as offering a better 'physical fit' than its homosexual counterparts, but at the feminisation of childbearing and rearing.)

Does this have any resonance in an era in which postmenopausal women desperately seek fertility treatment? One only has to read the recent discussion of pregnancy stimulated by the publication of Naomi Woolf and Rachel Cusk's maternal memoirs to conclude that it may well do.[30] Not only do the two mothers complain of trauma, exhaustion, depression, isolation and social subordination, but they do so in classic Firestonian prose. But where *The Dialectic* shocked its 1970s readers by announcing that 'pregnancy is the temporary deformation of the body of the individual for the sake of the species',[31] in 2001 Rachel Cusk could observe that 'childbirth and motherhood are the anvils upon which sexual inequality was forged' and be accused of stating the obvious. Commenting in the London *Evening Standard*, Zoe Williams replied that bourgeois literati like Cusk and Woolf could easily have taken evasive action, the increasing option of young, middle-class women in the West: fewer pregnancies, decreasing birthrates.[32] If the technology for external gestation was available for this generation might there be a significant change?

Although duplicating the functions of the uterus and placenta has proved far more daunting than simpler interventions in cellular biology, researchers at Cornell University's Centre for Reproductive Medicine and Infertility and Tokyo's Juntendo University now predict that artificial wombs capable of sustaining the full nine-months gestation of a human infant may be only years away. Again, this research - creating an artificial womb lining at Cornell and a oxygenated amniotic tank in Tokyo - is aimed at enabling traditional maternity for women prone to miscarriage or with damaged uteruses. And when such cybernetic pregnancy becomes available, it needn't lead to the dialectical outcome foreseen by Firestone. Setting aside the sheer cost of such procedures, as well as the largely non-feminist regime which still controls them, the consequences of prosthetic gestation would not necessarily differ

30. Naomi Woolf, *Misconceptions*, London, Chatto & Windus, 2001; Rachel Cusk, *A Life's Work*, London, Fourth Estate, 2001.

31. Shulamith Firestone, *The Dialectic of Sex*, op. cit., p198.

32. Rachel Cusk, *A Life's Work*, op. cit., p8. Zoe Williams, 'The Mother of all Bores', *Evening Standard*, 7.09.01, p15.

from those of surrogacy or adoption, if the child is reared by a primary caregiver without equally engaged co-parents and the appropriate institutional support. Whether the possibility of release from the physical burdens, or the dyadic bonds, of traditional motherhood would make group parenting appear a potentially less consuming, and thus more appealing enterprise remains to be seen - as does its effects on the cultural significance of genital difference.

Nevertheless, as the prospect of artificial pregnancy looms, science ethicists are convening conferences like the February 2002 event at Oklahoma State University titled 'The End of Natural Motherhood?'. Setting out its agenda, organiser Scott Gelfant suggested that the existence of artificial wombs might encourage the Moral Right to insist that all pregnancies proceed to term, but - if combined with cloning technology - could equally enable gay male reproduction.[33] Meanwhile, biotechnology commentator Jeremy Rifkind responded to the Cornell and Juntendo announcements by quoting Firestone's call for 'an honest examination of the ancient value of motherhood' and asking 'How will the end of pregnancy affect the way we think about gender and the role of women?'[34] Such speculations have outstripped present day feminist theory, which advises us to value gender as an attribute of individual diversity while somehow resisting the rigidities of sexual binarism. Paradoxically, while reproductive technologies develop which could subvert or perpetuate that order, and conventional maternity is increasingly criticised or refused, Firestone's ungendered utopia is virtually forgotten by the women's movement, as is the major attempt to give it imaginative expression, the American writer Marge Piercy's *Woman on the Edge of Time* (1976).

Like many of the more provocative attempts to think difference differently, Piercy's novel is a work of science fiction. And typically of that genre, the future imagined is very much of its writing's time, a 1970s-style commune of androgynous ecologists with names like Morningstar dressed in down jackets. Here, in Massachusetts of 2137, embryonic children gestate in acquarial brooders until they are delivered into a world of neutral pronouns, communal co-operation and three voluntary parents. The result, one character explains, is that '"All coupling, all befriending goes on between biological males, biological females, or both. That's not a useful set of categories. We tend to divvy up people by what they're good at and bad at, strengths and weaknesses, gifts and failings"'.[35] A century and a half from this idyll the novel's heroine, a poor Chicana woman forcibly committed to a present-day public mental ward, time travels to this contingent community. It is her story, and not the prosthetic maternity of the state abbreviated MA, that prefigures Firestone's own.

In 1998, the avant-garde publisher Semiotext(e) issued *Airless Spaces*, a collection of Firestone's stories set in and out of mental hospitals, a life she herself had lived for many of the silent years following the publication of *The Dialectic of Sex*. Like Piercy's Connie Ramos, Firestone's characters are

33. See Robin McKie, 'Men Redundant? Now We Don't Need Women Either', *Observer*, 10.02.02, p7.

34. Jeremy Rifkind, 'The End of Pregnancy', *Guardian*, 17.01.02, p17.

35. Marge Piercy, *Woman on the Edge of Time* [1976], London, the Women's Press, 1979, p116.

desperate inside the hospital and destitute when out. Years of medication and institutional routine have left one unable to read, write or 'care about anything, and love was forgotten':

> She was lucid, yes, at what price. She sometimes recognized on the faces of others joy and ambition and other emotions she could recall having had once, long ago. But her life was ruined, and she had no salvage plan.[36]

36. Shulamith Firestone, *Airless Spaces*, New York, Semiotext(e), 1998, p59.

Who is 'she' in this story? *Airless Spaces* contains 51 vignettes, divided into headings such as 'Hospitals', 'Losers', 'Obituaries', and 'Suicides I Have Known'. So recognisably autobiographical are elements of these that their status as fiction becomes suspect. (One rather vindictive obituary is for an actual feminist, dead at 50, who had helped to overthrow the founding principles of a woman's group that Firestone started in the East Village, the coup that finally provoked her withdrawal from the women's movement.) Such *romans-à-clef* reinforce the question still posed at Firestone's project: is their author's self-described 'madness' the fate reserved for those who would contest sexual difference?

If *Airless Spaces* is the tragic sequel to the utopian hopes of *Woman on the Edge of Time*, which ends with its heroine fiercely resistant, if captive in the asylum, it was not the only ambiguous biography of Firestone to emerge in the 1990s. Despite its publication, and the reissuing of *The Dialectic* in 1993, Firestone remains resolutely outside the public arena. At her insistence, the 1967 documentary portraying her as a member of the 'Now Generation' has never been released, but in the mid-1990s, while researching the left film collective that some of its makers subsequently formed, another young graduate of the Art Institute of Chicago discovered *Shulie*. Struck by Firestone's onscreen remarks about the voyeuristic pleasures of the cinema ('I always like to feel that I'm peeking into things that I wouldn't otherwise see') versus the ethical responsibilities of the artist ('You can go too far in using people's situations as subject matter'), as well as the historic significance of this portrait of a woman who would become so major a feminist figure, experimental director Elisabeth Subrin decided on a remake. The resulting work, also called *Shulie*, is a prosthetic documentary, a shot-by-shot copy of the original, with certain key differences. Casting look-alike Kim Suss as Shulie, Subrin returned to the Chicago locations of the 1967 film, inserting 'a deviation in every frame'.[37] Not least is the substitution of Subrin herself, its woman director, for Firestone's original off-screen interrogator, a man.

37. Elisabeth Subrin, quoted in Amy Kroin, 'Cases of Mistaken Identity', *The Valley Advocate*, 13 August 1998.

Subrin's own description of her film sees it as another 'sort of time travel, a means of forcing viewers to analyze, shot by shot, what constitutes now and then, across social, economic, racial, cultural and aesthetic terms ... *Shulie* (1997) is not necessarily about the young Firestone, but about the conditions of a woman's representation and the recognition that she, and many other women of her generation, survived, or even conquered that representation, often at enormous risk and sacrifice. It is also about the present. The amateur, sexist and self-aggrandising strategies of the original four male filmmakers and their positioning of her in the documentary; how she's treated by her painting teachers; how she articulates her subjectivity as a white, middle class Jewish woman: these moments represent critical and neglected evidence of a time that hasn't necessarily passed'.[38]

Such statements have not won Firestone's support for the second *Shulie*, although she has taken no action against its dissemination. Her reputed indignation at her own cinematic redoubling finds support in the film theory which begins with Metz's observations on the spectator's discovery of himself as 'the double of his double' in 'that other mirror, the cinema screen', and that screen's 'prosthetic' substitution for his 'primally dislocated limbs'.[39] Here the cinema performs what has been called the 'double logic'[40] of the prosthesis, technologically extending the agency of the spectator, while threatening bodily fragmentation and objectification. And as feminist critics have demonstrated since *The Dialectic*, these functions are not innocent of the sexual distinction which genders spectatorship masculine, while traditionally making the female spectacle - from Muybridge's moving women to *Metropolis*'s false Maria to *The Stepford Wives* - mechanical objects. Against this logic, Subrin's reanimated *Shulie* - however original in its simulation - may have no defence. As one viewer asked me after a recent screening, 'how amusing might you find an anachronistic puppet show of yourself, I wonder … ?'

But perhaps *Shulie*'s spectacularisation of its female subject only contributes to the strange sense of *Nachträglichkeit* with which the spectator subliminally registers its contemporary additions, such as the insertion of a demonstration at the 1996 Democratic Convention for a 1960s be-in, or the Starbucks coffee cup in a postal worker's hand, in its ostensible portrait of the faraway 1960s. For when the spectator discovers that this portrait from the Now Generation really is now, the deferred temporality of trauma is achieved, confronting us with the original experience of sexual difference which lead women like Firestone to become feminists, and which remains - in her life and our own - all too familiar.

Many thanks to Sarah Franklin for her extensive and enthusiastic advice.

38. Elisabeth Subrin, 'Shulie', paper for 1999 College Arts Association panel 'Trash: Value, Waste and the Politics of Legibility'.

39. Christian Metz, *Psychoanalysis and Cinema: The Imaginary Signifier*, London, Macmillan, 1982, *passim*.

40. Mark Seltzer, *Bodies and Machines*, New York and London, Routledge, 1992, p157.

THINKING EXPENDITURE: BATAILLE AND BODY ART

Kate Ince

I have always considered my woman's body, my woman-artist's body, privileged material for the construction of my work. My work has always interrogated the status of the feminine body, via social pressures, those of the present or in the past ... My body has become a site of public debate that poses crucial questions for our time (Orlan, 1996).[1]

Orlan's claim in her manifesto of 'carnal art'[2] is that through the project 'The Reincarnation of Saint Orlan', her female body has become a site of public debate raising questions crucial to our time. 'The Reincarnation of Saint Orlan' is the surgical performance project Orlan began in 1990, which has comprised the resculpting of her face and image to match a digitally designed template combining features from five of the greatest icons of female beauty in the Western art historical canon, including the Mona Lisa (the brow) and Botticelli's Venus (the chin). Orlan's operations of cosmetic surgery have been photographed, filmed, broadcast live to an international audience, and disseminated across the world in art galleries and a wide variety of art-related publications and magazine journalism. Her claim about the centrality of her woman's body to the project makes it apparent that she is engaged in feminist materialist critique. What I would like to do here is explore the kind of materialism her project stages, drawing parallels as I do so between Orlan and the group of mainly British and American artists whose work has inspired reviews of the 'revival' of body art in the 1990s,[3] in particular the performances and photographs of the Italian-born performance artist Franko B, now based in London.

To do so I shall explore the implications of Bataille's notions of base materialism, of expenditure, and of the *informe* for contemporary body art. One of my aims in linking Bataille's theories of culture and representation to contemporary artistic production is to extend the field of what he called 'intransigently' materialist images from Surrealism to the type of spectacularly cruel representations that feature prominently in much late twentieth-century art, whether it be the photographic plates of Orlan's operation-performances, Damien Hirst's sliced-up animals, or the grotesquely distorted mannequins of Jake and Dinos Chapman.

As philosopher and critic, Georges Bataille wrote extensively on the art of his own time. His notion of base materialism was particularly concerned to prevent materialism from being conceptualised as, ultimately, just another type of idealism, since according to Bataille, most materialists, despite their intention and wish to eliminate all spiritual entities, 'ended up positing an order of things whose hierarchical relations mark it as specifically idealist'.[4]

1. Orlan, 'Conférence', in Duncan McCorquodale (edited and produced), *Ceci est mon corps...ceci est mon logiciel/This is my body...this is my software*, London, Black Dog Publishing, 1996, pp81-93 (p84, p88).

2. Orlan, '"Carnal Art": Manifesto', inside front cover and pp2-3 in Orlan and Stéphane Place (eds), *Orlan: de l'art charnel au baiser de l'artiste*, Collection "Sujet Objet", Paris, Editions Jean-Michel Place, 1997.

3. Jeff Rian, 'What's All This Body Art?', *Flash Art*, XXVI, 168 (Jan/Feb 1993), 50-3.

4. Georges Bataille, *Visions of Excess: selected writings, 1927-1939*, Allan Stoekl (ed), Allan Stoekl, Carl R. Lovitt and Donald M. Leslie, Jr (trans), Minneapolis, MN, University of Minnesota Press, 1985, p15.

An account of how Bataille's materialism differs from the ordered, hierarchical kind he saw in the majority of materialist thinking is given by Denis Hollier in the essay 'The Dualist Materialism of Georges Bataille'.[5] What characterises Bataille's approach to materialism, Hollier points out, is a dualism that entails thinking (of) matter as 'a second principle, with its distinctive nature, different from that of the spirit, and not derived from it'.[6] In dualist philosophy and religion God and matter are not opposed to one another as mutually antagonistic constituents of the same hierarchically ordered system or totality; they are disjointed, separate principles. Dualist thinking is by definition not systematic thinking, but an attitude to thought that amounts to 'a resistance to system and homogeneity'.[7]

The form taken by the ordered, hierarchical type of materialism Bataille criticised as 'doddering idealism' was the pyramid.[8] Matter lay at the base of the pyramid, while its summit was the point of synthesis or closure of the system, the place in which its mutually opposing elements might be reconciled. Writing in 1929, Bataille announces that the word materialism should jettison this in-built reliance upon the pyramidal structure of idealist thought, and henceforth 'designate the direct interpretation, *excluding all idealism*, of raw phenomena and not a system founded on the fragmentary elements of an ideological analysis elaborated under the sign of religious relations'.[9] The materialism Bataille proposed was disconnected from any monistic theology, it was atheological, a-pyramidal. For Bataille, the only kind of materialism to have escaped systematic abstraction in the way it developed was dialectical materialism, which saw matter as containing within its own nature the tensions and contradictions which provide the motive force for change. In applying Hegel's dialectic to material reality, however, dialectical materialism nonetheless revealed Hegelian absolute idealism to be its original source.[10] The greater part of conventional materialism situated dead matter at the top of a hierarchy of facts, and in so doing retained an 'obsession' with the ideal form of matter, putting dead matter, pure ideas and God on the same plane.[11] In Bataille's atheological materialism, the absence of a summit-level at which these principles can come together implies a shifting mass of material tensions that is horizontal rather than vertical, if not unimaginably amorphous.

One obstacle to interpreting Orlan's surgical work according to Bataille's materialism as I have started to outline it here, is that, especially when its preparatory stages are taken into account, the 'Reincarnation' project seems to have involved a definite engagement with ideals. The representations of the Mona Lisa, Venus, Diana, Europa and Psyche from which Orlan's surgical template was cut and pasted are ideal images of feminine beauty. Orlan has repeatedly insisted that her work is not concerned to embrace or endorse these ideals, because straightforward mimetic desire - the desire to resemble (another image) - does not concern her.[12] Although her status as an artist of representation required the choice of visual images for her digital self-redesign, she selected the features of Mona Lisa, Venus, Diana, Europa and

5. Denis Hollier, 'The Dualist Materalism of Georges Bataille', in *Bataille: A Critical Reader*, Fred Botting and Scott Wilson (eds), Oxford, Blackwell, 1998, pp59-77.

6. Ibid., p62.

7. Ibid.

8. Ibid., p64.

9. Bataille, *Visions of Excess*, op. cit., p16

10. Ibid., p45

11. Ibid., p16

12. Orlan, '"I do not want to look like ... ": Orlan on becoming-Orlan', *Women's Art Magazine* 64 (May/June 1995), 5-10.

Psyche not for their appearance, but because of the mythical qualities and attributes these women possessed - the Mona Lisa for the androgyny resulting from the palimpsest of Leonardo da Vinci's self-portrait beneath her image, Venus because of her connection to fertility and creativity, Diana for her insubordination to men and aggressivity as the goddess of hunting, Europa because Gustave Moreau's painting of her is unfinished, and because her look to another continent showed her interest in an unknown future, and Psyche because of her need for love and spiritual beauty.[13] Orlan's own explanations of her surgical performances, as well as a proportion of the commentary about them, emphasise that 'Reincarnation' was never planned as a quest or pursuit of one ideal image of beauty. The very plurality of ideal images combined already seems to parody the notion of a unified ideal, as well as engaging in pastiche of the fetishistic fragmentation of the female body by male artists. This plural aesthetic is also a critically imitative repetition of the composition of a beautiful face practised by the Greek painter Zeuxis, who 'when painting his portrait of Helena in the city of Kroton, [chose] five virgins, so as to reproduce the most beautiful part of each one'.[14] There is thus no unquestioning or uncritical engagement with ideals in Orlan's surgical project, more a stopping-short of the points of resolution that they stand for. But at the same time, she is indisputably working in the space - or on the movement - between idealism and materialism. Rather than a deconstruction of the idealism/materialism binary, we can see in Orlan's carnal art a materialism that does not get 'as far' as idealism, that makes us question the relationship between these two mutually hostile philosophies, and requires that we theorise a materialism different from the kind on which materialist thought has usually depended.

In a short essay originally contributed to the art journal *Documents*, Bataille allies base materialism with Gnosticism.[15] Bataille states that although Gnosticism has been represented as a Hellenized intellectual form of a primitive Christianity, with its main protagonists (Basilides, Valentinus, Bardesanes, Marcion) appearing to be important religious humanists and Christians, in fact orthodox Christians were mainly responsible for destroying the writings of the Gnostic theologians. Whatever its later metaphysical developments, the origins of Gnosticism lay in the Egyptian tradition, in Persian dualism and in Eastern Jewish heterodoxy, all elements it introduced into Greco-Roman ideology in what Bataille calls 'an almost bestial way', as 'a most impure fermentation'.[16] The leitmotiv of Gnosticism, according to Bataille, also stands as the definition of base materialism; it is 'the conception of matter as an *active* principle having its own eternal autonomous existence as darkness which would not be simply the absence of light, but the monstrous *archontes* revealed by this absence'.[17] 'Present-day' materialism, by which Bataille means 'a materialism not implying an ontology, not implying that matter is the thing-in-itself',[18] and thus having no truck with Kantian idealism, resembles the psychological process of Gnosticism. The refusal to submit oneself or one's reason to any higher thing or principle means that

13. Orlan, 'Conférence', op. cit., pp88-9; Barbara Rose, 'Is it Art? Orlan and the Transgressive Act', *Art in America*, February 1993, pp82-87, 125.

14. Ernst Kris, Otto Kurz, *Die Legende vom Künstler. Ein geschichtlicher Versuch*, Frankfurt am Main, Suhrkamp, 1980, p68, quoted in Beate Ermacora, 'Orlan', *European Photography* 56 (1994), 16.

15. Hollier's exposition of dualism as a mode of thought notes that 'Manichean Gnosticism is considered to be [its] most striking manifestation', Hollier, 'The Dualist Materalism of Georges Bataille', op. cit., p62.

16. Bataille, 'Base materialism and Gnosticism', op. cit., p46.

17. Ibid., p47. Bataille's 'definition' of darkness as 'not [...] simply the absence of light' reconfirms the dualist character of his thinking.

18. Bataille, 'Base materialism and Gnosticism', op. cit. p49.

base materialism does not appeal to a higher authority of any kind. Not allowing one's reason to become the limit of matter, when matter is invoked, means that it does not take on the value of a superior principle - to God or to the idea. 'Base matter is external and foreign to ideal human aspirations, and it refuses to allow itself to be reduced to the great ontological machines resulting from these aspirations'.[19] By juxtaposing and comparing Gnosticism and base materialism, parallels are opened up between the figures of ancient art in which the 'bestial' influence of Gnosticism is apparent and the forms of the early part of the twentieth century in which certain plastic representations express an 'intransigent materialism'.[20] Bataille included in *Documents* figures from Asiatic and mythological art which illustrate these parallels with the Surrealist art of the late 1920s, and open up connections between Surrealism and base materialism. The prominence of 'intransigently' materialist images in the work of Orlan and other late twentieth century artists I mentioned in the introduction to this essay suggests that we are again living in a moment when base materialism can help to account for contemporary artistic production.

The potential of Bataille's notion of base materialism for contemporary art was explored recently, in an exhibition devised by Yve-Alain Bois and Rosalind Krauss, 'Formless: A User's Guide', that took place at the Centre Georges Pompidou in Paris from May to October 1996. The exhibition actually took its title from another of Bataille's terms, the formless or *informe* that entitled one of Bataille's entries for the 'Dictionnaire critique' of the review *Documents*, edited by Bataille between 1929 and 1930 (other entries, in addition to 'Base materialism and Gnosticism', include, 'Figure humaine', 'Les écarts de la nature', and 'The Notion of Expenditure'). In the introductory essay to the 'Formless' exhibition,[21] Bois and Krauss explain that 'the *informe* is an operation which consists of confusing, or rather confounding, classification. Resolutely anti-idealist, this attitude undermines and reverses every attempt at sublimation'.[22] The exhibition, like much of Krauss's recent work,[23] aimed to offer a critique of the understanding of modernist art according to which its development should be charted as the logical unfolding of stages of formal discovery, the now widely questioned but very influential line of argument put forward in the writings of Clement Greenberg. If the Greenbergian view puts the history of art in the service of a Hegelian developmental dialectic, Bataille's notions of 'formless' and of base materialism open up an alternative approach both to the history of modern art itself and to the dominance of the question of form within that history. One of the four parts of the 'Formless' exhibition was entitled 'Base Materialism' (the others were 'Horizontality', 'Pulse' and 'Entropy') and contained works by Piero Manzoni, an important early contributor to body art, with his 'living sculptures' of 1961, and the canning of his own excrement as 'artist's shit' in the same year. Taking my cue from Krauss and Bois, I would like now to pursue the links I have suggested between Bataille's *informe*, base materialism, and the performance art of Orlan and Franko B.

19. Ibid., p51.

20. Ibid.

21. Subsequently published as Rosalind E. Krauss and Yve-Alain Bois, *Formless: A User's Guide*, Zone Books, 1997. My source here is the exhibition leaflet: 'Formless: A User's Guide'.

22. Ibid., p2.

23. See Rosalind E. Krauss, *The Optical Unconscious*, Cambridge, Massachusetts, MIT, 1993.

24. Patrick ffrench, *The Cut/reading Bataille's Histoire de l'oeil*, A British Academy Postdoctoral Fellowship Monograph, Oxford, Oxford University Press, 1999, p18.

25. Ibid., pp19-20.

26. Apart from one early operation in which fat was extracted from her thighs through liposuction, Orlan's face has been the object of all her surgeries. It is now noticeably plumper and puffier than in 1990, and 'crowned' by two protuberances above her eyebrows that have been dubbed her 'horns' - silicone implants intended for the cheeks that have been inserted in imitation of the Mona Lisa's ridged forehead.

27. Kate Ince, 'Between the Acts: Orlan, performance and performativity', in Victoria Best and Peter Collier (eds), *Powerful Bodies: Performance in French Cultural Studies*, Peter Lang, 1999, pp51-69. Reprinted in modified form in Kate Ince, *Orlan: Millennial Female*, Oxford, Berg, 2000, pp111-116.

28. Judith Butler, *Bodies that matter: On the Discursive Limits of 'Sex'*, London and New York, Routledge, 1993, p9.

In a recent extended reading of Bataille's novel *Histoire de l'oeil*, Patrick ffrench acknowledges that Rosalind Krauss's project in *The Optical Unconscious* is 'possibly the most significant contemporary reading of Bataille, and has, moreover, proved productive of intense debate and reassessment of his work, and particularly the *Documents* period, in the field of art history'.[24] The importance of Krauss's rereading of Bataille relates particularly to her interpretation of the *informe*, which ffrench draws on and sets himself apart from in his discussion of the notion. Summarising selectively from ffrench's explanation of the *informe* will provide a slant with which I can view Orlan's carnal art:

> What does the word *informe* do? To say what it means is to go against the direction of its task - to declassify, it would be to give it form, to give form to a word whose task is to 'unform'. *Informe*, then, is a task ... The *informe* ruins mimesis, ruins resemblance, the possibility of saying what the universe is 'like' ... The *informe*, in my reading, designates an operation that resists the tendency to ascribe meaning, to interpret and to fix. Its task is to interrupt meaning, inscribe a cut, which ruins the possibility of form ...[25]

In 'The Reincarnation of Saint Orlan' ('Saint Orlan' was the persona Orlan adopted in 1971 and used for her 1970s and 1980s performances, installations and exhibitions), Orlan's initial objective was to alter the form of her face and body to match a digitally designed surgical template. In the view of most commentators, the changes have been to the detriment of her 'natural' (unmodified), well-proportioned, and even beautiful appearance. Is the material 'task' of modification (Bataille's word is 'besogne', which carries connotations of toil or drudgery) we see in Orlan's operations not the declassificatory, unfixing work of the *informe*? Performance is the primary artistic medium of live action, of tasks to be executed, though not usually life-changing ones: Orlan's surgical project has attracted worldwide attention in part because of the quasi-permanent changes to her body effected during her operations. I indicated earlier how Orlan is not concerned with mimesis or mimetic desire; instead, operations of deforming - or un-forming - the female body seem to be what her surgical project is all about. The repeated alterations to which she has subjected her face[26] mean that as an object of interpretation, it resists a fixed meaning or meanings. Its morphology is in flux, in process; the work of the *informe* can be understood in each cut of the surgeon's scalpel.

In an earlier reading of Orlan's surgeries that employed Judith Butler's theory of gender performativity,[27] I suggested that Butler's notion of materialisation, in which matter is thought of 'not as a site or surface, but as a process of materialisation that stabilises over time to produce the effect of boundary, fixity and surface we call matter',[28] might be the best way of elucidating Orlan's surgical work. But is it possible that the shifting and recasting of bodily matter displayed in Orlan's operations is being less externally (for example, discursively) shaped even than in the performative constructions of matter described by Butler, that what we are being shown is, rather, the unstable, ruining and unfixing reorganisation of the flesh suggested by Bataille's notions of the *informe* and of base materialism? The use of surgical instruments in the operating theatre might undermine this suggestion where Orlan's operation-performances are concerned, as it strongly implies modification by the institution and tools of medicine, but if so, my shift in reading would still apply to the series of post-operative pictures she has exhibited, in which the differences in the images in sequence - taken once a day for forty days after 'Omnipresence' (the seventh operation) - exhibit shocking bruising, but also the body's self-activating process of repair, a process not brought about by any external instrument.

The resistance to the closure and fixity of meaning in 'Reincarnation', best evinced by the permanently unfinished nature of the project (Orlan might always undergo further surgery), invites a poststructuralist reading. Bataille's notions of base materialism and of the *informe* - Bataille is now often regarded as a proto-poststructuralist, although protests have quite rightly been registered about the historical inappropriateness of this classification[29] - echo Orlan's work particularly well in the emphasis her artistic practice puts upon the material precarity of form. Orlan claims that her surgical work of the 1990s and more recent garish and distorted portraits composed by digital morphing of her features with those of pre-Colombian idols constitute a critique of beauty standards - a critique, amongst other things, of a certain grand narrative of the perfectibility of human form.[30] Orlan has maintained that some of her non-performance work is best understood as a riposte to Greenbergian formalist modernism,[31] and I would contend that the same can be said of 'Reincarnation', her major performance project. As Rosalind Krauss and Yve-Alain Bois say of pieces by Lucio Fontana and Bernard Réquichot included in the 'Base Materialism ' section of 'Formless: A User's Guide', in these works, 'matter, the material, never becomes figure or light'. The very constitution of form or figure is, rather, impeded by the interruption of the process by which lower becomes higher. This levelling up with one another of substances or values that traditionally each occupied a strict position in a hierarchy contests the supremacy of form in modern art, offers another way of understanding art works that insist on their un-sublatable material content, and critiques the formalist ideals and idealist forms in which much modernist art trades.

Patrick ffrench's commentary on the *informe*'s work upon human form in *Documents* runs as follows:

> In *Documents* the operation of the *informe* is brought to bear on diverse manifestations of human culture; the dislocation of the human more often than not takes the form of a foregrounding of the animalistic, not in order to propose an animal nature, a ground for the human in its

29. This issue is discussed by Fred Botting and Scott Wilson, *Bataille*, op. cit., pp6-8.

30. 'Self-Hybridation', Orlan at the Espace d'Art Yvonamor Palix, Paris, 3.11.98-30.1.99, and touring.

31. Personal communication, Paris, August 1998.

animality, but simply in order to depose the human from its sublime position. Krauss writes: 'In order to knock meaning off its pedestal, to bring it down in the world, to deliver it a low blow' (*The Optical Unconscious*, p137). The operation of the *informe* is a reminder of the body, of the *low* ('le bas'), but again, not in order to propose a primary physicality or sexuality, but for the purposes of desublimation.[32]

32. ffrench, *The Cut/ reading Bataille's Histoire de l'oeil*, op. cit., p21.

In ffrench's reading, *Histoire de l'oeil* is 'about the desublimation of the body as idea, as form', and I suggest, without being able to develop an argument here about the historical situatedness of this recurrence, that a similar deforming, desublimating movement can be detected across the work of a number of contemporary body artists. While dismembered body parts fabricated by Robert Gober protrude eerily from gallery walls, the performances of Orlan and Franko B both give a prominent place to the opening of the body, the puncturing or cutting of the skin that abolishes the body's spatial limits - extending it, in the instance of Franko B, to wherever his blood flows. (In his performance 'I Miss You', touring Britain in 2000, small taps were inserted into the veins in Franko's arms while he paced up and down the catwalk constructed at floor level, his blood spattering beneath him in an eerily violent counterpoint to the still, statuesque form of his naked and chalked body.) Severed or multiplied, free-floating genitalia are attached to the heads of Jake and Dinos Chapman's mannequins - and so on.[33]

33. Matthew Barney, Kiki Smith and Cindy Sherman are three artists whose respective contributions to this desublimation of human form are too extensive to allow me to begin to do them justice here.

A further dimension of the interrelationship of Bataille's thought with contemporary 'carnal' art is raised by a round-table discussion published in the review *October* in 1994, where Rosalind Krauss debates the notion of the abject with Yve-Alain Bois, Benjamin Buchloh, Hal Foster and Helen Molesworth.[34] The main topic of this discussion is Julia Kristeva's concept of the abject and the degree (if any) to which it emerges out of Bataille's understanding of abjection. As ffrench puts it, 'what Krauss objects to is the tendency she identifies within Kristeva's approach, to reify, to fetichize *certain* objects or states as subject to exclusion'.[35] In art involving the human body these 'certain objects' are bodily fluids and substances such as urine, blood, sperm and faeces, which have figured fairly regularly in performance and installation art since at least the 1960s, in the work of Warhol, Acconci, Gilbert and George, and Gina Pane, to name but a few. In the work of Orlan and Franko B, it is blood and tissue whose exteriorisation is important, and these substances are not simply capitalised upon for shock value. For both artists blood is (re-) used for representational purposes, while Orlan's tissue is encased in resin and mounted as 'relics', reinforcing the importance of the sacred and the body as sacred to her work. I therefore agree entirely with Krauss's opposition to the art history discourse on the abject as reified substance, and would seek, like her, to refute any moves to account for contemporary art's apparent obsession with the material body and its substances in terms of a 'return to the real' - a return to referentiality that is

34. 'The Politics of the Signifier II: A Conversation on the *Informe* and the Abject', *October* 67 (Winter 1994), 3-21.

35. ffrench, *The Cut/ reading Bataille's Histoire de l'oeil*, op. cit., p23.

a notable element of French poststructuralism. As ffrench concludes:

> Bataille's appeal, *now*, may be partly to do with this 'return to the real', a desire to dirty one's hands, to 'get down into the shit', as an eminent art historian has put it (Griselda Pollock, in discussion at a 1996 Institute of Romance Studies conference on Kristeva). Krauss's emphasis on the *structural* nature of Bataille's early work on the culture of his time is to this extent a welcome check to a potentially exploitative and redundant discourse.[36]

36. Ibid., p25.

Pursuing Krauss's emphasis on the the structural rather than the real-historical implications of Bataille's early work on base materialism and the *informe* provides a link to the one Bataillian reading of Orlan's work that has so far been made, and to some related suggestions I shall make about the work of Franko B. In an essay that focuses particularly on art as communication - in the specific sense in which Bataille uses this term - and on the multimedia dimension of the diverse projects Orlan has undertaken before and concurrently with 'Reincarnation', Isabelle Rieusset-Lemarié points out that in the bodily acts that make up Orlan's artistic practice, Orlan is not simply provisionally 'lending' her body to art as occurs with mimetic representationalism, but is giving it over wholesale, in a movement of Bataillian expenditure that reconnects with art's sacred origins.[37] For Bataille, communication and 'community' are to be understood not as the interconnection of well-defined individuals within a socially, geographically or ethnically bounded grouping, but as depoliticising collective experience and referring instead to often extreme and erotic communifying experiences. The experience of communication /community was associated with a sense of the sacred, and to be found above all in the human emotional states of excessive vitality, energy and *jouissance* in which he became increasingly interested. For Bataille, art could not be accomplished without this dimension of sovereignty that is inseparable from 'communication', expenditure and sacrifice.

37. Rieusset-Lemarié, Isabelle, 'Le corps d'Orlan et les arts multimédias', in *Une oeuvre de Orlan*, textes de Marie-Josée Bataille, Christian Gattinoni, Bernard Lafargue, Orlan, Lydie Pearle, Isabelle Rieusset-Lemarié, Joël Savary, Collection Iconotexte, Marseilles, Editions Muntaner, 1998, p97.

> This multimedia body, whether it is work made body or body become work, is a sovereign body, because it is, essentially, communication with other bodies ... It is no longer only a question of treating one's body as an artistic 'material', not even of giving it the status of a medium so that it becomes inscribed in an aesthetics of communication ... It is literally a question of giving a body to art, in other words of giving it to sovereign communication.[38]

38. Ibid., pp98-9.

Rieusset-Lemarié does not broach issues of materiality and materialism directly, but she makes the important advance of demonstrating that Orlan does something more than and decisively different from 'using her body as a canvas' - an oft-repeated critical appreciation of her work.[39] The gift of

39. Franko B also applies this idea to his work, in an interview given to Gray Watson on 13 June 2000, on Franko B's website <http://www.franko-b.com>.

the body to sovereign communication may be an apt description of the work of a number of performance artists, but none more so than Franko B, whose blood-letting performances engage perhaps even more strikingly than Orlan's in the aesthetics of extreme bodily and emotional states (Orlan is anaesthetised when she is being operated on, although visibly expresses pleasure and joy in the process):

> *I'm Not Your Babe Part I*, ICA Theatre, May 1996. The space is dungeon dark and the music is piercing, penetrating, hypnotising. White light spotlights a man, naked, at the centre of an expectant and anxious circle of spectators. Our attention is focused on him and him alone - the mute, motionless, monochromatic body before us, that is at once all powerful and utterly helpless as a steady stream of blood drips from his arms to a pool on the floor. The highly charged presence of this body disarms us, fascinates us, repels us and seduces us.[40]

40. Lois Keidan, 'Blood on the Tracks: The Performance Work of Franko B', in Lois Keidan and Stuart Morgan (text), Nicholas Sinclair (photographs), *Franko B*, London, Black Dog, 1998.

In *I'm Not Your Babe* Franko B both bled onto the white floor of the performance space from the veins of his inner arms, and poured over himself (from a metallic bowl of the kind used in operating theatres) blood drawn off beforehand. Having cupped his hands in the bowl of blood early in the performance, he proceeded to 'paint' abstract shapes across the floor with the pool of blood, and to move through these shapes in different foetal and prostrate positions. These movements left smears, smudges and marbled drips all over his head, shoulders, torso and limbs, carefully documented in Nicholas Sinclair's black and white photographs of the performance.[41] The most remarkable images in Sinclair's photographic study, however, are those in which the performer faces the audience/camera squarely, either standing or kneeling with his legs apart, his taped but blood-stained arms and hands opened to his spectators in a statuesque, dignified, compelling gesture of suffering, but also of joy, openness and connectedness - of sovereign communication.

41. Ibid.

In Franko B's performances, as in Orlan's, images of the opening of the body and of the gestures of cutting and blood-letting amount to a disruptive anti-aesthetic, a praxis of deformation of the human form. This practice is close to the violence done to the integrity of the human form in the images Bataille included in *Documents*, a violence that can be understood not as destructive, but as anti-idealist, in that it broke with traditional anthropocentric theories of resemblance having their foundation in the idea of man created in the image of God. In an idealist system of resemblance, 'the 'figure humaine' in art stands for the possibility of form and idea being coincident'.[42] Bataille's base materialism aims to break down the relationship of identity between form and idea, but as Johanna Malt's analysis of what she calls his 'epistemology of process' or 'performative knowledge model' shows, 'this is not to say that matter is to be made axiomatic in itself; it is not a question of replacing idealism with a materialist ontology'.[43] The

42. Johanna Malt, 'Montage in Surrealism as Political Metaphor', in Victoria Best and Peter Collier (eds), op. cit., pp138-9.

43. Ibid., p141.

images Bataille included in *Documents* 'confront[ed] the idealism of the 'figure humaine' with the inalienable presence of matter in a selection of its most unappealing and incomprehensible forms',[44] but not in a dualism resolvable into a synthesis by Hegelian dialectic. (In his 1929 *Documents* article 'Figure humaine', also discussed by Malt, Bataille 'describes the Hegelian dialectic, and particularly certain of his contemporaries' readings of the Hegelian dialectic, as a second kind of idealism'. The rejection of this position is evident in Bataille's veiled attack, in the same article, on André Breton, whose surrealism he viewed as upholding the traditional sublimatory function of the aesthetic.[45])

Johanna Malt's affirmation that 'Bataille's whole project aims to break down the relationship of identity between form and idea'[46] can best be seen in the practice of deformation evident in the images of *Documents*, which allow their viewer no conciliatory aesthetic synthesis of visceral materiality with the image of the human form, and in *Documents'* disruptive juxtapositions of images with text. It is in this practice of deformation and disruption that Bataille's own non-Bretonian brand of surrealism, an experimental base materialism, is revealed.[47] As will by now be clear, the aspect of this pre- or an-ontological materialism I most wish to bring out here, in order to relate it to contemporary carnal art, is its foreignness to anthropocentrism: as Denis Hollier puts it, 'with matter - the formless matter of Bataille's 'base materialism' - we can identify the generalized movement of cosmic expenditure, and with form, its miserly anthropocentric denial'.[48] The violence done to the human figure in the work of contemporary body artists Orlan and Franko B is not a gratuitous or destructive violence, but, as Georges Didi-Huberman says of Bataille's montages of images, a *work* of violence, a planned, prepared, methodical process of challenging the anthropocentrism of figural art. According to Hollier,

> Anthropocentrism, indeed, represses dehumanizing and decentring excesses; it is committed to saving 'the world we live in', a world organized around the human subject, against the world of expenditure, which Bataille also calls 'the world we die in', 'a world for nobody, a world from which subjects have been evacuated, the world of the non-I'.[49]

The questioning of anthropocentrism through contemporary performance and carnal art can, as with the discourses of 'posthumanity' triggered by Jeffrey Deitch's 1992 exhibition *Posthuman*, contribute to the rethinking of human subjectivity that has become an urgent priority in recent cultural criticism and theory. Thinking Bataille's concept of expenditure (*la dépense*), for which, according to Hollier, 'matter' is 'just another name', 'means first of all thinking of a scene from which he [the subject] has been evacuated'.[50] The 'rediscovery' of Bataille's base materialism by Rosalind Krauss and others in art criticism of the 1990s corresponds to the increasingly bold and invasive exploration of the material body by contemporary artists. In surrealist art,

44. Ibid.

45. Ibid., p140.

46. Ibid., p141

47. See ibid., pp141-2 on how Bataille's practice of montage can be understood as 'symptom made theory'.

48. Hollier, 'The Dualist Materalism of Georges Bataille', op. cit., p68.

49. Ibid., p69.

50. Ibid., p68, p71

the dominant new anti-sublimatory feature was the use of unmediated real objects in paintings and collages. By the 1990s and early twenty-first century, and in line with the (arguable) decline of painting and rise of a variety of other media, bodily 'reality' has been drawn into experimental artistic practice, and the materialist work surrealist artists did in images and collages is to be found instead in performance and installation art.

SEXING THE ECONOMY

Patrick Brantlinger

Regenia Gagnier, *The Insatiability of Human Wants: Economics and Aesthetics in Market Society*, Chicago and London, University of Chicago Press, 2000; 264 pp; £10.50 paperback.

In one of her earlier books *Idylls of the Marketplace: Oscar Wilde and the Victorian Public* (1986), Regenia Gagnier demonstrated the complex, ironic relations between Wilde's brand of aestheticism and late-Victorian consumerism. Her most recent book *The Insatiability of Human Wants* offers a much broader and more ambitious historical analysis of the relations between economic and aesthetic discourses from the Enlightenment to the present. Her analysis functions in part as a critique especially of neoclassical economics, which, after the so-called marginalist revolution of the 1870s and 1880s, abandoned much of the social-critical dimension of earlier economic thinking.

Symptomatic of the transition of economics to a mathematised social science focused on marginal utility as the standard of value was William Stanley Jevons's rejection of the word 'political' from the earlier name for the discipline: 'political economy'. As Gagnier puts it, in contrast to earlier economic thinking from John Stuart Mill back to Adam Smith, neoclassical economics has entailed 'the decoupling ... of wealth and welfare' (32). It has also entailed the decoupling of conceptions of economic demand or desire from aesthetic taste. As Gagnier notes, a book like *Accounting for Tastes* by Nobel Prize economist Gary Becker is precisely not about taste in the sense of aesthetic discrimination. Instead, as do the other neoclassical economists, Becker treats the capitalist marketplace as a level playing field in which equally equipped or moneyed individual consumers make equally valid rational choices among goods and services. Aesthetics has no more to do with this model than do social class, gender, or race. Individuals' supposedly rational choices or preferences can be measured as economic demand, but cannot be interpreted or explained in aesthetic, ethical, or for that matter political terms.

In part, Gagnier wants to restore an aesthetic dimension to economics. In so arguing, she follows in the tradition of what she calls, echoing John Ruskin, 'the political economists of art'. Ruskin was one, and so were William Morris and Oscar Wilde. Although she indicates, as she did earlier in *Idylls of the Marketplace*, some of the formal and thematic parallels between marginalist (or emergent neoclassical) economics and late-Victorian aestheticism, which to many of its interpreters has seemed also characterised by the attempt, at least, to divorce art from social, political, and moral critique (as suggested by the slogan, 'art for art's sake'), she argues persuasively that, in part through its emphasis on taste, aestheticism retained a socially critical function that economics was losing. This was certainly the case with Ruskin and Morris (the latter was a Marxist after all, albeit a romantic one, and Ruskin has figured in several histories of British socialism). Wilde, too, penned 'The Soul of Man under Socialism,' which is at least half-serious about socialism as an alternative to capitalism.

The Insatiability of Human Wants almost functions as a history of alternatives to orthodox economics, at least in the British context. If it is not quite that, it is because Gagnier is just as interested in tracing representations and patterns of economic rationalisation, consumerism, desire, and aesthetic taste in nineteenth- and twentieth-century literature (as, for example, in her fascinating albeit brief analysis of Virginia Woolf's *Orlando*). She brings to life, however, such intriguing figures as William Thompson and Anna Wheeler, whose 1825 *Appeal of One Half of the Human Race, Women, Against the Pretensions of the Other Half, Men, to Retain Them in Political, and Thence in Civil and Domestic Slavery* expressed both an early version of radical feminism and Owenite socialism. As Gagnier notes, 'This example from the Owenite socialists indicates how multifariously' early nineteenth-century intellectuals 'contested the values of market society' (76). By no means do the alternatives to orthodox economics boil down to Marx and Engels. Among those usually categorised as orthodox, both Thomas Malthus and David Ricardo understood (in contrast to today's neoclassical economists) that there were limits to economic growth or the expansion of capitalism and industrial production. And John Stuart Mill, also ordinarily categorised as orthodox, shed both his father's strict utilitarianism and equally strict belief in the virtues of unrestricted free trade to become an advocate both of cooperative socialism and of feminism. As Gagnier points out, both Adam Smith and Mill feared that 'the social emotions of sympathy and altruism ... would be obliterated by market society' (67), the theme also of Charles Dickens's industrial novel *Hard Times*, with its insistence on the interdependence of ethics and aesthetics.

As itself a version of alternative economics (or of Ruskin's 'political economy of art'), *The Insatiability of Human Wants* points to the consequences of economic rationalisation and reification in our own time. Economists neglect 'the aesthetic dimension' at their and our peril. As Dickens insisted in *Hard Times*, a just and humane society must also be one that allows for the expression of imagination and the exercise of taste. 'If we are prepared to say that Marxism is dead,' Gagnier writes in the conclusion to her challenging analysis, 'and that Smith's sympathy and Mill's progressivism are discredited, are we also prepared to make the image of our future ... [Francis] Fukuyama's "infinitely diverse consumer culture" or Pater's "flood of external objects", or just the solipsistic individualism of "each mind keeping as a solitary prisoner its own dream of a world"?' (234). It is that last dessicated image from Pater that *homo economicus* seems to have been reduced to in our era of relentless downsizing, outsourcing, and transnational corporate greed.

It would be good if economists, and not just literary and cultural historians like myself, would read Gagnier's study of the complex historical intertwinings and 'decouplings' of 'economics and aesthetics in market society'. Most neoclassical economists seem to be uninterested in the history of their discipline. They seem even less interested in alternative versions of economic theory. As feminist economist Dianne Strassman remarks, 'dissent' in today's college and university economics departments 'is labelled not economics and is suppressed'. This is unfortunate. Without an understanding of and, indeed, respect for alternatives, the outcome is what Friedrich Nietzsche for one insisted is a thoroughly irrational fetishising of 'the factual' and of the status quo. Gagnier's study opens many intellectual windows, revealing both the rich diversity of alternatives - most of them related in one way or another to aesthetics - and the limits of marginalist and neoclassical economics. It is a book that all economists could benefit from reading; I am going to purchase additional copies to send to Gary Becker and, perhaps, to the Chairman of the US Federal Reserve, Allen Greenspan.

MOBILE HOMES

Tony Bennett

David Morley, *Home Territories: Media, Mobility and Identity*, London and New York, Routledge, 2000, 340pp; £14.99 paperback.

1. Didier Maleuvre, *Museum Memories: History, Technology, Art*, Stanford CA, Stanford University Press, 1999, pp119-20.

'A home,' Didier Maleuvre writes, 'is not simply a house. It is an image of how we dwell, how we inhabit the world, how we view ourselves in the world'.[1] The context for these remarks is Maleuvre's discussion of the nineteenth-century bourgeois interior. He suggests we should treat this as an anthropological document which, in telling us what it was like to dwell in the nineteenth century, also tells us what it was like to *be* in the nineteenth century. It tells us, as he puts it, 'about the ontological (and therefore

2. Ibid., p120.

sociological, psychological, historical) self-grounding of a particular society at a particular historical juncture'.[2] This is so, however, only provided that we know how to read the idealisation of the bourgeois interior as a compensation for the new forms of homelessness that were produced by the massive relocations of rural populations associated with the first wave of industrialisation. Far from supporting stable patterns of domesticity, industrialisation 'prohibits dwelling permanently' in the unending uprooting of labour that its development entails. 'Only in the midst of such dire homelessness', Maleuvre concludes, 'does the image of the snow-blanketed, thatched-roofed cottage, windows aglow with the promise of a warm hearth,

3. Ibid., p120.

have a sentimental appeal'.[3]

The perspective informing these remarks derives from Maleuvre's view that how the home is constructed - how it is organised, viewed, and represented - offers an insight into different social and cultural forms of accommodation to (after Heidegger) the essential uprootedness of human existence. This is also Morley's concern in *Home Territories*, but with the important qualification that his application of this perspective to the relations between homes and the intensified and geographically extended forms of labour mobility prevailing at the end of the twentieth century throws light on a vastly expanded repertoire of the relations between home and movement. And not least because, in Morley's analysis, homes themselves become mobile. Although, in much of the earlier literature, the home had been seen as always connected to movement - as a place from whence movement initiates and to which it returns - it has often been viewed as itself a fixed and stable point of reference, affected by movement but not in movement itself. Agnes Heller's influential account of the role of home in providing an ontological grounding for everyday life is a case in point. 'Integral to the average everyday life is awareness of a fixed point in space, a firm position from which we "proceed" (whether every day or over larger periods of time) and to which we return in due course. This firm position is what we call "home".[4] For Morley, by contrast, an adequate approach to the full range of contemporary practices of home, as these are defined in relation to increasingly international patterns of movement, requires a deterritorialisation of home. Stressing the need for 'a more plurilocal concept of home', he suggests that we need to think about home less as 'a singular physical entity fixed in a particular place' and more as 'a mobile, symbolic habitat, a performative way of life and of doing things in which one makes one's home while in movement' (46-7).

It is, however, more than the household as home that is at issue for Morley here. He also has his eye on the wider set of questions prompted by the relations between movement and home that arise from the broader currency of 'home' associated with its application to the territory of a region or nation, as well as that of household. To put the point more accurately, it is the cross-overs between these different meanings of home - and the ways in which these inform one another in the different practices of home that are caught up in the histories of immigration, of refugees and asylum seekers, and of varied diasporas - that concern him. His focus, as he summarises it, 'is thus on the mutually dependent processes of exclusion and identity construction, in relation to the domestic home, the neighbourhood and the nation as "spaces of belonging"' (p4). And the political horizon informing these concerns is provided by Morley's assessment of the need for a postmodern geography that will be able to connect what, following Foucault, he calls the 'little tactics of the habitat' to the 'grand strategies of geo-politics' (p3). He seeks to do this by examining the dialectic between practices of home, their link to processes of identity formation and their dependence on practices of othering and exclusion operating across reciprocally reinforcing boundaries of nations, ethnicities, regions, religions, cultures and civilisations. And it is to his credit that he avoids the metropolitan bias that is often associated with these concerns by encompassing the practices of home of indigenous populations who have been obliged to reach an accommodation with the invasive movement of others in the history of colonialism.

Home Territories is, as a result, nothing if not ambitious in the scale of its conception. Morley is, of course, no stranger to issues focused on the relations between home and nation. This was an important focus of his and Charlotte Brunsdon's study of *Nationwide*,[5] while the use of the media in domestic settings was the central concern of *Family Television*.[6] The legacy of these earlier areas of work is evident in the attention he gives to the shifting relations between the media and practices of home (understood in their relations to domestic, national and regional territorialisations), especially insofar as these concern the changing dynamics of gender, both within the household and in relation to the varied gendered forms in which the nation-as-home is imagined. There is, though, also a significant broadening of Morley's focus as his discussion encompasses these issues in a wide range of

4. Agnes Heller, *Everyday Life*, London, Routledge and Kegan Paul, 1984, p239.

5. Charlotte Brunsdon and David Morley, *Everyday Television: Nationwide*, London, British Film Institute, 1979.

6. David Morley, *Family Television: Cultural Power and Domestic Leisure*, London, Comedia, 1986.

national contexts and, in the process, brings questions of ethnicity fully into play alongside those of gender and class. It is, however, Morley's insertion of this wider set of relations between the media and the formation of identities within a nuanced account of the relations between travel and dwelling in a world of fluid and changing boundaries that delivers a reach to match the ambition of his enterprise. For this allows him to connect his specific concerns to the more general re-orientations of contemporary social theory evident in the stress now placed on mobilities, borders and boundaries.

Home Territories is, in these respects, a book of its times, with - for me - a couple of general features that are especially valuable.[7] The first is the sense of theoretical and political balance that informs Morley's discussion throughout the book. If anxious to press the case for rethinking the home - as household and, metaphorically, as nation - from the point of view of new theories of travel, he is careful not to press that case too far. His discussion of the mobile practices of home that are evident in some diasporic formations thus does not result in any neglect of the senses in which, for many caught up in histories of travel, home remains elsewhere, serving as a place of origin and a place of imagined return and final rest. Nor does Morley fall into the trap of valorising movement over stasis: he is as robust in his criticisms of uncritical celebrations of cosmopolitanism as he is in his rebuttal of the tendency to latch diaspora theory onto standpoint epistemology as a means of generating - in the figure of the nomad - yet another in a long line of epistemologically privileged social positions. And if he rightly stresses the greater fluidity of borders that characterises some contexts - inter-state mobility within Europe, for example - he is careful to point to the emergence of new borders and boundaries in the phenomenon of 'white flight' and the emergence of gated communities, while also noting the contradictions between the putatively 'free air' rhetoric of globalisation and the increased policing of international boundaries that is evident in 'First-World' responses to the current refugee crisis.

It is also an extraordinarily accessible book. As I have already indicated, there are few concerns in contemporary social and cultural thought that *Home Territories* does not engage with. The politics of difference, Europe and its others, the changing forms of the city, the changing relations of space and time characterising postmodern geographies, the contested politics of diaspora, changing conceptions of citizenship: all of these are among the issues that Morley factors into his account of the changing and varied experience of being 'at home' in the modern world. But his mode of engagement with these issues is always concrete and vividly illustrated, allowing the reader to hook into and connect with a wide range of debates through the thread of home that connects them. And, in the extensive literature he draws on and quotes from, Morley has a good eye for the arresting image that will help drive his point home. Adorno's persistence in using German as a means of preserving some sense of home during his

7. There is much interesting common ground between *Home Territories* and John Urry, *Sociology Beyond Societies: Mobilities for the Twenty-first Century*, London and New York, Routledge, 2000 (reviewed in *new formations* no. 43).

exile in the United States (47); James Joyce's reference to his wife Nora as his 'portable Ireland' - his 'home away from home' - as a telling abbreviation of the gendered associations of home (65); and the Barbadian flag stuck to the door of an immigrant family's home to establish the boundary which said that 'whenever we entered the house we were not English - we were in Barbados and would behave accordingly' (Gary Younge, cited p52) are all examples of what I have in mind here.

That said, it's also true that Morley quotes too much and too often, so that his discussion often has the feel of a literature review. He rarely makes a point without putting it in someone else's name - which, while an eloquent tribute to his modesty, is a shame, for when he speaks in his own voice he is usually worth listening to. And, to complete my list of gripes, each chapter has too many sections, dividing the reader's attention between too many discrete issues at the price of some loss of flow and direction in the development of the argument. But, viewed in the round, *Home Territories* is a major accomplishment - and a very good read.

Philosophy Reflecting Culture

David Cunningham

Peter Osborne, *Philosophy in Cultural Theory*, Routledge, London and New York, 2000, 146pp; £40.00 cloth, £12.99 paperback.

In his *Introductory Lectures on Aesthetics*, Hegel marks a division within the modes of 'scientific consideration' applied to the subject of art, 'each of which appears to exclude the other, and so to hinder us from arriving at *any true result*'. On the one hand, he writes,

> we see the science of art merely, so to speak, busying itself about the actual productions of art from the outside, arranging them in series as a history of art ... or sketching out theories intended to provide the general points of view that are to govern both criticism and artistic production. On the other side we see science abandoning itself independently to reflection upon the beautiful, and producing mere generalities which do not touch the work in its peculiarity.

Few have been convinced by Hegel's own philosophical reconciliation of 'metaphysical universality with the determinateness of real particularity'.[1] Yet this unsatisfactory split between the torn halves of 'empirical method' and 'abstract reflection' has continued to trouble all post-Hegelian philosophies of art and culture. In the draft introduction to *Aesthetic Theory*, for example, Adorno refers to the seeming 'obsolescence of aesthetics', its 'antiquated quality' in the light of its continuing attachment to 'a universality that culminates in inadequacy to ... artworks'. With this situation, Adorno argues, the theorist finds herself caught in the 'miserable alternative' between a 'dumb and trivial universality', which reduces particularity to the mere 'status of exempla', and a slippage into the arbitrariness of a 'radical nominalism' which characterises the hegemonic practices of art and literary history.[2]

Despite the rather patchy influence of Adorno's own difficult brand of *Kulturkritik* on contemporary thought, if anything this 'situation' seems even more acutely our own today, particularly in relation to an 'Anglo-American' context in which philosophy is, for the most part, still governed by the narrow perspective of what Quine called a 'logical point of view'. It is of course true that the apparent chasm between the 'abstract' transcendentalism of philosophical aesthetics (such as it is) and the 'concrete' empiricism of cultural, literary and art historicism (self-styledly 'new' in character or otherwise) has in recent decades been seen as bridgeable through something called 'theory', taking its central terms from Continental 'post-structuralist'

1. G.W.F. Hegel, *Introductory Lectures on Aesthetics*, Bernard Bosanquet (trans), Michael Inwood (ed), Harmondsworth, Penguin, 1993, pp17, 25-6.

2. Theodor Adorno, *Aesthetic Theory*, Robert Hullot-Kentor (trans), London , Athlone, 1997, pp332-3, 343.

philosophy, psychoanalysis, or certain strands of Western Marxism. In practice, however, these alternate theoretical vocabularies have tended to be engaged only as a means of recasting them as decontextualised 'sources' either for standardised interpretative models - the 'general points of view' of which Hegel writes - or, even more commonly, for new 'objects' or 'thematics' of empirico-historicist enquiry ('the body', 'writing', 'desire' etc.). To the extent that such approaches are *themselves* theorised, it is in terms of the increasingly tired metaphorics of *bricolage* or - that most persistent cliché of contemporary positivisms - the critical 'toolbox'.

If traditional aesthetics has indeed become obsolete, one of the beneficiaries of its demise has undoubtedly been cultural studies, which, as Peter Osborne notes in his excellent new book, has partially defined itself through an 'antipathy' to 'anything connected to "aesthetics"' (30), positioning itself, more generally, as 'one of philosophy's most stridently *non*-philosophical - indeed, proudly "post-philosophical" - others' (2). Such antipathy has not, it should be said, been without its justifications - an understandable suspicion of dehistoricising generalisation and lofty abstraction - but it has itself risked giving way, as Hegel also recognised, to reliance upon 'abstract principles and categories ... without being aware of it', resulting in an *unreflective* philosophy which is placed beyond critical interrogation.[3]

3. Hegel, *Introductory Lectures on Aesthetics*, op. cit., p24.

It is in this context that the importance of Osborne's book reveals itself. For the ambiguity of its title reflects the dual task involved in any demand to reconfigure the relationship between the disciplinary 'fields' of philosophy and cultural theory today, insofar as the critical role of philosophy *in* cultural theory may be read both as an 'interpretation' of the philosophy which already (consciously or otherwise) underwrites 'really existing' cultural studies, and as a more directly interventionist 'critique' of that unreflective philosophy, from the point of view of more explicitly articulated alternatives (chiefly, here, the thought of Benjamin and Peirce). At the same time - lest this be thought to be a question of philosophy merely correcting the misapprehensions of a slightly simple-minded younger cousin - such a project must also, Osborne argues, entail a rethinking of the historical character of 'philosophy' itself as a cultural form, and of the 'legitimate range of application' of its concepts.

Osborne's setting out of the 'task to which the essays in this book aim to contribute' (19) may therefore, on the basis of his argument in the eponymous first chapter, be divided into two parts. First, an account of the implicit philosophical underpinnings of cultural studies as it evolved from the 1960s; most crucially, its roots in Marxism, which appears here as the 'vanishing mediator' in its disciplinary formation, and (more contentiously) a developing conception (or at least 'attitude') of 'pragmatism' as that which constitutes the 'philosophical unconscious of post-Marxist cultural studies' (p9). Second, a rethinking of what might be the most productive role for philosophy itself as a kind of 'anti-disciplinary specialism, excessive in relation to each and every disciplinary field, yet without a determinate field of its own' (p6). The meeting point for these two strands lies in the exploration of those specific kinds of concept which might be seen to belong to a 'cross-disciplinary type of generality' necessarily straddling the domains of both philosophy and cultural theory. As explored in the other six essays of the book, such concepts include 'sign', 'image', 'modernism', 'modernity', 'art', and (in the final chapter on Laplanche) a range of psychoanalytic categories.

For those who have read Osborne's 1995 book, *The Politics of Time*, the most familiar work here will be that on the concepts of 'modernism' and 'modernity' elaborated in the three central chapters of this collection. Extending the analyses of the political significance of particular conceptual forms of historical temporalisation carried out in that earlier work, Osborne develops a persuasive account of modernism as a term whose most fundamental meaning is limited to neither a literary/art period style nor a philosophical 'discourse' (in Habermas's sense), but which 'displays the universality of a philosophical concept ... in its transcendental or quasi-categorial status as a temporal form' (57). It is the distinctive character of this 'universality' which generates its significance for a rethinking of cultural theory in general. For, as Osborne states, it is a peculiarity of the 'general concepts of cultural theory'- particularly when they are extended or 'translated' beyond the restricted spatial ground of the nation-state - that they apparently 'have the universality of the *categorial* in the Kantian sense ... [but] are nonetheless "historical" in the sense that their universality has historical conditions of existence' (18). Thus a focus upon the concept of modernism 'raises in a particular instance the general question of the relationship of philosophical to historical form' (58). The implicit *promise* here is that of marking out a passage beyond the kind of 'miserable alternative' Adorno locates in the torn halves of traditional aesthetics and art history.

To a large extent Osborne makes good on this promise, or at least he shows the path which future work might take in this respect. This is not to say that there are not several arguments here with which one might take issue. Deleuzians will no doubt find much to question in the rather hasty critique of their master in the second chapter entitled 'Sign and Image'. Derrideans, meanwhile, would have good reason to dispute the claim - in the context of a welcome re-reading of Peirce *contra* Saussure - that *différance* is little more than a 'refinement' of the Saussurean semiotic 'paradigm' (22-3). (Surely the Heidegger of *Identity and Difference* is at least as important a precursor, if not more so. Typically, however, Osborne's writing does seem to be governed by a regulative principle of being as hard on Derrida as possible, sometimes to the point of misleading simplifications - as in his comments on *Specters of Marx*). Yet, none of this should distract from his achievement in outlining plausible theoretical criteria for the construction and philosophical mediation of concepts which would be 'analytically adequate to action on a par with the educational-political project from which cultural studies set out' (16).

Osborne's own philosophical master in this is - explicitly enough - Walter Benjamin, who, as he says, 'sets the theoretical course, with his concern for the conjointly historical, metaphysical and political experience of cultural form' (ix). Fascinating as is the attempt to use Peirce's respective theories of 'pragmatism' and the 'sign' to bridge the division between 'Continental' and 'Anglo-American' thought, it is finally Benjamin's conceptions of the 'messianic' - as 'the practical moment of Benjamin's thought' - and of the 'image-space' that provide the crucial models for Osborne's delineation of both philosophy and cultural theory's potential as 'speculative anti- and cross-disciplinary specialisms'. Such potential is demonstrated in Osborne's own engagements with particular problematics in cultural studies and art theory. If there is any criticism to be made here it is only, I suppose, in terms of the limitations of his choice of topics. In the preface, while recognising that 'for a certain German tradition, philosophy simply *is* the ideal reflexive form of modern culture as a whole', he rightly criticises this tradition's somewhat Arnoldian conception of what 'culture' in this instance might mean, excluding as it does 'vast bodies of significant practice and experience within Western capitalist societies' as well as non-Western cultural forms (viii). Yet, one might argue, Osborne's own focus, (however brilliant his individual readings might be), is itself directed upon a rather restricted cultural terrain: Greenberg, conceptual art, the *Communist Party Manifesto*. That said, more important is the fact that Osborne provides - in, for example, his reworking of the concept of modernism or (in his discussion of photography) of the relation of image to text - the basis for an extension of theory, without loss of philosophical sophistication, into areas of cultural practice that Critical Theory characteristically ignored. More than anything, perhaps, the value of this book lies in its impetus for work to come, demanding of both philosophers and cultural theorists that they finally take as their true object of analysis 'cultural *experience* in the full sense of the term' (118). It is for this reason that *Philosophy in Cultural Theory* seems to me to be such an important and timely book.

THE SERIOUS PLAY OF CONSPIRACY

Clare Birchall

Peter Knight, *Conspiracy Culture: From Kennedy to The X-Files*, London, Routledge, 2000, 287pp; £45.00 hardback, £12.99 paperback.

Martin Waller in *The Times* recently reported a conspiracy theory doing the rounds: 'The first signs of foot-and-mouth can be dated to a short time after we last bombed Iraq. It was, as was reported at the time, a Middle Eastern strain. And which rogue state is most advanced in biological warfare?' Waller is quick to point out that he '[does] not vouch for this one, but at least you read it here first'.[1] Although Waller's reportage is tongue-in-cheek, the theory does bring to the surface a Western fear of Middle Eastern military capability. And therein lies conspiracy theory's paradoxical significance: it entertains us, to be sure, but repeats back, through a certain suggestibility, something we recognise as our own. The cultural circuit of conspiracy theory is at work.

1. Martin Waller, 'City Diary,' *The Times*, Thursday, 22.03.01.

Peter Knight's *Conspiracy Culture* marks a significant contribution to the growing research into conspiracy theory. Knight situates conspiracy theory within its socio-historic context (from 1960s countercultural interest to today's ironic and demotic use of it), while reading it at a close textual level. In this way, he manages both to introduce and interrogate the rhetorical manoeuvres utilised by this form of popular knowledge.

As introduction and interrogation, *Conspiracy Culture* caters to a variety of readers familiar or otherwise with the research. As with any academic specialism, conspiracy studies has its seminal texts, and Knight is as careful to point towards these as he is to position the conspiracy theories themselves within their socio-historic framework. Key voices include the progressive historian Richard Hofstadter, who analysed the Right's employment of a paranoid rhetoric. Other historians such as Bernard Bailyn suggested that conspiracy theory had played a major role in the founding of the American Republic and national identity. Novelists such as Don DeLillo, Thomas Pynchon and Ishmael Reed responded creatively to the register of conspiracy theory and paranoia that they observed around them, and influenced the concerns of a whole area of literary study. John Fiske highlighted the positive role of popular knowledges in the articulation of power and privilege differentials between the upper echelons and the working class. Fredric Jameson suggested ways of thinking about conspiracy narratives as attempts to represent or map out the ever elusive social totality. More recently, there have been arguments by Daniel Pipes, Elaine Showalter, Robert Robins and Jerrold Post that seek to warn us against the dangers of conspiracy thinking.

Indeed, conspiracy theory offers an object of interest for many different disciplines. It has been lauded as subversive social formation, and criticised as failed intervention into the political sphere. Both tendencies, as Knight recognises, assess conspiracy theory against an ideal of political action. Knight explains how many cultural studies approaches 'end up insisting that other (usually less sophisticated) people's everyday cultural practices fulfil one's own political agenda - and then chastising them for failing at what they never intended in the first place' (21). Like conspiracy theory itself, the academic study of conspiracy theory has been used and abused to various political ends.

More interesting is how conspiracy theory exceeds or complicates this (either positive or negative) narrowly defined political interest in popular practices and texts. For conspiracy theory appears (to varying degrees in different contexts) *both* politically engaged *and* deeply ineffectual in the realm of democratic politics. Knight relates this apparently contradictory status to the way in which conspiracy theory is employed in both an ironic and earnest fashion. In this way, conspiracy theory is characterised by a continual oscillation between the figural and the literal. Because the effects of institutionalised racism, for example, make it look *as if* there has been a conspiracy, exactly how these theories are being invoked by African-American communities becomes undecidable. Do such conspiracy theories refer to actual conspiracies or merely something *like* conspiracy?

Knight has an eye for cultural movements and discursive moments - for the way in which tropes substantiate a socio-political climate. He is careful not to get bogged down in the details of specific conspiracy theories, although he provides enough of an outline to convey the playfulness and passion of these vivid narratives. He also avoids the trap of attempting to correct conspiracy theory's 'mistakes'. What commands Knight's interest, rather, are firstly a diachronic movement from 'secure' to 'insecure' paranoia that has apparently taken place over the past half century, and secondly a synchronic play between the literal and the figural in conspiracy theory. With reference to DeLillo's *Underworld*, Knight writes of 'the relatively secure paranoia of the Cold War years, through the countercultural hopes of the 1960s and after, and into the as yet unconfigured work of insecure paranoia beyond the end of the Cold War' (226). Insecure paranoia emerges alongside the vertigo of interpretation or an overriding structure of connectedness inherent in contemporary economic and technological encounters. *Underworld's* mantra, 'everything is connected', becomes the guiding logic of conspiracy culture, but it also suggests something about contemporary experience in general. Knight advises us to read this movement from secure to insecure paranoia in economic terms: we should interpret the anxiety produced by this movement as prompted equally by a 'loss of a sense of control over national ... economic destiny that previously allowed governments to guarantee the social contract between the state, capital, and labor' (235). However, Knight falls short of a totalising theory of conspiracy theory, stressing instead how it performs different functions in different situations (for example, it could be used as a way to understand institutional sexism or racism in one context, and as the glue that holds America together in another).

Knight has well-researched chapters on the Kennedy assassination, the trope of conspiracy in popular and academic feminism, paranoia in African-American communities, the role of conspiracy theories in body panics (especially AIDS and food scares), and technologies and theories of connectedness in late capitalism. A range of media is addressed throughout this study, along with a number of key events and texts in the underground and mainstream histories of conspiracy theory. Occasionally, Knight has to skim over complex issues and texts (such as conspiracy thinking in rap music), but the benefits which accrue from an all-encompassing study outweigh the detrimental effects of a lack of detail. His footnotes are generous too, pointing us to other interesting studies in the field.

Occasionally, his desire to present a genealogical shift in conspiracy thinking (such as his overriding schema from secure to insecure paranoia, or what he calls 'the secret history of conspiracy culture') appears too neat. Just as there is an oscillation between ironic and earnest elements of conspiracy theory, or between its figural and literal status (as Knight points out), post-fordist, postmodern paranoia operates in other ways as well - for example, as *a play between* secure and insecure paranoia, or even involving a third term such as solipsism - an internally assured knowledge system that has nothing to do with our relation to outside structures; or countless other terms that those nominal positions might not encompass. In fact, a different model altogether might be in play, one that traces the conditions of possibility of conspiracy, paranoia, etc., back to a prior, generative agency of discourse and knowledge. In this view one moves away from Knight's 'genealogical' view to an atemporal, though equally political, approach. Nevertheless, Knight's identification of a definite shift in paranoia as both thought-structure and trope in the light of post-Cold War politics, post-fordist models of production, and globalised commerce, does help to account for the unprecedented popularity of conspiracy theory that we have seen at the turn of the century.

Perhaps the least interesting thing to say about conspiracy theory is that it signals an aberration in an otherwise functional code of interpretation (such a position has been put forward in one guise or another by commentators including Elaine Showalter and Umberto Eco). This only serves to pathologise conspiracy theorists, ignoring the relationship we all have to such structures of interpretation - and for his part Knight recognises too the common structure of connectedness between legitimate and 'illegitimate' discourses: 'Everything Is Connected could function as the operating principle not just for conspiracy theory, but also for epidemiology, ecology, risk theory, systems theory, complexity theory, theories of globalization, boosterism for the Internet, and even poststructuralist literary theories about intertextuality' (205). In my view, what is critical when thinking about conspiracy theory is to recognise the way it puts on display a general condition of reading. Once we recognise how conspiracy theory (or 'overinterpretation' as Umberto Eco terms it) shares characteristics with - and even structures - the idea or possibility of an accepted paradigm of interpretation (what, we might ask, would interpretation be without the idea of overinterpretation?), many other ways of writing about conspiracy theory in an academic sphere suddenly become particularly precarious.

Those studies that want to decry the presence of conspiracy theorists as a symptom of an individual and social ailment fail to take on board the relationship between the conditions on which their own statements depend and the discourse they wish to denigrate. Conspiracy theory perfectly highlights the value of cultural studies at its best, when it analyses both the institutional anxiety that attends popular phenomena and the social significance of those phenomena themselves. Knight's book is an impressive attempt at coming to terms with the significance of a discourse that plays with the limits of textuality - how conspiracy narratives work on a figural and literal level simultaneously. That this is precisely why it becomes such a problematic discourse in the everyday realm points towards the problem of how to read cultural phenomena at all (and consequently the anxieties produced by disciplines, such as cultural studies, that draw on a range of methodologies). In considering textual effects, *Conspiracy Culture* loses nothing of the socio-political significance of conspiracy theory. In fact, the textual comes centre stage in order to comment on a shift in interpretative practices. The cognitive subject is not incidental to this process, but our access to him or her derives from the textual effects he or she produces, rather than any psychological state that creates those texts. Pathologising falls away.

When, on occasion, my own research into the subject of conspiracy theory has been frostily received, I have wanted a book such as this in order to justify my enquiry. This might make it sound like the groundwork I didn't want to do myself. This is not the case. Knight has a particular American Studies angle on a phenomenon that can support many methodologies and approaches from various disciplines. While his is not the only approach, it is certainly a much needed one if we are to make headway in assessing the confrontation between 'legitimate' or official and 'illegitimate' or popular knowledges.

DANCING WITH REFLECTION

Bob Bennett

Valerie A. Briginshaw, *Dance, Space and Subjectivity*, Basingstoke and New York, Palgrave, 2001; 233pp. £45 hardback.

In Britain, Valerie Briginshaw and Ramsay Burt have maintained the vibrancy of the New Dance movement in scholarship after its collective commitments to the *New Dance* periodical - a movement which poignantly addressed issues related to gender and sexuality. Latterly Burt edited the journal, then went on to write *The Male Dancer* (1995); and now Briginshaw has produced *Dance, Space and Subjectivity*.

As her rather plodding introduction makes clear, Briginshaw is no less committed today to issues related to gender, sexuality and race than she was in those heady days of post-1960s fervour. She might be forgiven for having taken on the stateside, postmodern-inflected vocabulary of New York's Judson Dance Theatre, but this has involved her overlooking its British equivalences in 'New Dance'.

That introduction gives us a false sense that we are heading for a mix and match of 'dances' (by which Briginshaw indicates choreographed performance events) with contemporary cultural theorists. In the chapters that follow comment abounds, interweaving the case for engagement in a kinaesthesia of tactility - a 'proprioception' - with theoretical reflection. Take for instance the following, from a chapter on 'Dance that can be Read as Lesbian': 'Desire can be seen to be spatialised differently. This different spatialisation is not based on lack, or space seen as distance, but rather on surfaces, intensities, interfaces and touching' (80).

'Dance' and dance scholarship in Britain, however, are the product of a higher educational system which placed the physicality of the arts subordinately, and has only lately, and begrudgingly, admitted writing about dance into its canon. Briginshaw's book serves well those of us who are educators, and who want our performing arts students to understand what cultural theory has to do with their 'creative' projects.

In the last decade, writing about dance from North America has overtaken the liveliness of the New Dance engagements in Britain, despite the kickstart of Angela McRobbie's brilliant 'Dance and Social Fantasy'. McRobbie's 1984 essay, originally published in *Gender and Generation*, theorised dance as 'the one pleasurable arena where women have some control and know what is going on in relation to physical sensuality and to their own bodies'.

Dance was much less regulated in North America through dedicated institutions, and thus has been more generally positioned, particularly in state/provincial universities. For this reason, perhaps, it is instructive to read

Briginshaw alongside Marta Savigliano's *Tango and the Political Economy of Passion* (1995, Westview). Where Briginshaw labours to make explicit how theory is related to dance - that sense of having to justify dance as academically worthwhile - and in doing so, for instance, takes on postmodernity somewhat uncritically, Savigliano blasts away at postmodernity's coldness and distancing, showing it to be inadequate for nuancing the passion of tango, say. She demands of her readers that they realise what being placed with a remit for 'autoexoticism' might mean in the lives of Argentinians subordinated to Northern European/North American hegemonies.

Savigliano remains the only dance scholar to have produced a sustained and coherent book-length argument for a 'whole life' engagement with dance as the basis for wide political and cultural reflection. Briefer but equally intense articles in edited volumes, especially from the States, are now rapidly accumulating (Jane Desmond's recent *Dancing Desires: Choreographing Sexualities On and Off the Stage* being an excellent example), and the news of a new journal edited by Susan Leigh Foster and Ramsay Burt, *Discourses in Dance*, bodes well for dance scholarship becoming much more critically adventuresome.

There is the possibility of an explosion in dance writing of the quality of Savigliano's in Britain, too. McRobbie continues to produce occasional essays on dance and popular culture. Why not a volume commensurate with Briginshaw's which brings these essays together and reinstates the primacy of that 1984 essay referred to above? Maria Pini incorporates ethnographies of ravers into a dynamic of what space might mean to the subjectivities of young women in *Club Cultures and Female Subjectivity* (Palgrave 2001). As someone who has collected well over a thousand 'dancing' memories from students during the past ten years, I know there is a wealth of reflection to come from sustained work in this area. To return to Briginshaw, for women the refiguring of desire within that distance can take place not only on the stage or in the studio but also in the ravers' field or on the club dance floor. Mirroring and response as danced by women in these spaces has a long tradition and needs to be honoured as such.

DIFFERENCE: SPORTS THEORY AND STRUCTURAL TRANSFORMATION

Grant Farred

Ben Carrington and Ian McDonald (eds), *'Race', Sport and British Society*, London, Routledge, 2001, 256pp; £55.00 hardback, £16.99 paperback.

The effects of racism have impacted upon every aspect of black (African, Afro-Caribbean) and brown (South Asian) life in post-imperial Britain. From campaigns against racist policing to protests against prejudicial housing and educational policies, diasporic communities in different parts of Britain have struggled to obtain redress against the state - or local government structures. Like any other sphere of minority life in London or Glasgow, sport has not been immune to racist practices and, like many cultural struggles, it has seen the rise of popular anti-racist movements. The major sports - football and cricket - have, over the last three decades, seen the founding of 'Kick it Out' and 'Hit Racism for a Six' respectively, both multi-racial organisations publicly committed to identifying, attacking, and eradicating racism from the playing field, from amongst the spectators, and from the media.

Ben Carrington and Ian McDonald's *'Race', Sport and British Society* is a thoughtful collection of essays. It is a timely contribution to a growing discipline which explores the difficult, frequently unarticulated relationship between sport, race and the nation - sport seen, as the editors and some of the contributors suggest, as the enunciation of a (nostalgically) raced national identity. (These loaded conjunctures are taken up most directly in the essay by Les Back et al on the notoriously racist history of Millwall F.C.) Conceived as an attempt to determine how sport creates, shapes, and informs the public's perceptions of race and racism, *'Race', Sport and British Society* is also a critique of a conspicuous absence in British sociology: a theoretical paradigm which could initiate and sustain a rigorous investigation into the connection between racism and sport, a disciplinary framework which could simultaneously offer itself as an intervention into the day-to-day machinations of sports organisation. Carrington and McDonald want to 'advance the debate about "race" and sport within sociology itself to a more self-reflexive critical positioning' (13). Revealing their transformative political vision, the editors also want *'Race', Sport and British Society* to participate in the process of procuring structural transformation. They want to produce a praxis out of critical sports race sociological theory: 'we hope that this book will contribute to an emerging policy focus on tackling racial inequality amongst sport governing bodies'.

The second of the book's goals, the production of programmatic suggestions that would allow for structural reform, is a project not always kept in view by the various contributors. This is an understandable lack, since the range of essays offers a rich account of the variegated experiences of racism in British sport that would require an expansive, reflexive paradigm to accommodate the nation's several articulations of discrimination and prejudice against people of colour, women, and different ethnicities and religions.

In their essay on football 'north of the border', Paul Dimeo and Gerry Finn provide a convincing refutation of Scottish 'exceptionalism' (racism is exclusively English, Scottish sectarianism does not equal racism), while Sheila Scraton calls for an engagement with other (mainly literary) black feminist theories in order to rethink sport sociology's inattention to the role of black women, and in the process offers a useful suggestion for enriching and recalibrating one discipline through the history of another. Scott Fleming and Sanjiev Johal raise the important and under-researched issue of sport in the South Asian community, in essays sharpened by their willingness to confront the demeaning, historically inaccurate public images of the role sport plays for subcontinentals. Carrington and McDonald's contribution on 'recreational cricket', as direct a challenge as any in the collection to the notion of post-imperial white ownership of a sport that has long since been claimed and remade by black and brown ex-colonials (both in the metropolis and abroad), is the best of three chapters on the game. (Mike Marqusee's and Chris Searle's are too anecdotal to offer much in the way of theoretical insight, a shortcoming shared by Emma Lindsey's essay on the condition of being a black, feminist journalist.)

'Race', Sport and British Society, however, is less wanting in terms of structural suggestions than it is cognisant of the deeply embedded nature of racism in British sport. This text calls for a polyvocal, multi-accentual paradigm in which race theory (so necessary to rethinking sport's sociology), will be attentive to the specificities of context and will be applied strategically and selectively.

All sport racism may be equal, but one theory will fit neither all sport's codes nor all experiences. It is for this reason that the collection's structural lack is not so much a conceptual shortcoming as a recognition, albeit an unacknowledged one, that different racisms call for particularised responses. The recreational cricketers in Yorkshire and the female Muslim *kabbadi* players in London all experience discrimination and racism; they are all denied access to equal facilities, but their encounters with racism require that they make their different demands on the state, or the local governing authority, if they are to transform their sporting lives. It is by bringing difference into such keen focus that 'Race', Sport and British Society is most likely to produce both a racially conscious discourse in sociology and improved conditions for the various communities its contributors champion.

READING IMPERIALISM: COMPLEXITY VS HYBRIDITY

Carolyn Burdett

Laura Chrisman, *Rereading the Imperial Romance: British Imperialism and South African Resistance in Haggard, Schreiner and Plaatje*, Oxford, Clarendon, 2000; 241pp, £40 hardback.

Chilling accounts of the twenty-first-century death of the humanities monograph are a not uncommon feature of academic publishing gossip. It is reassuring, therefore, to find a work such as Laura Chrisman's appearing in the Oxford English Monographs series. Consisting of extensive readings of four fictional texts, three of which are not well known, authored by three interestingly marginal writers, this is a scholarly study which brings together writing on South Africa in a new and distinctive way. It is committed, as the book's final phrase has it, to 'historically specific' readings of its selected fictions and of the late-nineteenth and early-twentieth-century imperial contexts with which they engage. This detailed work aims to exemplify a number of theoretical issues explicitly addressed in the book's introduction.

These issues are ones that have been raised before in Chrisman's shorter criticism, and they concern the dominance, at least through the 1980s and part of the 1990s, of certain practices and assumptions associated with 'the postcolonial theory industry' which she wishes to counter. An over-exclusive focus on India and mid-Victorian missionary ideology as the paradigmatic sites of imperialism, associated with the work of Gayatri Spivak, for example, must be resisted in order to understand the 'stubbornly local' writing of Rider Haggard's *Nada the Lily* or Olive Schreiner's *Trooper Peter Halket of Mashonaland*. Similarly, Edward Said is taken to task for seeing 'the imperial metropolis as unified', while overused postcolonial concepts such as mimicry and hybridity are rejected as inadequate tools with which to understand the complex rewriting of the imperial romance undertaken in Sol Plaatje's *Mhudi*. Chrisman's theoretical friends here are the Frankfurt School writers, particularly the Adorno and Horkheimer of *Dialectic of Enlightenment*, and Hannah Arendt. Thus the introduction serves as a commentary on where theoretical postcolonial studies might be going, while much of the book's strength lies in its preparedness to allow this theoretical argument to be exemplified via the detailed readings in which it is engaged.

In a book about the imperial romance it is perhaps no surprise that the writer who occupies most space is Rider Haggard, 'King Romance' of the Age of Empire. Haggard has attracted a good deal of critical attention in recent years, and Chrisman uses the novel which made his name, *King Solomon's Mines*, to explore the emergence of gold and diamond mining in

South Africa. A more compelling illustration of the aim to historicise imperialism comes, however, when she turns to a much lesser-known work, *Nada the Lily*, Haggard's fictionalised account of the rise and fall of the Zulu nation, written during 1889-90 just after the British annexation of Zululand. Read in conjunction with Haggard's 1881, pre-annexation commentary on South African affairs, *Cetywayo and His White Neighbours*, Chrisman explores the fraught metropolitan response to the Zulu nation across the decade during which the conquest of Zululand takes place. Haggard's attempt to write Britain out of responsibility for the demise of the Zulu kingdom in *Nada* is central to Chrisman's assessment and critique of his 'contradictory but ultimately affirmative imperialist articulations' (20).

Haggard knew and admired Olive Schreiner, and Schreiner herself was friendly with Sol Plaatje. Chrisman's book in fact suggests a whole web of subtle connections between her three writers as she uses their fictions to explore 'important moments of South African transformation' (4). The two chapters dealing with *Trooper Peter Halket of Mashonaland* - which provide the fullest critical treatment yet published of this extraordinary 1897 novella - concern Schreiner's attempt to intervene in and halt the rapacious colonising activities of Cecil Rhodes during the violent making of Rhodesia. Schreiner was a writer all too keenly aware of the importance of audience, and Chrisman's subtle reading of *Trooper Peter*'s rhetorical strategy produces a nuanced and intelligent account of Schreiner's humanitarian and radical position. The historical sharpness here also means that Chrisman corrects critical assessments of Schreiner which see her as an apologist for white liberalism, pointing out rightly that neither English nor South African liberalism 'was at this time readily reducible to a single, identifiable, belief system or practice' (125). Similarly, Chrisman's sustained reading of Sol Plaatje's *Mhudi* uncovers a far more complex and dynamic picture than is often associated with the early black nationalists in South Africa. *Mhudi* 'dramatically revises, and critiques, the imperialist textual politics of *Nada*' (163), producing a proto-nationalism in which the central character of Mhudi herself is an active, self-affirming agent. For Plaatje, there is no 'escape' from history into a mythic past.

The chronology of these chapters clearly echoes a move from the 'imperialism' of Chrisman's sub-title, towards 'South African resistance', with consequent implications about the villains and heroes of the book. *Mhudi* in particular emerges as an extraordinarily positive portrait of a 'constitutively multiple' understanding of nation and its 'diverse ethnic, gender, and political implications' (208). This affirmative reading works so well, however, because Chrisman is scrupulous in interrogating all the texts with which she is concerned at their strongest and most complex points.

BECOMING STUART

Jeremy Gilbert

Paul Gilroy, Lawrence Grossberg and Angela McRobbie (eds), *Without Guarantees: In Honour of Stuart Hall*, London, Verso, 2000, 433pp; £17 paperback, £45 hardback.

Stuart Hall: the most public and yet the most enigmatic intellectual of the British left in recent decades. Admired far and wide, many things to many people, this man, whose only single-authored book is a relatively overlooked collection of political essays, seems at times to be famous largely just for 'being Stuart'. A leading theorist who has always made explicit his own distaste for theoretical systematisation, he still has not offered us, three years after his retirement from the chair in Sociology at the Open University, any system which bears his name, any coherent way of nailing him down, any hostage to posterity's modish cruelties. A speaker, an essayist, an editor, a mentor - but never a writer of Big Books - it is ironic that his retirement should be the occasion for one of the biggest books to come out of cultural studies for some time.

This tributary volume contains no less than thirty-four essays, ranging from one-and-a-half to twenty-three pages in length, and taking many different forms: poetry, personal reflections, essays using Hall's ideas to work through theoretical and empirical topics (including Jamaican post-war politics and struggles over the meaning of globalisation in South Korea). It includes contributions from many of the leading figures of Anglo-American cultural studies and theory, and some from other areas (criminology, social policy) to which Hall's oeuvre remains relevant, as well as from writers that I had not encountered before.

Celebrity is no guarantee of quality, and very often the essays by the better known contributors consist of lyrical but inconsequential rehearsals of well-worn cultural studies themes. From Iain Chambers we learn, for instance, that music culture is, like, all about identity, and identity is, you know *fluid* and, well, you shouldn't go around making rigid distinctions between the cultural and the economic. This is hardly front page news.

Valuable as these contributions may be in their own right, far more interesting at the present moment, and more appropriate to the occasion they mark, are those which challenge the complacencies of mid-Atlantic cultural studies with concrete reminders of what, following Hall, cultural studies was always supposed to be about. For example, John Clarke - once a contributor to *Policing the Crisis*, now Professor of Social Policy at the Open University - offers a fascinating set of reflections on the premise that Hall's work holds great relevance for his own field. In the process, he reminds us that something has gone desperately wrong with cultural studies, that this should be a statement which surprises - indeed, which needs to be made at all.

Perhaps the most striking difference between the various pieces is the nature and extent of their engagement with Hall's work. The fact that the book is not, nominally, *about* Stuart Hall but merely *for* him can technically excuse a complete lack of such engagement on the part of the contributors. However, this hardly lessens the embarrassment of noting that Judith Butler's seven-page exposition of her own work demonstrates no direct knowledge of Hall's, apart from one minor essay in which he happens to cite her. Similarly, Gayatri Spivak presents a characteristic deconstructive reading of Jamaica Kincaid's novel *Lucy*, the relevance of which to Hall's projects can best be described as tangential.

This reviewer would emphasise - despite his editor's distaste for such pleasantries - that there are no living intellectuals he holds in greater awe than Butler and Spivak. Nevertheless, it is hard to resist the conclusion that their contributions tell us something about the individualistic culture of American - and to some extent all - academic life which goes some way towards explaining the reverence in which Hall is held.

In comparison with him, these are figures whose brilliance lies largely in their capacity to fill whole books with their own ideas (often in the form of commentaries on the Great Traditions of literature and philosophy). This is the classical mode of intellectual life, and it is unavoidable for most of us. Hall's genius has always been to avoid it. It is the pithy essay, the concise analysis, the momentary synthesis, the rousing speech, the timely collection, the concern for the popular and the immersion in the contemporary for which he is famous. In other words, it is always - *always* - for the sake of some tactical intervention, in the name of some collective project, at the moment of some precise conjuncture, that Hall has acted, written and spoken.

Perhaps, after all, the contrast which the work of these quite different scholars provides is a necessary part of any such collection. It is in the nature of Hall's methods that they should be mobile, polysemic, and often unpredictable in their effects. Thought in these terms, we can see that only a collection as rich and varied as this could possibly be a fitting tribute to a man who has always said exactly what needed to be said, and no more.

Reading
Benjamin's Arcades

For full details and registration information
contact Merrick Burrow - M.Burrow@wkac.ac.uk

King Alfred's College, Winchester
Saturday July 13ᵗʰ 2002

*An international one-day conference
dedicated to Walter Benjamin's* Arcades
Project. *Supported by* New Formations.

Keynote speakers: Andrew Benjamin
                      Esther Leslie

Reading Benjamin's Arcades
School of Cultural Studies
King Alfred's College
Winchester
UK SO22 4NR

BACK ISSUES

1 Peter Wollen on fashion and orientalism / **Denise Riley** on 'women' and feminism / **Dick Hebdige**'s sociology of the sublime / **Laura Marcus** on autobiographies / **John Tagg** should art historians know their place? / **Franco Bianchini** on the GLC's cultural policies / **Homi K Bhabha, Stephen Feuchtwang** and **Barbara Harlow** on Fanon.

2 Mary Kelly, Elizabeth Cowie and Norman Bryson on Kelly's Interim / **Greil Marcus** on subversive entertainment / **Georgina Born** on modern music culture / **Geoffrey Nowell-Smith** on popular culture / **Ien Ang** on 'progressive television' / **Alan Sinfield** on modernism and English Studies in the Cold War / **Tony Bennett** on Eagleton.

3 TRAVELLING THEORY – **Julia Kristeva** on the melancholic imaginary / **David Edgar** on carnival and drama / **Kobena Mercer** black hair – style politics / **Jacques Ranciere** on journeys into new worlds / **Peter Hulme**'s Caribbean diary / **Bill Schwarz** on travelling stars / **Ginette Vincendeau** on *chanteuses realistes* / **Steve Connor** on Springsteen / **Christopher Norris** on Gasché's Derrida.

4 CULTURAL TECHNOLOGIES **Out of print**

5 IDENTITIES **Out of print**

6 THE BLUES – **Jacqueline Rose** on Margaret Thatcher and Ruth Ellis / **James Donald** how English is it? / **Benita Parry** on Kipling's imperialism / **John Silver** on Carpentier / **Mitra Tabrizian** and **Andy Golding**'s blues / **Barbara Creed** on *Blue Velvet* / **Joseph Bristow** on masculinity / **Graham Murdock** on Moretti's *Bildungsroman* / **Edmond Wright** on post Humptydumptyism.

7 MODERNISM/MASOCHISM – **Victor Burgin**'s Tokyo / **Linda Williams** on feminine masochism and feminist criticism / **John Tagg** on criticism, photography and technological change / **Geoff Bennington** *l'arroseur arrose(e)* / **Emilia Steuerman** on Habermas vs Lyotard / **Paul Crowther** on the Kantian sublime, the avant-garde and the postmodern / **Mark Cousins** on Levi Strauss on Mauss / **Iain Chambers** being 'British' / **Adrian Forty** on lofts and gardens / **Lisa Tickner** on Griselda Pollock.

8 TECHNO-ECOLOGIES – **Peter Wollen** cinema: Americanism and the robot / **John Keane** on the liberty of the press / **S.P. Mohanty** on the philosophical basis of political criticism / **David Kazanjian** and **Anahid Kassabian** naming the Armenian genocide / **Paul Théberge** the 'sound' of music / **David Tomas** the technophilic body / **Felix Guattari** the three ecologies / **Margaret Whitford** on Sartre.

9 ON ENJOYMENT – **Slavoj Zizek** the undergrowth of enjoyment / **Peter Osborne** aesthetic autonomy and the crisis of theory / **Rachel Bowlby** the judgement of Paris (and the choice of Kristeva) / **Joseph Bristow** being gay: politics, identity, pleasure / **Gail Ching-Liang Low** white skins black masks / **Christine Holmlund** I Love Luce / **Line Grenier** from diversity to indifference / **Mark Cousins** is chastity a perversion? / **Simon Critchley** review of Christopher Norris.

10 RADICAL DIFFERENCE – **McKenzie Wark** on the Beijing demonstrations / **Paul Hirst** on relativism / **Cindy Patton** African AIDS / **Anna Marie Smith** Section 28 / **Tracey Moffatt** something more / **Susan Willis** Afro-American culture and commodity culture / **Hazel V. Carby** on C.L.R.James / **David Lloyd** on materialist aesthetics / **Peter Redman** Aids and cultural politics.

Back issues cost £14.99 each
Make cheques payable to *Lawrence & Wishart* and send to:
Lawrence & Wishart, 99a Wallis Road, London E9 5LN

Why not Subscribe?

New Formations is published three times a year. Make sure of your copy by subscribing.

SUBSCRIPTION RATES FOR 2002 (3 ISSUES)

Individual Subscriptions
UK & Rest of World   £40.00

Institutional Subscriptions
UK & Rest of World   £120.00

Back issues: *£14.99 plus £1 post and packing for individuals*
£34.99 plus £1 post and packing for institutions

Please send one year's subscription
starting with Issue Number ⎯⎯⎯⎯⎯⎯⎯⎯

I enclose payment of ⎯⎯⎯⎯⎯⎯⎯⎯⎯

Please send me ⎯⎯⎯ copies of back issue no. ⎯⎯⎯⎯

I enclose total payment of   ⎯⎯⎯⎯⎯⎯⎯

Name ⎯⎯⎯⎯⎯⎯⎯⎯⎯⎯⎯⎯

Address ⎯⎯⎯⎯⎯⎯⎯⎯⎯⎯⎯

⎯⎯⎯⎯⎯⎯⎯⎯ Postcode ⎯⎯⎯⎯

Please return this form with cheque or money order (sterling only) payable to *Lawrence & Wishart* and send to:
Lawrence and Wishart, 99a Wallis Road, London E9 5LN

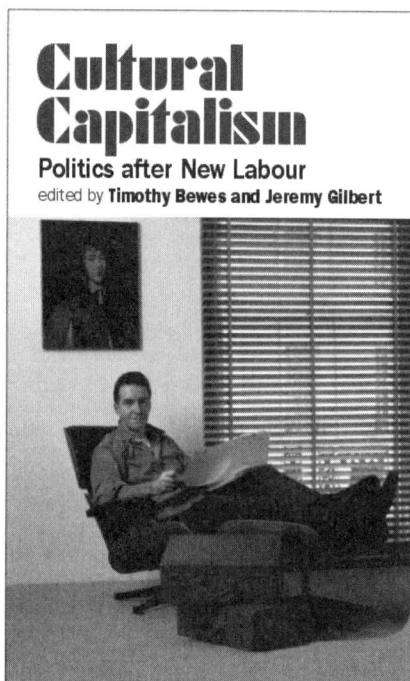

The Political Subject develops some of the themes from Wendy Wheeler's previous book *A New Modernity?*, gathering together essays which explore the complex nature of the contemporary 'self'; this, she argues, should be the starting point for politics. Wheeler's contributors show that, through looking creatively and imaginatively across the different disciplines, we can see the emergence of new ideas about the nature of politics, and of the human beings which are the subject of politics. In particular we can see the poverty of much contemporary political discourse, which tends to lose sight of human beings in its focus on managerialism, efficiency and a rather narrowly defined realism. By rethinking fundamental questions about the nature of political subjects, we can begin to develop a new and more humane politics.

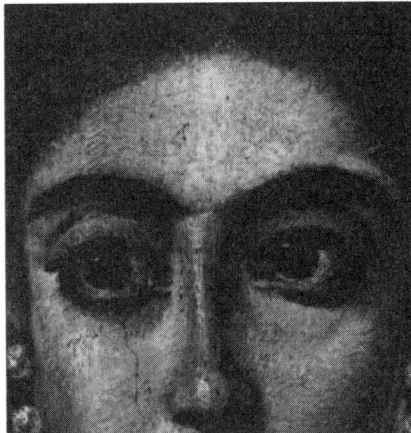

The Political Subject

Essays on the Self from
Art, Politics and Science

Wendy Wheeler (ed)

Contributors: *Erica Fudge, Colin Counsell, Paul McSorley, Mary Peace, Jenny Bourne Taylor, Carolyn Burdett, Sebastian Kraemer, Stuart Murray, James Park, Stephen Reicher, Alan Finlayson, Ashok Bery, Peter Middleton, Paul Cilliers, Tanya de Villiers, Jonathan Rutherford, Kevin Warwick.*

Each book is available at £11.99, a saving of £3 on the recommended retail price, or you can buy both books for £20, giving you a saving of £10.

For more information and offers on L&W books and journals, visit our website at www.l-w-bks.co.uk

Send orders to Lawrence & Wishart, 99a Wallis Road, London, E9 5LN. Please enclose full payment with order. Send Visa/MasterCard details, or cheques payable to Lawrence & Wishart Ltd. Postage is free in the UK. Alternatively, you can email us at lw@l-w-bks.demon.co.uk

A COMPLETE FIFTY VOLUME SET OF MARX & ENGELS COLLECTED WORKS

The publication of the definitive English language edition of the *Collected Works of Marx and Engels*, in 50 volumes, will be completed by 2003, when the last volume will be released. The series contains all the works of Marx and Engels, whether published during their lifetimes or since, and includes their complete correspondence as well as many works previously unpublished in English.

To mark the completion of this long term project, Lawrence and Wishart is offering special discounts to people who want to purchase the whole set. Each volume normally costs £45.00 making a complete set £2,250. But you can pay now and get Volumes 1-49 for just £1,250.00 (plus £100.00 UK post and packing - for overseas rate contact L&W). We will then send you Volume 50 **free** when it is published next year.

To take advantage of this offer, simply send your cheque or Visa/MasterCard details to Lawrence and Wishart, or visit our website for more information. You can also pay for and receive your volumes in instalments – for more information contact the L&W office.

> *'Indispensable to anyone with a serious interest in Marx, Marxism and the nineteenth century ... It is unlikely that this edition of the Collected Works will ever need to be replaced.'*
> **E. J. Hobsbawm**

> *'The translation is masterly; not only faultless but immensely readable and displaying a fine ingenuity in making sense of the more abstruse – or merely tougher Teutonic – constructions.'*
> **Yvonne Kapp, Sunday Times**

> *'The series still represents at least twice the value for money of any comparable product on offer elsewhere. Not only does it maintain a consistently good standard of production, it is beautifully indexed and presented.'*
> **Ken Coates, Tribune**

LW Lawrence & Wishart Ltd, 99a Wallis Road, London, E9 5LN.
Tel: 020 8533 2506 Fax: 020 533 7369 www.l-w-bks.co.uk

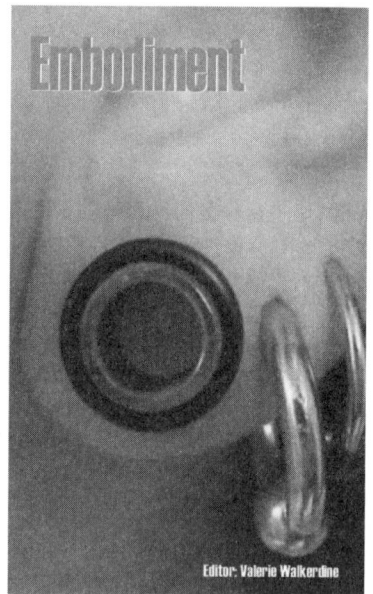